Distinguished Recipes from Distinguished Cooks

Northwood Institute
National Women's Board
Dallas Chapter

Herme de Wyman's Favorite Recipe
Recipe for Happiness

A heaping cup of Kindness   One cup of Gracious Listening
Two cups of Love and Caring   One cup of Sweet Forgiving
One cup of Understanding   Mix ingredients together
One cup of Joyful Sharing   Toss in Smiles and Laughter
A level cup of Patience   Serve to everyone you know
One cup of Thoughful Insight   with Love forever after

Herme de Wyman
Distinguished Woman
Palm Beach, Florida

Published by Favorite Recipes® Press
P. O. Box 305142, Nashville, TN 37230

Copyright© 1990 Northwood Institute
3100 Monticello, Suite 775 LB7
Dallas, Texas 75205

Library of Congress Number: 89-71454
ISBN: 0-87197-271-9

Printed in the United States of America
First Printing: 1990, 11,000 copies

Cover: *Kristina Bowman Photography*
Dallas, Texas

This cookbook is dedicated to
Joan and Doc Swalwell
and
Eloise Johnson
*for their heartfelt diligence
in preserving a piece of Texas History
to be appreciated and enjoyed by
those to come.*

Northwood: America's Business College

Free Enterprise is the spirit, the essence of the United States of America. It encompasses the right to choose one's own path, to tap individual strengths and talents, to succeed, to achieve due to one's own decisions and actions - and be rewarded for those achievements. Northwood Institute is a college unique to the country. And, because it is conceived in the very spirit of America, it is a college unique to the world.

Founded in 1959, Northwood was from the first dedicated to the principles of American Free Enterprise. Drs. Arthur E. Turner and R. Gary Stauffer recognized that a void existed between teaching conceptual theory and teaching the practical application of theory in America's colleges. Nowhere was that void more evident than in business education.

Business is the engine that moves this country and the world. And the fuel that powers America's great engine is Free Enterprise – that unique combination of the determination and the opportunity to win, coupled with a sense of honesty, integrity, accountability and an ability to make sound decisions; Free Enterprise – the core of business, of entrepreneurship, the idea upon which America was conceived, founded and built. But how is this idea "taught"?

Northwood's founders had the answer: capitalize on the experience of key figures in industry, commerce and finance; provide the opportunity to experience how the community, the arts and business are all integrally linked; and offer a thoroughly practical education in specific career fields. Beyond the classroom, offer experiences to provide a hands-on working knowledge of the business specialty field into which a student is determined to enter.

Northwood's practical approach to business education – instilling the *ability* to succeed with the *will* to win – has proven successful. Industry leaders avidly seek Northwood graduates. And Northwood *graduates* are successful, because, as they enter the real business world, they are better prepared to compete and contribute than their counterparts from any other college in this country.

Northwood Institute – the college of business management, a training ground for leaders. An investment in the future of America.

Contents

The Chapel

A symbol of the past, present and future, the relocated Northwood Chapel represents:

> historical significance
>
> viable re-use
>
> spiritual blessings
>
> and business acumen

not only for students of Northwood Institute, but also for an entire community and metroplex.

Originally a much-loved church and the most significant structure in Eureka, Texas, the chapel's relocation to the Northwood campus adds an educational dimension by becoming a visible lesson on the importance of our historic past for the students of Northwood's entrepreneurial business education system.

Mrs. C. E. (Joan) Swalwell

Foreword

Good food is like a good education–both must be sought after with much time and effort. And so the idea was born to create a cookbook that would provide wonderful recipes while supporting education. In this book, you will find delicious menus and recipes from distinguished individuals who have supported Northwood Institute through their efforts.

For years, the Texas Campus was without a church, but through the dream and vision of Joan and Doc Swalwell, long-time supporters and friends of Northwood, an old church building was located and moved to the campus in Cedar Hill. With the purchase of this cookbook, you will be helping to provide funds dedicated to the renovation and completion of the church.

As chairman of the Dallas Women's Board, I am most appreciative of all of the support given to Northwood Institute and especially to those of you who have contributed to make this book possible. To those of you who use this book, I say thank you for continuing to support good education and BON APPETIT!

Beverly Holmes

Beverly Holmes, Dallas
Women's Board Chairman
1989 – 1990

Accolades

To the Northwood Cookbook Committee

Mrs. R. William (Nancy) Barker
Vice-President, External Affairs
Midland, Michigan

Mrs. Reid (Martha) Calcott
Chapter Chairman
Saginaw-Bay City, Michigan

Mrs. Sy Clark
Cookbook Committee
Dallas, Texas

Ms. Leslie A. Gowan
Director of External Affairs/Dallas
Dallas, Texas

Mrs. Lou (Evie) Grubb
Chapter Chairman
Valley of the Sun, Arizona

Mrs. Leonard (Jane) Haber
Chapter Chairman
New York City, New York

Mrs. Robert H. (Beverly) Holmes
Chapter Chairman
Dallas, Texas

Mrs. Ronald (Linda) Hopton-Jones
Chapter Chairman
Cedar Hill, Texas

Mrs. William (Sue) Ignatowski
Chapter Chairman, Town & Campus
Midland, Michigan

Mrs. Don (Julie) Ingram
Cookbook Committee
Dallas, Texas

Mrs. Jack S. (Gretchen) Josey
Chapter Chairman
Houston, Texas

Mrs. Leonard (Shirley) Kleckner
Chapter Chairman
Palm Springs, California

Mrs. Joseph O. (Evelyn) Lambert
International Chairman
Vicenza, Italy

Mrs. John J. (Gini) Marston, Jr.
Cookbook Committee
Dallas, Texas

Mrs. Jess R. (Beth) Moore
Senior Development and External Affairs Officer
Director of National Costume Collection
Houston, Texas

Ms. Lynn O'Brien
Cookbook Committee
Dallas, Texas

Mrs. Edward (Carolyn) Rabidoux, Jr.
Chapter Chairman
Palm Beach, Florida

Miss Willie Mae Rogers
Chapter Chairman
New York City, New York

Mrs. Larry (Dinghy) Sharp
Chapter Chairman
Greater Detroit, Michigan

Ms. Nancy Sipes
Chapter Chairman
Southern Indiana

Mrs. David (Maureen) Smith
Chapter Chairwoman
Fort Lauderdale, Florida

Mrs. William (Harriet) Stout
National Chairman
Northwood National Women's Board

Mrs. C. E. (Joan) Swalwell
Cookbook Committee
Dallas, Texas

Mrs. Ralph (Bonnie) Tomioni
Chapter Chairman-Elect
Valley of the Sun, Arizona

Mrs. Benjamin (Audrey) Weinberg
Chapter Chairman
Greater Detroit, Michigan

Mrs. Murray F. (Janet) Wilson
Chapter Chairman
Valley of the Sun, Arizona

We wish to express our most sincere thanks to all of our supporters who contributed recipes for this cookbook project.

Nutritional Analysis Guidelines

The editors have attempted to present these family recipes in a form that allows approximate nutritional values to be computed. Persons with dietary or health problems or whose diets require close monitoring should not rely solely on the nutritional information provided. They should consult their physicians or a registered dietitian for specific information.

Abbreviations for Nutritional Analysis

Cal — Calories   Chol — Cholesterol   Potas — Potassium
Prot — Protein   Carbo — Carbohydrates   gr — gram
T Fat — Total Fat   Sod — Sodium   mg — milligram

Nutritional information for recipes is computed from values furnished by the United States Department of Agriculture Handbook. Many specialty items and new products now available on the market are not included in this handbook. However, producers of new products frequently publish nutritional information on each product's packaging and that information may be added, as applicable, for a more complete analysis. If the nutritional analysis notes the exclusion of a particular ingredient, check the package information.

Unless otherwise specified, the nutritional analysis of these recipes is based on the following guidelines.

- All measurements are level.
- Artificial sweeteners vary in use and strength so should be used "to taste," using the recipe ingredients as a guideline.
- Artificial sweeteners using aspertame (NutraSweet and Equal) should not be used as a sweetener in recipes involving prolonged heating which reduces the sweet taste. For further information on the use of these sweeteners, refer to package information.
- Alcoholic ingredients have been analyzed for the basic ingredients, although cooking causes the evaporation of alcohol thus decreasing caloric content.
- Buttermilk, sour cream, and yogurt are commercial types.
- Cake mixes prepared using package directions include 3 eggs and 1/2 cup oil.
- Chicken, cooked for boning and chopping, has been roasted; this method yields the lowest caloric values.
- Cottage cheese is cream-style with 4.2% creaming mixture. Dry-curd cottage cheese has no creaming mixture.
- Eggs are all large.
- Flour is unsifted all-purpose flour.
- Garnishes, serving suggestions and other optional additions and variations are not included in the analysis.
- Margarine and butter are regular, not whipped or presoftened.
- Milk is whole milk, 3.5% butterfat. Lowfat milk is 1% butterfat. Evaporated milk is produced by removing 60% of the water from whole milk.
- Oil is any type of vegetable cooking oil. Shortening is hydrogenated vegetable shortening.
- Salt and other ingredients to taste as noted in the method have not been included in the nutritional analysis.
- If a choice of ingredients has been given, the nutritional analysis reflects the first option.

Menus

Dinner at the Mansion on Turtle Creek

Grilled Gulf Red Snapper
Tomatillo And Serrano Chili Vinaigrette
Corn Bread Oysters
Crème Brûlée
Sauvignon Blanc, Robert Pecota, 1985

Dean Fearing
Executive Chef at the Mansion on Turtle Creek
Dallas, Texas

GRILLED GULF RED SNAPPER

Yield: 4 servings   *Preheat: grill*

4   7-ounce red snapper fillets
3 tablespoons peanut oil

Salt and freshly ground black
pepper to taste

Brush grill lightly with oil. Dip fillets in peanut oil. Place skin side up on grill; season with salt and pepper. Grill for 2 minutes. Turn fillets; sprinkle with salt and pepper. Grill for 2 minutes longer or just until fish flakes easily; do not overcook. Ladle Tomatillo and Serrano Chili Vinaigrette onto 4 warm serving plates. Place 1 fillet on each plate. Arrange 3 Corn Bread Oysters around each fillet. Serve immediately.

Approx Per Serving: Cal 288; Prot 41 g; Carbo 0 g; T Fat 13 g;
    Chol 73 mg; Potas 828 mg; Sod 127 mg.

CORN BREAD OYSTERS

Yield: 4 servings   *Pan Size: deep saucepan*   *Preheat: oil to 375 degrees*

1¹/₂ cups yellow cornmeal
¹/₂ cup flour
2 teaspoons baking powder
Salt to taste
2 eggs, slightly beaten
¹/₄ cup bacon drippings

2 cups milk
2 tablespoons fresh oyster
   liquid
12 fresh oysters
3 cups peanut oil

Mix first 4 ingredients in bowl. Add eggs, bacon drippings and milk; mix well. Add just enough oyster liquid to make of corn bread batter consistency. Dip oysters into batter. Place in single layer in hot peanut oil in saucepan. Fry until golden brown. Drain on paper towels. Store unused batter in refrigerator for up to 3 days. Keep oysters warm until serving time.

Approx Per Serving: Cal 514; Prot 17 g; Carbo 61 g; T Fat 22 g;
    Chol 238 mg; Potas 405 mg; Sod 454 mg.
    Nutritional information does not include oil for deep frying.

TOMATILLO AND SERRANO CHILI VINAIGRETTE

Yield: 4 servings   *Pan Size: medium bowl*

1 pound tomatillos, husks
  removed, chopped
1/2 cup chopped jicama
1/2 cup chopped mango
2 tablespoons chopped red
  bell pepper
2 tablespoons chopped yellow
  bell pepper
2 serrano chilies, seeded,
  finely chopped

1 cup peanut oil
2 tablespoons virgin olive oil
1/4 cup white wine vinegar
2 tablespoons balsamic
  vinegar
Juice of 1/2 lime
2 teaspoons lemon juice
1/4 cup chopped fresh cilantro
1 clove of garlic, minced
Salt to taste

Combine tomatillos, jicama, mango, bell peppers and chilies in medium bowl; mix well. Mix peanut oil, olive oil, vinegars, lime juice and lemon juice in bowl. Stir in cilantro, garlic and salt. Pour over tomatillo mixture; mix well. Let stand at room temperature until ready to serve.

Approx Per Serving: Cal 589; Prot 2 g; Carbo 13 g; T Fat 61 g;
  Chol 0 mg; Potas 353 mg; Sod 19 mg.

CRÈME BRÛLÉE

Yield: 6 servings   *Pan Size: double boiler*   *Preheat: broiler*

1 cup fresh raspberries, puréed
1/2 cup sugar
6 egg yolks
1/2 cup sugar
3 cups whipping cream

1 vanilla bean, split
1 cup fresh raspberries
Puff Pastry Shells (see
  page 172)
3/4 cup sugar

Strain purée through fine sieve to remove seed. Combine with simple syrup in bowl. Chill for up to 24 hours. Combine egg yolks and 1/2 cup sugar in double boiler. Cook over hot water until lemon-colored and the consistency of mousse, whisking or beating constantly. Remove from heat. Combine cream and vanilla bean in heavy saucepan. Bring to a boil over medium heat; remove from heat. Strain through fine sieve into egg yolks, whisking constantly. Cook for 10 minutes or until very thick, stirring constantly. Set top of double boiler in bowl of ice. Cool until of consistency of thick custard, stirring occasionally. Sprinkle 1 cup fresh raspberries into Puff Pastry Shells. Fill shells with cooled crème. Chill for 3 to 8 hours. Sprinkle 2 tablespoons sugar over each serving; place on baking sheet. Broil 6 inches from heat source for 3 minutes or just until sugar is caramelized. Do not overcook as crème will melt. Spoon raspberry sauce onto 6 serving plates. Place 1 Crème Brûlée on each plate. Serve immediately.

Approx Per Serving: Cal 718; Prot 6 g; Carbo 66 g; T Fat 50 g;
  Chol 376 mg; Potas 169 mg; Sod 54 mg.
  Nutritional information does not include Puff Pastry Shells.

Southern Sunday Brunch

Honey Baked Ham
Rolls or Biscuits
Southern Grits
Savory Spinach Loaf
Fruit Salad
Gigi's Crumbles
Liz's "Never The Same" Iced Tea

Mrs. C. E. Swalwell
Distinguished Woman, Past National Women's Board Chairman
Dallas Women's Board
Dallas, Texas

LIZ'S "NEVER THE SAME" ICED TEA

Yield: variable   *Pan Size: pitcher*

Freshly brewed tea	Small amount of apricot juice
Lemon juice	Sliced lemon and orange rinds
Orange juice	1/4 teaspoon cloves
Pineapple juice	1/8 teaspoon cinnamon

Combine tea with juices, rinds and spices in pitcher. Chill overnight to improve flavor. Serve over ice. Garnish with mint leaves. Adjust juices to suit individual tastes, taking care that tea remains the main ingredient. May be served hot if preferred.

Nutritional information for this recipe is not available.

SOUTHERN GRITS

Yield: 8 servings   *Pan Size: 9x13 inch*   *Preheat: 350 degrees*

2 cups quick-cooking grits	1 teaspoon Tabasco sauce
Salt to taste	2 tablespoons Worcestershire
8 cups boiling water	sauce
1 cup butter	Red pepper to taste
1 8-ounce roll garlic cheese	2 eggs, beaten
1/4 cup Sherry	Cayenne pepper to taste

Cook grits in salted boiling water in saucepan until fairly dry. Add butter, cheese, Sherry, Tabasco sauce, Worcestershire sauce and red pepper; mix well. Stir in eggs. Spoon into greased baking dish. Sprinkle with cayenne pepper. Bake for 1 hour or until set. Serve hot.

Approx Per Serving: Cal 485; Prot 12 g; Carbo 32 g; T Fat 34 g;
    Chol 142 mg; Potas 159 mg; Sod 656 mg.

SAVORY SPINACH LOAF

Yield: 8 servings   *Pan Size: 1¹/₂ quart*   *Preheat: 350 degrees*

3 slices bacon
3 tablespoons chopped onion
2 tablespoons butter
3 tablespoons flour
1 10-ounce package frozen
  chopped spinach, thawed
¹/₄ to ¹/₂ cup low-fat milk
5 eggs

3 tablespoons low-fat milk
1 teaspoon instant beef
  bouillon
¹/₂ teaspoon salt
¹/₂ teaspoon lemon pepper
¹/₂ teaspoon nutmeg
1 pimento, sliced

Cut bacon into 1-inch pieces. Cook with onion in saucepan until bacon is crisp. Remove with slotted spoon. Add butter to pan drippings. Stir in flour. Cook for several minutes over medium heat. Squeeze liquid from spinach into measuring cup. Add enough milk to measure ³/₄ cup liquid. Add liquid to flour. Cook until thickened, stirring constantly. Stir in spinach; remove from heat. Beat eggs with 3 tablespoons milk, beef bouillon, salt, lemon pepper and nutmeg in bowl. Add to spinach. Stir in bacon. Spoon into greased baking dish. Bake for 50 to 60 minutes or until set. Garnish with sliced pimento. Slice to serve.

Approx Per Serving: Cal 121; Prot 7 g; Carbo 6 g; T Fat 8 g;
    Chol 144 mg; Potas 211 mg; Sod 385 mg.

GIGI'S CRUMBLES

Yield: 8 servings   *Pan Size: 8x8 inch*   *Preheat: 350 degrees*

2 cups finely crushed vanilla
  wafers
1 14-ounce can sweetened
  condensed milk
1 cup chopped pecans

1 cup semisweet chocolate
  chips
Salt to taste
1 tablespoon vanilla extract

Combine cookie crumbs, condensed milk, pecans, chocolate chips, salt and vanilla in bowl; mix well. Press into lightly greased baking pan. Bake for 20 minutes or until light brown on top. Cool for several minutes. Cut into squares; remove from pan. May substitute graham cracker crumbs for vanilla wafers if preferred.

Approx Per Serving: Cal 468; Prot 7 g; Carbo 58 g; T Fat 26 g;
    Chol 31 mg; Potas 344 mg; Sod 149 mg.

General Motors Executive Dinner

Crab Dip Spread
Tenderloin of Beef Au Jus
Potatoes and Onions Au Gratin
Broccoli and Artichoke Bake
Bing Cherry Salad
Macaroon Ladyfinger Pudding
Champagne

Mrs. William W. (Lorraine) Bland
*Distinguished Woman, Houston Women's Board
Houston, Texas*

CRAB MEAT SPREAD

Yield: 10 servings   *Pan Size: 10-inch plate*

1 7-ounce can dark crab meat
1 7-ounce can white crab meat
1 green bell pepper, chopped
1 red bell pepper, chopped

2 stalks celery, chopped
10 green olives, chopped
8 ounces cream cheese
2 tablespoons (about) milk
1 8-ounce bottle of chili sauce

Mix crab meat, peppers, celery and olives in bowl. Beat softened cream cheese with milk in mixer bowl until smooth. Add ⅓ of the crab mixture; mix well. Spread cream cheese mixture on plate; make hole in center. Pour ½ cup chili sauce in hole. Sprinkle remaining crab mixture over cream cheese. Drizzle remaining chili sauce over top.

Approx Per Serving: Cal 156; Prot 11 g; Carbo 8 g; T Fat 9 g; Chol 65 mg; Potas 308 mg; Sod 584 mg.

POTATOES AND ONIONS AU GRATIN

Yield: 10 servings   *Pan Size: 9x13 inch*   *Preheat: 325 degrees*

3 tablespoons butter
3 tablespoons flour
2 cups milk
8 Number 1 white potatoes, thinly sliced

2 medium onions, thinly sliced
1 cup shredded Cheddar cheese

Melt butter in saucepan. Blend in flour. Add milk gradually. Cook until thick and smooth, stirring constantly. Layer potatoes, onions, white sauce and cheese ½ at a time in greased baking dish. Bake for 1 hour.

Approx Per Serving: Cal 301; Prot 9 g; Carbo 47 g; T Fat 9 g; Chol 28 mg; Potas 805 mg; Sod 133 mg.

BROCCOLI AND ARTICHOKE BAKE

Yield: 10 servings   *Pan Size: 9x13 inch*   *Preheat: 350 degrees*

2 4-ounce jars marinated
   artichoke hearts
1 20-ounce package frozen
   broccoli flowerets
8 ounces cream cheese

1/2 cup margarine
1 8-ounce can water
   chestnuts, drained
1/4 cup Italian bread crumbs
1/4 cup Parmesan cheese

Drain artichoke hearts; cut into bite-sized pieces. Place in baking dish. Cook broccoli using package directions; drain. Layer over artichokes. Melt cream cheese with margarine in saucepan over low heat. Stir in water chestnuts. Pour over layers. Top with bread crumbs and Parmesan cheese. Bake until bubbly and golden brown on top.

Approx Per Serving: Cal 229; Prot 5 g; Carbo 10 g; T Fat 20 g;
   Chol 27 mg; Potas 225 mg; Sod 366 mg.

MACAROON LADYFINGER PUDDING

Yield: 9 servings   *Pan Size: 9x9 inch*

4 egg yolks
1/3 cup sugar
Salt to taste
2 cups milk
1 teaspoon vanilla extract
Macaroons

Sherry
Ladyfingers
Raspberry or strawberry jam
Vanilla ice cream
Whipped cream

Beat egg yolks with sugar and salt in bowl. Scald milk in double boiler. Stir a small amount of hot milk into egg yolks; stir egg yolks into hot milk. Cook over hot water until mixture coats spoon, stirring constantly; remove from heat. Stir in vanilla. Dip macaroons into Sherry. Arrange 1 layer in dish. Split ladyfingers; spread split sides with jam. Arrange single layer over macaroons. Top with second layer of macaroons. Pour warm custard over layers. Chill for 8 hours. Cut into squares. Place on serving plates. Serve with ice cream and whipped cream.

Nutritional information for this recipe is not available.

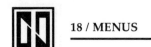

Thatched Cottage Pantry Tea

Cucumber Sandwiches
Bombay Chicken Sandwiches
Raisin Scones with Clotted Cream
Red Currant Jam and Strawberry Jam
English Trifle
Lady Primrose Teas:
Lady Caroline Tea — Rose Pouchon Tea
Lady Vivian Tea — Christmas Tea
Herbal Garden Tea — Secret Garden Iced Tea

Caroline Rose Hunt
Distinguished Woman, Dallas Women's Board
Dallas, Texas

RAISIN SCONES

Yield: 12 servings	Pan Size: baking sheet	Preheat: 350 degrees

2 cups flour
2 teaspoons baking powder
1/2 teaspoon soda
1/2 teaspoon salt
1/2 teaspoon freshly ground
  nutmeg

1/2 cup butter
1 cup raisins
2 tablespoons sugar
3/4 cup low-fat yogurt
1 egg yolk, beaten
1 egg white, slightly beaten

Mix flour, baking powder, soda, salt and nutmeg in mixer bowl. Add butter; mix until mixture resembles fine meal. Add raisins and sugar; mix well. Add mixture of yogurt and egg yolk; mix well. Knead on floured surface until smooth. Roll and cut as desired. Place on baking sheet. Brush with egg white; sprinkle with additional sugar. Bake for 20 to 25 minutes or until golden brown. Serve with clotted cream and jam.

Approx Per Serving: Cal 209; Prot 4 g; Carbo 30 g; T Fat 9 g;
  Chol 39 mg; Potas 165 mg; Sod 260 mg.

ENGLISH TRIFLE

Yield: 12 servings	*Pan Size: three 9 inch*	*Preheat: 400 degrees*

3/4 cup plus 2 tablespoons
  cake flour
1 tablespoon baking powder
1 teaspoon salt
8 egg yolks
1/2 cup oil
1 cup plus 2 teaspoons sugar
2 teaspoons vanilla extract
1 teaspoon lemon emulsion
1/2 cup water
3/4 cup egg whites
1/2 teaspoon cream of tartar

6 egg yolks
1 cup sugar
1/4 cup all-purpose flour
2 tablespoons cornstarch
4 cups milk
2 tablespoons vanilla extract
3/4 cup Sherry
4 cups strawberry halves
1/2 cup raspberry jam
4 cups raspberries
2 cups whipped cream

Mix cake flour, baking powder and salt in bowl. Combine 8 egg yolks, oil, 1 cup plus 2 teaspoons sugar, 2 teaspoons vanilla and lemon emulsion in mixer bowl; mix well. Add to dry ingredients; mix well. Add water; mix for 10 minutes, scraping bowl after 5 minutes. Beat eggs whites with cream of tartar in mixer bowl until stiff peaks form. Fold gently into batter. Spoon into 3 greased and floured cake pans. Bake for 25 minutes. Remove to wire rack to cool. Mix 6 egg yolks and 1 cup sugar in bowl. Add all-purpose flour and cornstarch; mix well. Heat milk to the simmering point in saucepan. Stir a small amount of hot milk into egg yolks; stir egg yolks into hot milk. Cook for 2 to 5 minutes or until thickened, stirring constantly. Stir in 2 tablespoons vanilla. Place 1 cake layer in trifle bowl. Sprinkle with 1/4 cup Sherry. Spread with 1/3 of the custard. Arrange half the strawberries cut side out around outside of container. Spoon raspberry jam between spaces of strawberries. Arrange single layer of raspberries over custard. Repeat layers. Top with remaining cake layer, Sherry and custard. Pipe whipped cream in decorative design over top. Garnish with additional raspberries.

Nutritional information for this recipe is not available.

Wine Connoisseur's Dinner

Chicken Puffs
Light Cheeses and Crackers
Light Champagne, Fumé Blanc, Sauvignon Blanc,
Paul Cheneau Blanc de Blanc

Shrimp Remoulade
Chalone Vineyards 1986 Pinot Blanc - Estate Bottled

Cherry Tomato Salad
Horseradish and Chive Dressing
Gerard Chavy 1985 Puligny Montrachet

Steaks with Roquefort Butter
Green Beans in Onion Sauce
French Bread
BV Private Reserve 1974 Cabernet or 1966 Margaux

Lemon Roll
Brut 1979 Verve Clicquot Ponardine-Rosé Champagne

Bill Burford
TAG Wines, Proprietor and Connoisseur; Friend of Northwood
Dallas, Texas

WINE GLASSES

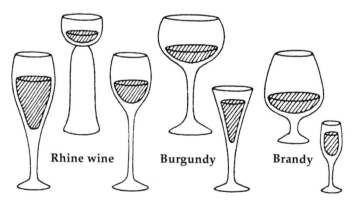

Rhine wine   Burgundy   Brandy

All-purpose   Champagne   Sherry   Liqueur

CHICKEN PUFFS

Yield: 36 servings *Pan Size: saucepan*

1 cup finely chopped pecans
2 tablespoons butter
3 ounces cream cheese,
  softened
1½ cups finely chopped
  cooked chicken
⅓ cup mayonnaise

½ teaspoon grated lemon rind
¼ teaspoon nutmeg
¼ teaspoon salt
36 small cream puffs
3 tablespoons finely chopped
  parsley

Sauté pecans in butter in saucepan over low heat until toasted. Cool. Add cream cheese, chicken, mayonnaise, lemon rind, nutmeg and salt; mix well. Spoon into cream puffs. Garnish with parsley.

Approx Per Serving: Cal 62; Prot 2 g; Carbo 1 g; T Fat 6 g;
  Chol 11 mg; Potas 33 mg; Sod 44 mg.

SHRIMP REMOULADE

Yield: 8 servings *Pan Size: medium bowl*

⅓ cup horseradish mustard
2 cloves of garlic, chopped
½ cup olive oil
⅓ cup tarragon vinegar
½ cup chopped green onions
  with tops

3 tablespoons paprika
½ teaspoon cayenne pepper
1 teaspoon salt
1 pound shrimp, cooked,
  peeled

Combine mustard, garlic, olive oil, vinegar, green onions, paprika, cayenne pepper and salt in bowl; mix well. Add shrimp; toss to coat well. Marinate in refrigerator for several hours. Serve on lettuce leaves.

Approx Per Serving: Cal 185; Prot 12 g; Carbo 2 g; T Fat 14 g;
  Chol 111 mg; Potas 153 mg; Sod 463 mg.

CHERRY TOMATO SALAD WITH HORSERADISH AND CHIVE DRESSING

Yield: 8 servings   *Pan Size: large bowl*

1/2 cup sour cream
1/4 cup mayonnaise
1 tablespoon lemon juice
1 tablespoon prepared
  horseradish

2 tablespoons chopped chives
Salt and pepper to taste
36 cherry tomatoes
Sprigs of 1 bunch watercress

Combine sour cream, mayonnaise, lemon juice, horseradish, chives, salt and pepper in bowl; mix well. Chill in refrigerator. Pour enough boiling water over tomatoes to cover in bowl. Let stand for 1 minute; drain. Remove skins. Combine with watercress in bowl. Pour dressing over tomatoes and watercress; toss lightly to mix.

Approx Per Serving: Cal 90; Prot 1 g; Carbo 3 g; T Fat 9 g;
    Chol 10 mg; Potas 127 mg; Sod 52 mg.

STEAKS WITH ROQUEFORT BUTTER

Yield: 8 servings   *Pan Size: broiler pan*   *Preheat: broiler*

1/3 cup butter, softened
1/3 cup crumbled Roquefort
  cheese
Juice of 1/2 lemon

2 tablespoons finely chopped
  chives
Salt and pepper to taste
4 pounds tenderloin steaks

Cream butter and cheese in mixer bowl until light. Add lemon juice, chives, salt and pepper; mix well. Let steaks stand at room temperature for 1 hour or longer. Pat dry with paper towel. Place on rack in broiler pan. Broil to desired degree of doneness 3 inches from heat source, turning once. Season with salt and pepper. Serve on heated platter. Scoop small balls of Roquefort butter around steaks with melon ball scoop.

Approx Per Serving: Cal 382; Prot 43 g; Carbo 0 g; T Fat 22 g;
    Chol 152 mg; Potas 419 mg; Sod 218 mg.

GREEN BEANS IN ONION SAUCE

Yield: 8 servings   *Pan Size: 2 quart*   *Preheat: 350 degrees*

1/4 cup butter
1/4 cup flour
3 cups warm milk
3/4 cup shredded Cheddar
cheese

2 16-ounce cans whole green
beans, drained
1 3-ounce can French-fried
onions

Melt butter in saucepan. Blend in flour. Cook over medium heat for 1 minute, stirring constantly; remove from heat. Stir in milk. Cook until thickened, stirring constantly; remove from heat. Stir in cheese until melted. Alternate layers of green beans and onions in greased baking dish until all ingredients are used. Pour sauce over layers. Bake for 30 minutes.

Approx Per Serving: Cal 221; Prot 8 g; Carbo 16 g; T Fat 15 g;
     Chol 43 mg; Potas 262 mg; Sod 455 mg.

LEMON ROLL

Yield: 8 servings   *Pan Size: 10x15 inch*   *Preheat: 400 degrees*

4 eggs
3/4 teaspoon baking powder
1/4 teaspoon salt
1 cup sugar
3/4 cup cake flour
1/4 cup confectioners' sugar

3 eggs
1 cup sugar
Juice and grated rind of 2
lemons
1/2 cup butter

Combine 4 eggs, baking powder and salt in mixer bowl; beat until thick and lemon-colored. Add 1 cup sugar gradually, beating constantly for 15 minutes. Sift in cake flour; mix well. Spread in greased cake pan lined with greased waxed paper. Bake for 15 minutes or just until cake pulls away from sides of pan. Invert onto towel sprinkled with 1/4 cup confectioners' sugar; remove waxed paper. Roll as for jelly roll in towel. Let stand until cool. Mix 3 eggs, 1 cup sugar, lemon juice, lemon rind and butter in double boiler. Cook over simmering water for 25 to 30 minutes or until very thick, stirring constantly. Cool completely. Unroll cake. Spread with lemon filling. Roll as for jelly roll, enclosing filling. Chill, wrapped in waxed paper. Slice roll to serve. Garnish with additional confectioners' sugar and whipped cream.

Approx Per Serving: Cal 417; Prot 6 g; Carbo 63 g; T Fat 17 g;
     Chol 217 mg; Potas 91 mg; Sod 256 mg.

Christmas Brunch

Quail, Bacon, Sausage, Ham
Egg Casserole
Grits Soufflé
Creamed Spinach
Fried Apples or Applesauce
Charlotte Russe
Orange Juice, Coffee, Champagne

Edna Woodard Van Riper
Distinguished Woman
Indianapolis, Indiana

EGG CASSEROLE

Yield: 6 servings   *Pan Size: 7x12 inch*   *Preheat: 350 degrees*

8 slices bread	3 cups milk
2 cups shredded sharp cheese	1 teaspoon dry mustard
6 eggs	Salt and pepper to taste

Trim bread and cut into cubes. Layer bread and cheese in greased baking dish. Beat eggs and milk in bowl. Add dry mustard, salt and pepper. Pour over layers. Chill overnight. Bake for 50 to 55 minutes or until set.

Approx Per Serving: Cal 406; Prot 23 g; Carbo 25 g; T Fat 24 g;
    Chol 269 mg; Potas 307 mg; Sod 546 mg.

CHARLOTTE RUSSE

Yield: 12 servings   *Pan Size: 2 quart*

2 tablespoons unflavored gelatin	2 teaspoons vanilla extract
1/4 cup cold water	4 egg whites, stiffly beaten
2 cups milk	2 cups whipping cream, whipped
1/2 cup sugar	1 8-ounce package ladyfingers
4 egg yolks	

Soften gelatin in cold water in saucepan. Stir in milk. Cook over medium-low heat until gelatin is dissolved, stirring constantly. Add sugar; mix well. Stir a small amount of hot mixture into egg yolks; stir egg yolks into hot mixture. Cook over low heat until thickened, stirring constantly. Cool. Stir in vanilla. Fold egg whites and whipped cream gently into custard. Line bowl with ladyfingers. Fill with custard. Chill until serving time.

Approx Per Serving: Cal 290; Prot 6 g; Carbo 24 g; T Fat 19 g;
    Chol 198 mg; Potas 127 mg; Sod 73 mg.

Appetizers,
Beverages & Accompaniments

Dalby Commons
West Palm Beach, Florida

ARTICHOKE DIP

Yield: 10 servings   *Pan Size: medium bowl*

1 package chicken-flavored Rice-A-Roni	1 cup mayonnaise
2 7-ounce jars marinated artichoke hearts	1 cup chopped green onions
	¼ teaspoon curry powder
	¼ cup Spanish peanuts

Cook Rice-A-Roni using package directions. Cool. Drain artichokes, reserving liquid. Mix reserved liquid with mayonnaise in bowl. Add green onions and artichokes; mix well. Add Rice-A-Roni; mix well. Chill until serving time. Sprinkle with curry powder and peanuts.

Approx Per Serving: Cal 277; Prot 3 g; Carbo 16 g; T Fat 23 g; Chol 13 mg; Potas 161 mg; Sod 537 mg.

Ms. Yvonne Watkins, Dallas, Texas
Distinguished Woman/Chapter Advisor, Cedar Hill
Dallas Women's Board

THE BEST CON QUESO

Yield: 24 servings   *Pan Size: medium saucepan*

2 pounds Velveeta cheese	2 cups sour cream
2 cups shredded Cheddar cheese	2 10-ounce cans Ro-Tel tomatoes with chilies

Combine Velveeta cheese, Cheddar cheese, sour cream and tomatoes in saucepan. Heat over low heat until cheeses are melted, stirring to mix well. Serve with tostado chips. May serve over vegetables if desired.

Approx Per Serving: Cal 225; Prot 12 g; Carbo 3 g; T Fat 19 g; Chol 54 mg; Potas 150 mg; Sod 647 mg.

Paula Ulmer, Dallas, Texas
Northwood Arts Programs Administrator/Distinguished Woman
Campus Arts Coordinator, Texas/Dallas Women's Board

CHICK-PEA DIP

Yield: 12 servings   *Pan Size: 2 quart*

2 cups dried chick-peas
2¹/2 cups water
¹/3 cup tahini
1 large clove of garlic, crushed
¹/3 cup lemon juice

1 tablespoon salt
Chopped parsley to taste
Paprika to taste
2 tablespoons olive oil

Soak chick-peas in water in saucepan overnight. Cook in same liquid until tender. Drain, reserving 3 tablespoons liquid. Reserve several whole chick-peas for garnish. Place remaining chick-peas in bowl or blender container. Purée with mixer or in blender. Combine with tahini and reserved cooking liquid in bowl; mix well. Mix garlic, lemon juice and salt in small bowl. Add to chick-peas; mix well. Spoon into serving plate. Top with reserved chick-peas, chopped parsley and paprika. Drizzle with olive oil.

Approx Per Serving: Cal 183; Prot 8 g; Carbo 22 g; T Fat 8 g;
    Chol 0 mg; Potas 331 mg; Sod 543 mg.

Mrs. Robert (Millie) Hamady, Flint, Michigan
Distinguished Woman

PIÑA COLADA DIP

Yield: 32 servings   *Pan Size: small bowl*

8 ounces Neufchâtel cheese,
    softened
¹/4 cup flaked coconut

1 8-ounce can crushed
    pineapple in syrup

Combine cheese, coconut and undrained pineapple in bowl; mix well. Serve with fruit, water wafers or wheat crackers. Neufchâtel cheese, named for Neufchâtel-en-Bray in France, has fewer calories and less fat than cream cheese and can be substituted for it in your favorite recipes.

Approx Per Serving: Cal 27; Prot 1 g; Carbo 2 g; T Fat 2 g;
    Chol 5 mg; Potas 17 mg; Sod 30 mg.

Northwood Cookbook Committee, Dallas, Texas

SIX-LAYER DIP

Yield: 12 servings   *Pan Size: 10-inch plate*

1 16-ounce can refried beans	1 envelope taco seasoning mix
1 avocado	1 cup shredded Cheddar
1 envelope avocado dip mix	cheese
6 green onions, chopped	1 cup chopped tomatoes
1 cup sour cream	

Spread refried beans in serving dish. Mash avocado in small bowl. Add avocado dip mix; mix well. Spread over beans. Sprinkle with green onions. Mix sour cream and taco seasoning mix in small bowl. Spread over green onions. Top with Cheddar cheese and tomatoes. Serve with taco chips or corn chips.

Approx Per Serving: Cal 183; Prot 7 g; Carbo 17 g; T Fat 11 g;
    Chol 18 mg; Potas 381 mg; Sod 930 mg.
    Nutritional information does not include dip mix.

Shirley Kleckner, Palm Springs, California
Chairman, Palm Springs Chapter

ARTICHOKE CUPS

Yield: 48 servings   *Pan Size: miniature muffin cups*   *Preheat: 325 degrees*

2 loaves Pepperidge Farm	¼ cup bread crumbs
very thin bread	4 eggs, beaten
2 8-ounce jars marinated	8 ounces Cheddar cheese
artichoke hearts	Salt and pepper to taste
1 small onion	

Flatten slices of bread with rolling pin. Cut into circles. Press each piece into muffin cup to form cup. Drain 1 jar artichoke hearts. Pour liquid from remaining jar artichoke hearts into food processor container fitted with metal blade. Add artichoke hearts, onion, bread crumbs, eggs, cheese, salt and pepper, processing until smooth. Spoon into bread cups. Bake for 30 minutes or until set.

Approx Per Serving: Cal 63; Prot 3 g; Carbo 6 g; T Fat 3 g;
    Chol 23 mg; Potas 50 mg; Sod 137 mg.

Marilyn A. Boll, New York City, New York
New York Women's Board

CAVIAR PIE

Yield: 16 servings   *Pan Size: 9-inch springform*

8 hard-boiled eggs 3 tablespoons mayonnaise 1 large onion, finely chopped ²/₃ cup sour cream	8 ounces cream cheese, softened 7 ounces lumpfish caviar

Mash eggs with mayonnaise in bowl. Spread evenly over bottom of greased springform pan. Sprinkle with onion. Blend sour cream and cream cheese in bowl until smooth. Spread over onion. Cover tightly with plastic wrap and foil. Chill overnight. Place on serving plate; remove side of pan. Top with lumpfish caviar. May use both red and black caviar in decorative pattern if desired.

Approx Per Serving: Cal 162; Prot 8 g; Carbo 2 g; T Fat 14 g;
    Chol 200 mg; Potas 102 mg; Sod 282 mg.

Susan Golick, New York, New York
Distinguished Woman

MARY JOHN'S SCRUMPTIOUS CAVIAR MOUSSE

Yield: 30 servings   *Pan Size: 4-cup mold*

2 envelopes unflavored gelatin ¹/₄ cup cold water 2 cups sour cream	2 cups mayonnaise 2 tablespoons fresh lime juice 6 tablespoons grated onion 1 3-ounce jar black caviar

Soften gelatin in cold water in small bowl. Heat sour cream in saucepan just to the simmering point; do not boil. Whisk in mayonnaise. Add gelatin, stirring until dissolved. Add lime juice and onion; mix well. Pour into mold which has been rinsed with cold water. Chill overnight. Unmold onto lettuce-lined serving tray. Top with caviar. Serve with Melba rounds or crackers. Lumpfish caviar should be washed and well drained in cold water 2 or 3 times.

Approx Per Serving: Cal 148; Prot 2 g; Carbo 1 g; T Fat 15 g;
    Chol 32 mg; Potas 37 mg; Sod 135 mg.

Dr. Mary John, Dallas, Texas
Vice President, Texas/Distinguished Woman
National Director of Northwood Arts Program

TARAMA

Yield: 96 servings	Pan Size: 6-cup mold

4 ounces trimmed sour dough bread	1/2 cup soda water
1/2 cup milk	41/2 cups corn oil
4 ounces tarama or Russian-style carp roe caviar	1/2 cup soda water
	11/2 teaspoons lemon juice
	1 small onion, finely chopped

Soak bread in milk in bowl. Squeeze dry; place in mixer bowl. Mix until of consistency of paste. Add tarama. Mix slowly until thickened, checking consistency with spatula. Add 1/2 cup soda water; mix well. Add enough oil gradually until mixture stiffens, beating constantly and testing consistency with spatula. Add 1/2 cup soda water; mix well. Add enough remaining oil gradually to make of consistency of stiffly beaten egg whites. Add lemon juice and onion; mix well. Spoon into mold lined with waxed paper. Chill until firm. Unmold onto serving plate. Garnish with black olives. Serve with black bread or Russian rye bread.

Approx Per Serving: Cal 98; Prot 0 g; Carbo 1 g; T Fat 11 g;
Chol 7 mg; Potas 7 mg; Sod 25 mg.

Marge Predeteanu, Bloomfield Hills, Michigan
Greater Detroit Women's Board

CITRUS CUPS SUPREME

Yield: 4 servings	Pan Size: medium bowl

2 large grapefruit	2 or 3 tablespoons sugar
1 large cucumber	

Cut grapefruit into halves crosswise. Remove pulp, reserving shells. Cut pulp into bite-sized pieces, discarding seed and membrane. Place in bowl. Peel cucumber; cut into bite-sized pieces, discarding seed. Mix with grapefruit. Sprinkle with sugar. Chill for 4 hours or longer. Spoon into grapefruit shells. Serve cold.

Approx Per Serving: Cal 83; Prot 1 g; Carbo 21 g; T Fat 0 g;
Chol 0 mg; Potas 270 mg; Sod 2 mg.

Mrs. Fred C. (Betty) Hardy, Houston, Texas
Houston Women's Board

BAKED AVOCADO WITH CRAB MEAT

Yield: 8 servings *Pan Size: baking sheet* *Preheat: 325 degrees*

4 avocados
2 tablespoons lemon juice
1/2 cup chopped mushrooms
2 tablespoons butter
2 tablespoons flour
1 cup light cream
Sugar, salt and white pepper
   to taste

1 egg yolk
1/4 cup chopped black olives
2 tablespoons Sherry
1 pound crab meat
2 tablespoons butter
1/4 cup Parmesan cheese

Cut avocados into halves lengthwise, discarding seed. Brush with lemon juice. Place on baking sheet. Add water to depth of 1/4 inch. Sauté mushrooms in 2 tablespoons butter in skillet. Sprinkle with flour. Add cream. Cook until thickened and smooth, stirring constantly. Season with sugar, salt and white pepper. Add egg yolk, olives and Sherry; mix well. Sauté crab meat in 2 tablespoons butter in small skillet. Add to cream sauce. Spoon into avocados. Top with cheese. Bake for 20 minutes. Serve on bed of shredded iceberg lettuce. Garnish with black olives.

Approx Per Serving: Cal 351; Prot 16 g; Carbo 11 g; T Fat 28 g;
   Chol 106 mg; Potas 887 mg; Sod 353 mg.

Mrs. Robert (Genie) Parker, Phoenix, Arizona
Founding Member and 1985-1988 Chairman, Valley of the Sun Chapter

CRAB APPETIZER

Yield: 4 servings *Pan Size: 1 1/2 quart* *Preheat: 400 degrees*

2 6-ounce cans crab meat
1 cup Hellman's mayonnaise

2 tablespoons capers
8 ounces Velveeta cheese

Drain crab meat. Mix with mayonnaise in bowl. Add capers; mix well. Spoon into baking dish. Top with cheese. Bake for 15 minutes or until bubbly; mix well. Serve with crackers or bagel chips. May substitute Velveeta hot Mexican cheese if preferred.

Approx Per Serving: Cal 690; Prot 31 g; Carbo 2 g; T Fat 63 g;
   Chol 162 mg; Potas 429 mg; Sod 1407 mg.

Mrs. Bill (Pat) Burford, Dallas, Texas
Dallas Women's Board

CRAB BITES

Yield: 48 servings	Pan Size: baking sheet	Preheat: 400 degrees

1/2 cup butter, softened
1 1/2 tablespoons
  mayonnaise-type salad
  dressing

1/4 teaspoon garlic powder
1 7-ounce can crab meat
1 3-ounce jar old English
  process cheese

Combine butter, salad dressing and garlic powder in bowl; mix well. Add crab meat and cheese; mix well. Spread on English muffin halves. Cut into bite-sized pieces. Place on baking sheet. Bake for 10 minutes.

Approx Per Serving: Cal 30; Prot 1 g; Carbo 0 g; T Fat 3 g;
  Chol 11 mg; Potas 19 mg; Sod 59 mg.

Feather Buchanan, Orchard Lake, Michigan
Northwood Alumna/Detroit Women's Board

LA JOLLA CRISPIES

Yield: 24 servings	Pan Size: baking sheet	Preheat: 350 degrees

1/2 cup butter, softened
1 cup flour
Tabasco sauce to taste

1 cup shredded Cheddar
  cheese
1 cup crisp rice cereal

Combine butter, flour, Tabasco sauce, cheese and cereal in bowl; mix well. Shape into small wafers. Place on baking sheet. Bake for 10 to 15 minutes or until crisp.

Approx Per Serving: Cal 77; Prot 2 g; Carbo 5 g; T Fat 5 g;
  Chol 15 mg; Potas 12 mg; Sod 76 mg.

Mrs. George (Jodie) Biddle, Dallas, Texas
Distinguished Woman/Dallas Women's Board

CHEESE WAFERS

Yield: 18 servings　　　*Pan Size: baking sheet*　　　*Preheat: 375 degrees*

½ cup butter, softened
1½ cups flour
13 ounces shredded Cheddar
　cheese, at room temperature

½ teaspoon baking powder
½ teaspoon cayenne pepper
　(optional)
1 teaspoon salt

Combine butter, flour, cheese, baking powder, cayenne pepper and salt in bowl; knead until well mixed. Shape into roll ¾ inch in diameter. Chill for 2 hours. Cut into thin slices. Place close together on ungreased baking sheet. Bake for 10 minutes or just until wafers begin to brown. Cool on baking sheet. These are better if served the same day.

Approx Per Serving: Cal 166; Prot 6 g; Carbo 8 g; T Fat 12 g;
　　Chol 35 mg; Potas 32 mg; Sod 298 mg.

June Hunt, Dallas, Texas
Northwood Arts Programs Administrative Assistant

MONTEREY JACK WAFERS

Yield: 40 servings　　　*Pan Size: baking sheet*　　　*Preheat: 400 degrees*

1 pound Monterey Jack
　cheese

Cut cheese into slices ¼ inch thick and 1½ inches in diameter. Arrange 2 to 3 inches apart on nonstick baking sheet. Bake for 10 minutes; do not overbake. Remove immediately to wire rack to cool. Store in airtight container. Do not substitute other kinds of cheese for Monterey Jack.

Approx Per Serving: Cal 42; Prot 3 g; Carbo 0 g; T Fat 3 g;
　　Chol 10 mg; Potas 9 mg; Sod 61 mg.

Mrs. George Randolph (Rosalie) Hearst, Palm Springs, California
Distinguished Woman

Rosalie Hearst

NOW THAT'S A MEATBALL! AND SAUCE

Yield: 12 servings   *Pan Size: 1¹/₂ quart*   *Preheat: 350 degrees*

2 pounds ground beef	Salt and pepper to taste
1 egg, slightly beaten	1 12-ounce jar chili sauce
1 large onion, grated	1 10-ounce jar grape jelly
¹/₂ cup bread crumbs	Juice of 1 lemon

Combine ground beef, egg, onion, bread crumbs, salt and pepper in bowl; mix well. Shape into small balls. Place in baking dish. Bake for 30 minutes. Combine chili sauce, jelly and lemon juice in saucepan. Simmer for 10 minutes. Add meatballs. Simmer for 10 minutes longer.

Approx Per Serving: Cal 275; Prot 16 g; Carbo 28 g; T Fat 12 g;
    Chol 67 mg; Potas 334 mg; Sod 465 mg.

Phyllis Diller, Los Angeles, California
Achievement in the Arts Awardee

NUTS AND BOLTS

Yield: 40 servings   *Pan Size: large roasting pan*   *Preheat: 325 degrees*

1 15-ounce package Cheerios	2 12-ounce cans mixed nuts
1 8-ounce package Rice Chex	without peanuts
1 12-ounce package Corn Chex	2 10-ounce cans sesame nut mix
2 9-ounce packages pretzels sticks	4 pounds butter
2 12-ounce cans cashews	3 4-ounce jars garlic purée
1 24-ounce can peanuts	1 6-ounce bottle of Worcestershire sauce
1 pound pecan halves	Garlic salt to taste

Combine cereals, pretzels, nuts and sesame nut mix in large bowl; mix well. Spoon enough mixture to fill roasting pan 2 inches deep. Melt butter in saucepan. Add garlic purée and Worcestershire sauce, whisking until smooth. Ladle about ³/₄ cup of the seasoning mixture over cereal. Sprinkle with garlic salt; stir until coated. Bake for 20 minutes. Add ³/₄ cup seasoning mixture; mix gently. Sprinkle with garlic salt. Bake for 20 minutes longer. Spread on paper towels to cool. Repeat with remaining cereal and seasoning mixture until all ingredients have been used. Cool for 30 minutes. Store in airtight container for up to 30 days.

Approx Per Serving: Cal 935; Prot 18 g; Carbo 52 g; T Fat 78 g;
    Chol 99 mg; Potas 588 mg; Sod 1182 mg.

David Wilson, Dallas, Texas
Old Spaghetti Warehouse
Friend of Northwood

PAPA JOHN'S TEX-MEX TORPEDOES

Yield: 12 servings	*Pan Size: 9x13 inch*	*Preheat: 325 degrees*

This recipe won the American Regional Cuisine Award at the Gourmet Gala Cook-Off in Dallas.

The Mushrooms: Wash quickly, "dusting" off with a mushroom brush. Dry on paper towels. Open stem hole as much as possible by trimming with a very sharp pointed knife. This allows lots of goodies to be stuffed.

The Beans: In medium saucepan, sauté together 4 or 5 slices of bacon (cut up very small before cooking) and 2 slices from a large onion—also chopped up in small pieces. When cooked, add 1 can of Progresso black beans and 2 tablespoons of water. Stir well together, and *mash* thoroughly while beans are heating. Add 1 scant teaspoon of ground cumin seed, 1/2 teaspoon finely chopped cilantro (NO MORE!!!), 2 heaping teaspoons diced Ro-Tel with plenty of the liquid. Salt and pepper to taste. Add a dash or 2 of either Tabasco or Texas Champagne (by Jardin). Will fill 25+ mushroom caps.

The Pork: Use a 1/2-inch slice of pork tender. Cut into chunks and make ground pork by use of the trusty food processor (may I say F.P.?).

The Chicken: Being 1 of the most important parts, use the skinless, boneless breasts by *TYSON*—SO tender! Each breast will flavor 15 mushroom caps. We marinate our C.B. for an hour or so in a mixture of 1 part Kikkoman Soy sauce/4 parts Steen's Pure Ribbon Cane Syrup. Cook C.B. for 3 to 4 minutes on each side over a hot barbecue grill (top rack). This leaves C.B. about half done and soft enough to slice into "shoestring potato" size strips 3/4 to 1 inch long. You'll lay 3 or 4 of these across top of mushroom later.

The Crumb Mixture: This is about 10 Ritz crackers and a big handful of Tostito chips ground into a delightfully tasty bunch of "bread" crumbs.

The Green Chilies: They are just that. Chopped, peeled green chilies.

The Layers: Now you're creating! In your clean, raw mushroom cap, smear a light layer of the bean mixture, leaving the top still concave. Sprinkle 1/4 teaspoon of the crumb mixture over beans and lightly mash into the beans. Put *tiny* amount of green chilies over crumbs, and spread evenly over the chilies about 1/4 teaspoon of the ground pork. Place 3 or 4 of the chicken strips across the pork and top the masterpiece with as much Monterey Jack cheese as you can sprinkle into the pile (you should be about overflowing by now). The tip-top pièce de resistance is the thin slice of jalapeño, which we put on now—just before baking in a *covered* Pyrex dish for 25 to 30 minutes at 325 degrees or until the caps get tender. They are big, they are tasty, and they are filling. Don't serve more than 2 per person or your entrée could suffer neglect.

Nutritional information for this recipe is not available.

Gini and John Marston, Dallas, Texas
Dallas Women's Board

ITALIANA POTIZZAS

Yield: 12 servings	Pan Size: baking sheet	Preheat: 425 degrees

2 cups milk
4 cups water
1/2 cup butter
12 ounces instant potato
  flakes
2 ounces chopped green
  onions
1 ounce chopped garlic

12 ounces Fontina cheese,
  shredded
2 eggs, beaten
1 teaspoon salt
1 teaspoon pepper
1 cup cornmeal
3 tablespoons olive oil

Bring milk, water and butter to a boil in saucepan; remove from heat. Add potato flakes, green onions, garlic, cheese, eggs, salt and pepper; mix well. Shape into 24 pancakes 3 inches in diameter. Coat with cornmeal. Brown on both sides in olive oil in skillet. Place on baking sheet. Add favorite toppings such as pizza sauce, pesto sauce, shredded cheese, sliced pepperoni, chopped ham, sausage, mushrooms, sliced tomatoes, small shrimp, green peppers, zucchini, blanched asparagus, black olives, red pepper flakes and seasonings. Bake for 5 minutes or until heated through.

Approx Per Serving: Cal 403; Prot 14 g; Carbo 38 g; T Fat 22 g;
  Chol 95 mg; Potas 401 mg; Sod 312 mg.
  Nutritional information does not include toppings.

Andrew F. Stasio, Dallas, Texas
Texas Board of Governors, Northwood Institute

DELICIOUS DISAPPEARING SPINACH BALLS

Yield: 50 servings	Pan Size: baking sheet	Preheat: 350 degrees

2 10-ounce packages frozen
  chopped spinach, thawed
2 cups herb-seasoned
  stuffing mix
1 large onion, chopped

1/2 cup Parmesan cheese
4 eggs, beaten
3/4 cup melted margarine
1/2 teaspoon garlic salt
1/4 teaspoon pepper

Combine spinach, stuffing mix, onion, cheese, eggs, margarine, garlic salt and pepper in bowl; mix well. Chill for 1 hour to overnight. Shape into balls; place on baking sheet. Bake for 5 minutes or until light brown.

Approx Per Serving: Cal 49; Prot 2 g; Carbo 3 g; T Fat 4 g;
  Chol 18 mg; Potas 51 mg; Sod 121 mg.

Ms. Nancy J. Klein, Dallas, Texas
Bloomingdale's Corporate Gifts Department
Friend of Northwood

CHILLED CHERRY SOUP À LA BUDAPEST

Yield: 12 servings   *Pan Size: 4 quart*

2 1-inch sticks cinnamon
6 whole cloves
6 allspice
2 16-ounce cans pitted tart
   cherries
Juice from 1 16-ounce can
   pitted tart cherries

1 16-ounce can water
1 lemon slice
Salt to taste
1 tablespoon flour
1/2 cup sugar
2 cups cream
3 cups dry red wine

Tie cinnamon, cloves and allspice in cheesecloth bag. Combine with undrained cherries, cherry juice, water, lemon slice and salt in saucepan. Bring to a boil. Whisk flour and sugar into cream in small bowl. Add to cherries. Add wine. Bring to a boil, stirring constantly. Cool to room temperature. Chill until serving time. Remove spice bag. Ladle into serving bowls. Garnish with whipped cream. The recipe is from the Café Budapest in the Copley Square Hotel in Boston, Massachusetts.

Approx Per Serving: Cal 157; Prot 2 g; Carbo 18 g; T Fat 5 g;
   Chol 15 mg; Potas 193 mg; Sod 25 mg.

Cora Beard Mayne, Palm Beach, Florida
Palm Beach Women's Board

CHILLED CUCUMBER SOUP

Yield: 4 servings   *Pan Size: blender*

1 large cucumber, peeled,
   seeded, chopped
2 tablespoons chopped green
   onions
1 tablespoon margarine
2 teaspoons cornstarch

1 1/4 cups skim milk
1 teaspoon chicken-flavored
   instant bouillon
1/4 teaspoon dillweed
1/2 cup plain low-fat yogurt

Sauté cucumber and green onions in margarine in saucepan. Blend cornstarch and 1/4 cup milk in small bowl. Add cornstarch mixture, remaining 1 cup milk, bouillon and dillweed to saucepan. Cook over medium heat until thickened, stirring constantly. Pour into blender container; blend until smooth. Cool slightly. Combine with yogurt in bowl. Chill, covered, for 2 hours. Ladle into serving bowls. Garnish with cucumber slices and parsley.

Approx Per Serving: Cal 88; Prot 5 g; Carbo 10 g; T Fat 4 g;
   Chol 3 mg; Potas 362 mg; Sod 382 mg.

Mrs. Jim (Barbara) Lake, Dallas, Texas
Dallas Women's Board

GAZPACHO

Yield: 10 servings	Pan Size: large bowl

1/2 cup olive oil	2 teaspoons salt
1/4 cup lemon juice	1/4 teaspoon freshly ground
6 cups tomato juice	pepper
2 cups beef broth	2 green bell peppers, finely
1/2 cup finely minced onions	chopped
2 tomatoes, chopped	2 cucumbers, chopped
2 cups finely minced celery	1 cup croutons
1/8 teaspoon Tabasco sauce	

Beat olive oil and lemon juice in bowl until smooth. Add tomato juice, beef broth, onions, tomatoes, celery, Tabasco sauce, salt and pepper; mix well. Chill for 3 hours. Pour into soup tureen. Serve with bowls of chopped green peppers, chopped cucumbers and croutons.

Approx Per Serving: Cal 160; Prot 3 g; Carbo 14 g; T Fat 11 g; Chol 0 mg; Potas 621 mg; Sod 1178 mg.

Mrs. M.S. (Scottie) Buehler, Dallas, Texas
Distinguished Woman/Dallas Women's Board

TOMATO BOUILLON

Yield: 8 servings	Pan Size: medium saucepan

3/4 cup chopped onion	1 bay leaf
2 teaspoons butter	1/2 teaspoon oregano
1/2 cup chopped celery with	1/4 teaspoon seasoned salt
leaves	1/4 teaspoon pepper
1 48-ounce can tomato juice	

Sauté onion in butter in saucepan for 3 to 5 minutes. Add celery, tomato juice, bay leaf, oregano, seasoned salt and pepper; mix well. Bring to a boil; reduce heat. Simmer for 15 to 20 minutes, or to desired consistency, stirring occasionally. Strain into bowl. Serve hot or chilled.

Approx Per Serving: Cal 44; Prot 2 g; Carbo 9 g; T Fat 1 g; Chol 3 mg; Potas 419 mg; Sod 696 mg.

Mrs. William W. (Margot) Winspear, Dallas, Texas
Dallas Women's Board

CREAM OF PARSLEY SOUP

Yield: 2 servings   *Pan Size: small saucepan*

3/4 cup fresh parsley leaves
1 tablespoon butter
1/2 cup grated potato
2 teaspoons fresh chervil or
    1/2 teaspoon dried chervil
1 cup chicken broth

3/4 cup half and half
1/8 teaspoon freshly grated
    nutmeg
Salt and freshly ground
    white pepper to taste

Sauté parsley in butter in heavy saucepan over medium-low heat for 5 minutes or until wilted. Add potato, chervil and chicken broth. Increase heat. Bring soup to a boil; reduce heat. Simmer for 20 minutes. Cool to room temperature. Pour into blender container; process until smooth. Add half and half, nutmeg, salt and white pepper. Reheat over low heat. Ladle into bowls. Garnish with additional sprigs of parsley. Serve immediately with sour cream. May serve chilled if preferred.

Approx Per Serving: Cal 251; Prot 7 g; Carbo 19 g; T Fat 17 g;
    Chol 49 mg; Potas 556 mg; Sod 486 mg.

Mrs. Jack S. (Gretchen) Josey, Houston, Texas
Chairman, Houston Women's Board/Distinguished Woman

VICHYSSOISE

Yield: 2 servings   *Pan Size: medium bowl*

1 teaspoon instant chicken
    bouillon
1 cup warm water

1 cup buttermilk
Pepper to taste
2 teaspoons chopped chives

Dissolve bouillon in warm water in bowl. Add buttermilk and pepper. Chill until serving time. Ladle into soup bowls. Top with chives. My mother learned to put together lovely low-cost meals during the Great Depression and I inherited that zeal from her.

Approx Per Serving: Cal 54; Prot 4 g; Carbo 6 g; T Fat 1 g;
    Chol 5 mg; Potas 282 mg; Sod 704 mg.

Phyllis Diller, Los Angeles, California
Achievement in the Arts Awardee

MULLED CIDER

Yield: 20 servings	Pan Size: large saucepan

1 gallon apple cider	1/4 cup honey
2 oranges, sliced	2 sticks cinnamon
1 lemon, thinly sliced	12 whole cloves
4 maraschino cherries, chopped	6 whole allspice

Combine apple cider, oranges, lemon, cherries, honey, cinnamon, cloves and allspice in saucepan. Simmer for 45 minutes. Strain into mugs. May add 1 quart orange juice and 2 tablespoons lemon juice if desired.

Approx Per Serving: Cal 101; Prot 0 g; Carbo 25 g; T Fat 0 g; Chol 0 mg; Potas 273 mg; Sod 6 mg.

Nancy Barker, Midland, Michigan
Northwood Vice President/Distinguished Woman

WOMEN'S BOARD HOT ALMOND TEA

Yield: 90 servings	Pan Size: 3 gallon

12 cups water	Juice of 15 lemons
18 tea bags	2 tablespoons vanilla extract
6 cups sugar	6 tablespoons almond extract
24 cups water	

Bring 12 cups water to a boil in saucepan. Add tea bags; steep for 10 minutes. Bring sugar and 24 cups water to a boil in saucepan. Boil for 5 minutes. Combine with tea, lemon juice, vanilla and almond extract in large container; mix well. Store in refrigerator. Reheat to serve. This tea is very popular at Women's Board meetings.

Approx Per Serving: Cal 53; Prot 0 g; Carbo 14 g; T Fat 0 g; Chol 0 mg; Potas 10 mg; Sod 0 mg.

Northwood Cookbook Committee, Dallas, Texas

PERCOLATOR PUNCH

Yield: 8 servings   *Pan Size: 8-cup percolator*

2¼ cups pineapple juice
2 cups cranberry juice
1¾ cups water
1 tablespoon whole cloves

½ cup packed light brown
  sugar
½ teaspoon allspice
3 cinnamon sticks, broken

Combine pineapple juice, cranberry juice and water in bottom of percolator. Combine cloves, brown sugar, allspice and cinnamon in basket of percolator. Perk for 10 minutes. Serve hot.

Approx Per Serving: Cal 127; Prot 0 g; Carbo 32 g; T Fat 0 g;
  Chol 0 mg; Potas 153 mg; Sod 8 mg.

Donna Curry Miller, Waxahachie, Texas
Northwood External Affairs Assistant, Dallas, Texas

HOMEMADE KAHLUA

Yield: 32 servings   *Pan Size: 5 quart*

2 cups sugar
1 vanilla bean, split
  lengthwise

2 cups water
⅓ cup instant coffee
1 fifth 100 proof vodka

Bring sugar, vanilla bean and water to a boil in saucepan over high heat. Cook for 30 minutes; reduce heat to low. Stir in coffee and vodka. Simmer for 15 minutes; do not boil. Pour into bottles. Store in cool dark place for 30 days before serving, shaking occasionally. Store indefinitely. We make this at Halloween and it is just right for gift giving at Christmas.

Approx Per Serving: Cal 99; Prot 0 g; Carbo 13 g; T Fat 0 g;
  Chol 0 mg; Potas 22 mg; Sod 1 mg.

Mrs. Rick (Lori) Bregger, Grapevine, Texas
Northwood Alumna/Cedar Hill Women's Board

IRISH CREAM

Yield: 20 servings   *Pan Size: blender*

1³/4 cups Irish whiskey
1 14-ounce can sweetened
   condensed milk
1 cup whipping cream
4 eggs

2 tablespoons chocolate syrup
2 teaspoons instant coffee
1 teaspoon vanilla extract
¹/2 teaspoon almond extract

Combine all ingredients in blender container. Process until smooth. Store in airtight container in refrigerator for up to 1 month.

Approx Per Serving: Cal 169; Prot 3 g; Carbo 12 g; T Fat 7 g;
    Chol 66 mg; Potas 105 mg; Sod 45 mg.

Sandy Flanery, Cedar Hill, Texas
Cedar Hill Women's Board

VENETIAN PEACH BELLINIS

Yield: 8 servings   *Pan Size: blender*

4 cups chopped fresh peaches
1 cup sugar

Juice of 1 lemon
4 cups chilled champagne

Sprinkle peaches with sugar and lemon juice. Let stand until sugar dissolves. Process in blender until smooth. Chill in refrigerator. Fill champagne flutes half full with purée. Add chilled champagne.

Approx Per Serving: Cal 225; Prot 1 g; Carbo 37 g; T Fat 0 g;
    Chol 0 mg; Potas 270 mg; Sod 8 mg.

Mrs. R.H. (Beverly) Holmes, Dallas, Texas
Chairman, Dallas Women's Board

SIMPLY DIVINE SANGRIA

Yield: 15 servings   *Pan Size: punch bowl*

1 gallon red wine
¹/2 cup Brandy
1 quart orange juice
1 cup lemon juice

2 oranges, sliced
2 limes, sliced
1 quart club soda

Combine first 4 ingredients in punch bowl. Add half the fruit. Chill for 1 hour. Replace fruit. Add club soda.

Approx Per Serving: Cal 244; Prot 1 g; Carbo 19 g; T Fat 0 g;
    Chol 0 mg; Potas 473 mg; Sod 15 mg.

Mrs. David M. (Natalie) Taylor, Dallas, Texas
Dallas Women's Board

RASPBERRY BUTTER

Yield: 64 servings   *Pan Size: medium bowl*

1 cup butter, softened
2 cups confectioners' sugar

1 10-ounce package frozen
   raspberries, thawed

Cream butter and confectioners' sugar in mixer bowl until light and fluffy. Add raspberries; mix well. Store in refrigerator.

Approx Per Serving: Cal 42; Prot 0 g; Carbo 4 g; T Fat 3 g;
    Chol 8 mg; Potas 6 mg; Sod 24 mg.

Ms. Gwen Pharo, Dallas, Texas
Dallas Women's Board

PORT WINE JELLY FOR DUCK OR GAME

Yield: 80 servings   *Pan Size: double boiler*

3 cups Port
3 cups sugar

1/2 teaspoon rosemary
6 tablespoons liquid pectin

Combine wine, sugar and rosemary in double boiler. Cook over boiling water for 2 minutes, stirring constantly; remove from heat. Strain through cheesecloth into bowl. Stir in pectin. Pour into hot sterilized jars, leaving 1/2-inch headspace; seal with 2-piece lids.

Approx Per Serving: Cal 35; Prot 0 g; Carbo 8 g; T Fat 0 g;
    Chol 0 mg; Potas 10 mg; Sod 1 mg.

Mrs. Robert H. (Beverly) Holmes, Dallas, Texas
Chairman, Dallas Women's Board

TEXAS PEPPER JELLY

Yield: 96 servings   *Pan Size: 3 quart*

1/2 cup chopped jalapeño
   peppers
1/2 cup chopped green bell
   peppers

1 cup cider vinegar
6 cups sugar
1 bottle of liquid pectin
Green food coloring

Combine peppers, vinegar and sugar in saucepan. Bring to a rolling boil, stirring occasionally. Boil for 3 minutes; remove from heat. Cool for 5 to 10 minutes. Stir in pectin. Boil for 1 minute longer. Add food coloring. Strain into hot sterilized jars, leaving 1/2-inch headspace; seal with 2-piece lids. Serve over cream cheese with water biscuits or wheat crackers.

Approx Per Serving: Cal 49; Prot 0 g; Carbo 13 g; T Fat 0 g;
    Chol 0 mg; Potas 5 mg; Sod 0 mg.

Northwood Cookbook Committee, Dallas, Texas

HOT MUSTARD

Yield: 32 servings   *Pan Size: double boiler*

1 cup dry mustard
1 cup vinegar

2 eggs, beaten
1 cup sugar

Blend dry mustard and vinegar in bowl; let stand overnight. Combine with eggs and sugar in double boiler. Cook over hot water for 45 minutes or until thickened, stirring frequently. Store in refrigerator. Use to glaze baked ham or on sandwiches.

Approx Per Serving: Cal 30; Prot 0 g; Carbo 7 g; T Fat 0 g; Chol 13 mg; Potas 12 mg; Sod 5 mg.

Lynn O'Brien, Dallas, Texas
Dallas Women's Board

HORSERADISH CREAM SAUCE

Yield: 32 servings   *Pan Size: medium bowl*

1 cup whipping cream
1 teaspoon salt

¹⁄₄ cup prepared horseradish

Beat whipping cream with salt in mixer bowl until soft peaks form. Fold in horseradish gently. Serve with sliced beef tenderloin on cocktail breads.

Approx Per Serving: Cal 26; Prot 0 g; Carbo 0 g; T Fat 3 g; Chol 10 mg; Potas 11 mg; Sod 71 mg.

Mrs. John (Ginny) Eulich, Dallas, Texas
Dallas Women's Board

TEXAS JEZEBEL SAUCE

Yield: 64 servings   *Pan Size: blender*

1 18-ounce jar orange
marmalade
1 18-ounce jar apple jelly
2 ounces dry mustard

1 4-ounce jar creamed
horseradish
1 jalapeño pepper, seeded
Cracked pepper to taste

Combine all ingredients in blender. Blend until smooth. Store in glass container in refrigerator. Serve with broiled chicken, ham, pork or game; spread generous amount on cream cheese or Neufchâtel cheese and serve with Melba rounds. May substitute pineapple preserves for marmalade if preferred.

Approx Per Serving: Cal 43; Prot 0 g; Carbo 11 g; T Fat 0 g; Chol 0 mg; Potas 64 mg; Sod 5 mg.

Ms. Jan Greene, Dallas, Texas
Dallas Women's Board

Salads

& Salad Dressings

Church Family Administration Building
Midland, Michigan

FRUIT SALAD

Yield: 12 servings   *Pan Size: large glass bowl*

2 teaspoons (heaping) sugar	2 cups fresh chopped pears
2 egg yolks	2 cups chopped apples
2 teaspoons cornstarch	2 cups sliced bananas
1 teaspoon dry mustard	2 cups fresh chopped peaches
1/4 teaspoon salt	2 cups whipping cream,
1/4 cup vinegar	whipped
1 cup milk	2 cups miniature
2 cups fresh pineapple	marshmallows
chunks	1 cup chopped pecans

Blend sugar and egg yolks in medium saucepan. Add cornstarch, mustard and salt; mix well. Stir in vinegar and milk. Bring just to the boiling point over low heat, stirring constantly; remove from heat. Cool completely. Alternate layers of fruit, dressing, whipped cream, marshmallows and pecans in bowl until all ingredients are used. Chill until serving time.

Approx Per Serving: Cal 267; Prot 3 g; Carbo 32 g; T Fat 16 g;
    Chol 65 mg; Potas 329 mg; Sod 71 mg.

Rosabel Chandler, Houston, Texas
Houston Women's Board

HONEYDEW MELON SALAD

Yield: 2 servings   *Pan Size: salad plates*

1/3 honeydew melon, chilled	2 teaspoons chopped fresh
3/4 cup plain yogurt	mint
1 tablespoon honey	2 tablespoons chopped
1 1/2 teaspoons fresh lime juice	walnuts
4 fresh figs	

Cut melon into 2 slices; remove and discard rind and seed. Place on lettuce-lined plates. Combine yogurt, honey, lime juice, figs, mint and walnuts in small bowl; mix well. Spoon along edges of melon slices. Chill until serving time. Garnish each melon slice with fresh mint leaves and whole strawberry.

Approx Per Serving: Cal 284; Prot 7 g; Carbo 55 g; T Fat 6 g;
    Chol 5 mg; Potas 1061 mg; Sod 85 mg.

Ruth Van Otteren, Palm Beach, Florida
Palm Beach Women's Board

MANGO MOUSSE

Yield: 8 servings   *Pan Size: 1¹/₂ quart mold*

1 15-ounce can mangos
8 ounces cream cheese,
  softened
2 3-ounce packages orange
  gelatin

1 3-ounce package lemon
  gelatin
2 cups boiling water

Combine mangos and cream cheese in blender container. Process until smooth. Dissolve orange and lemon gelatins in boiling water in bowl. Add mango and cream cheese mixture; mix well. Pour into mold. Chill until firm. Unmold onto serving plate. Garnish center with strawberries or top with curried mayonnaise.

Approx Per Serving: Cal 252; Prot 5 g; Carbo 38 g; T Fat 10 g;
    Chol 31 mg; Potas 117 mg; Sod 186 mg.

Mrs. Cam (Evelyn) Dowell, Jr., Dallas, Texas
Dallas Women's Board

PASSION FRUIT CUP

Yield: 2 servings   *Pan Size: salad bowl*

1 large kiwifruit
1 small banana
2 ripe passion fruit
1 tablespoon honey

1 teaspoon lime juice
1 cup seedless red grape
  halves

Peel kiwifruit. Cut into halves lengthwise; slice into semicircles. Slice banana diagonally into thin slices. Cut tops from passion fruit; scoop out and reserve pulp. Combine passion fruit pulp, honey and lime juice in bowl; mix well. Add kiwifruit, banana and grape halves; toss gently.

Approx Per Serving: Cal 183; Prot 2 g; Carbo 46 g; T Fat 1 g;
    Chol 0 mg; Potas 571 mg; Sod 10 mg.

Elizabeth Collinson, Ft. Lauderdale, Florida
Ft. Lauderdale Women's Board

PORTOFINO MOLD

Yield: 12 servings   *Pan Size: 2 quart*

2 3-ounce packages raspberry gelatin	1 16-ounce can whole cranberry sauce
1/4 cup boiling water	1 cup chopped pecans
1 20-ounce can crushed pineapple	8 ounces cream cheese, softened
3/4 cup Port wine	1 cup sour cream

Dissolve gelatin in boiling water in medium bowl. Stir in pineapple, wine and cranberry sauce. Chill until partially set. Fold in pecans. Spoon into rectangular dish. Chill until firm. Blend cream cheese and sour cream in small bowl. Spread over gelatin mixture. Serve on lettuce-lined salad plates.

Approx Per Serving: Cal 330; Prot 4 g; Carbo 40 g; T Fat 17 g;
     Chol 29 mg; Potas 164 mg; Sod 124 mg.

Mrs. W. W. (Jane H.) Browning, Jr., Dallas, Texas
Dallas Women's Board

BEV'S STRAWBERRY GELATIN SALAD

Yield: 9 servings   *Pan Size: 8x8 inch*

2 3-ounce packages strawberry gelatin	2 10-ounce packages frozen strawberries
3 cups boiling water	1 cup sour cream
2 bananas, mashed	1/2 cup chopped pecans

Dissolve gelatin in boiling water in bowl. Stir in bananas and frozen strawberries. Spoon half the gelatin mixture into glass dish. Chill until set. Spread with mixture of sour cream and pecans; pour remaining half gelatin mixture over top. Chill until firm. Cut into squares; serve on lettuce leaves. Best when prepared a day ahead of serving. I serve this at Thanksgiving and Christmas because my family prefers it to cranberry sauce.

Approx Per Serving: Cal 214; Prot 4 g; Carbo 31 g; T Fat 10 g;
     Chol 11 mg; Potas 256 mg; Sod 75 mg.

Mrs. Robert H. (Beverly) Holmes, Dallas, Texas
Dallas Women's Board Chairman

CHICKEN ARTICHOKE SALAD

Yield: 8 servings   *Pan Size: large salad bowl*

5 whole chicken breasts
1 clove of garlic
Thyme and basil to taste
1 5-ounce package
   Rice-A-Roni
2 9-ounce jars marinated
   artichoke hearts

1 16-ounce can pitted black
   olives, sliced
4 green onions, chopped
1/2 cup (or more) mayonnaise
Lemon juice to taste

Combine chicken, garlic, thyme and basil in water to cover in large saucepan. Cook until tender, stirring frequently. Remove from heat; cool in broth. Bone chicken; cut into chunks. Chill in refrigerator. Prepare Rice-A-Roni using package directions; drain and fluff. Drain artichoke hearts, reserving liquid. Add artichoke hearts, olives and onions to rice; mix well. Combine reserved artichoke liquid with enough mayonnaise to make of desired consistency in small bowl; mix well. Stir in lemon juice. Pour over chicken; toss lightly. Chill rice and chicken mixture for several hours to overnight. Combine in serving bowl just before serving.

Approx Per Serving: Cal 445; Prot 28 g; Carbo 21 g; T Fat 31 g;
     Chol 69 mg; Potas 470 mg; Sod 1145 mg.

Kimula S. Holmes, Dallas, Texas
Dallas Women's Board

CHICKEN CURRY SALAD

Yield: 8 servings   *Pan Size: skillet*

1 5-ounce package
   Rice-A-Roni fried rice
4 chicken breasts, cooked,
   chopped
1 9-ounce jar marinated
   artichoke hearts, chopped
5 green onions, chopped
1 4-ounce can sliced black
   olives

1 4-ounce jar stuffed green
   olives
1/2 teaspoon garlic powder
1/2 teaspoon curry powder
1/4 teaspoon dry mustard
1/3 cup mayonnaise-type
   salad dressing
1/4 cup slivered almonds

Prepare Rice-A-Roni using package directions. Add chicken; mix well. Add artichoke hearts, onions, olives, garlic powder, curry powder and mustard; toss lightly. Fold in salad dressing. Sprinkle with almonds. Serve warm or cold. Store in refrigerator.

Approx Per Serving: Cal 300; Prot 23 g; Carbo 20 g; T Fat 15 g;
     Chol 52 mg; Potas 367 mg; Sod 972 mg.

Ms. Nancy J. Klein, Dallas, Texas
Friend, Bloomingdale's Corporate Gifts Department

GRAPE AND CHICKEN SALAD

Yield: 4 servings   *Pan Size: salad bowl*

2 cups cooked macaroni	1 cup buttermilk
2 cups sliced cooked chicken	1/4 teaspoon dillweed
1 1/2 cups seedless green grapes	Onion powder and garlic powder to taste
1/2 cup chopped celery	1/2 teaspoon soy sauce

Combine macaroni, chicken, grapes and celery in bowl; mix well. Mix buttermilk, dillweed, onion powder, garlic powder, and soy sauce in small bowl. Pour over chicken mixture; toss lightly.

Approx Per Serving: Cal 298; Prot 26 g; Carbo 34 g; T Fat 6 g;
    Chol 65 mg; Potas 455 mg; Sod 182 mg.

Mrs. Bert (Lucille) Robertson, Dallas, Texas
Dallas Women's Board

SALAD VALENTINO

Yield: 6 servings   *Pan Size: salad plates*

1 small head radicchio	Whites of 2 hard-boiled eggs, chopped
1 small head Bibb lettuce	2 tablespoons water
1 small head Boston lettuce	1 teaspoon Dijon mustard
8 ounces thinly sliced prosciutto	1/4 cup (or more) olive oil
1/4 cup butter	Salt and pepper to taste
3 tablespoons red wine vinegar	2 tablespoons minced flat leaf parsley

Rinse radicchio and lettuce; pat dry. Tear into pieces; place on salad plates. Cut prosciutto into julienne strips. Heat butter in skillet until brown and bubbly. Add prosciutto. Sauté for 2 minutes. Add vinegar. Cook until vinegar evaporates. Combine egg whites, water, mustard, olive oil and salt and pepper in small bowl; mix well. Sprinkle prosciutto over salad greens; spoon dressing over top. Sprinkle with parsley.

Nutritional information for this recipe is not available.

Mrs. W. W. (Jane H.) Browning, Jr., Dallas, Texas
Dallas Women's Board

CRAB AND AVOCADO SALAD

Yield: 4 servings   *Pan Size: large salad plate*

Red lettuce leaves
2 avocados, pitted, peeled,
  cut into wedges
2 tomatoes, peeled, cut into
  wedges
12 ounces black-fin crab meat

1 cup mayonnaise
2 tablespoons lemon juice
1 tablespoon horseradish
1 tablespoon Worcestershire
  sauce
1 tablespoon chili sauce

Arrange lettuce leaves on plate. Arrange avocado and tomato wedges in fan pattern over lettuce. Cover bases of fans with crab meat. Blend mayonnaise, lemon juice, horseradish, Worcestershire sauce and chili sauce in small bowl. Pour over salad. Garnish with lemon wedges and chives. May add capers and minced red onion.

Approx Per Serving: Cal 663; Prot 21 g; Carbo 14 g; T Fat 60 g;
    Chol 108 mg; Potas 1133 mg; Sod 709 mg.

Mardi Schma, Dallas, Texas
Owner of City Cafe/Distinguished Woman

SALADE DE SEPTEMBRE (SEPTEMBER SALAD)

Yield: 4 servings   *Pan Size: skillet*

1 pound sea scallops
2 tablespoons salad oil
Sherry to taste
Salt and pepper to taste
1 cup broccoli flowerets
1/2 cup finely chopped
  cucumber

1/2 cup finely chopped
  tomatoes
1 large carrot, grated
1/2 cup finely chopped onion
1 teaspoon dillweed
1/2 cup Italian salad dressing

Wash scallops thoroughly; drain and pat dry. Heat oil in medium skillet; add scallops. Sauté for 5 to 10 minutes or until cooked through. Add Sherry and salt and pepper; mix well. Drain; place on plate. Chill in refrigerator. Place broccoli in glass dish. Microwave for 1 minute and 15 seconds. Combine broccoli, cucumber, tomatoes, carrot and onion in salad bowl; toss lightly. Add dillweed, salad dressing and salt and pepper; toss lightly. Chill for 1 hour, tossing frequently. Stir in scallops just before serving. Serve on lettuce-lined salad plates. Garnish with minced parsley. This nutritious yet delicate salad is delicious for lunch or a light supper on a hot September day.

Approx Per Serving: Cal 326; Prot 21 g; Carbo 12 g; T Fat 26 g;
    Chol 37 mg; Potas 619 mg; Sod 341 mg.

Mrs. Robert R. (Carine) Blair, Dallas, Texas
Dallas Women's Board

FRENCH QUARTER SHRIMP SALAD

Yield: 4 servings *Pan Size: large salad plate*

1 cup mayonnaise
1/2 cup chopped green onions
1/2 cup chopped parsley
2 tablespoons lemon juice
1/4 teaspoon salt

1 tomato, cut into wedges
1 avocado, cut into wedges
1 pound cooked shelled
shrimp

Combine mayonnaise, green onions, parsley, lemon juice and salt in bowl; mix well. Chill, covered, for 2 hours or longer. Alternate wedges of tomato and avocado around outer edge of lettuce-lined plate. Arrange shrimp in center. Serve with chilled dressing.

Approx Per Serving: Cal 601; Prot 26 g; Carbo 8 g; T Fat 53 g;
Chol 254 mg; Potas 672 mg; Sod 711 mg.

Mrs. M. S. (Scottie) Buehler, Dallas, Texas
Dallas Women's Board/Distinguished Woman

SPICY MACARONI SALAD

Yield: 8 servings *Pan Size: glass bowl*

1 12-ounce package salad
macaroni
1 medium onion, chopped
1 cup chopped celery
1 cup shredded Cheddar
cheese
1 2-ounce jar chopped
pimento

6 sweet pickles, chopped
10 black olives, chopped
Salt and pepper to taste
1/2 cup picante sauce
1 teaspoon chili powder
2 tablespoons (or more)
mayonnaise

Prepare macaroni using package directions; rinse and drain. Combine macaroni, onion, celery, cheese, pimento, pickles, olives, salt and pepper, picante sauce and chili powder in bowl; mix well. Stir in mayonnaise. Chill for several hours before serving.

Approx Per Serving: Cal 281; Prot 10 g; Carbo 40 g; T Fat 9 g;
Chol 17 mg; Potas 234 mg; Sod 326 mg.

Mrs. Alphonso (Tricia) Ragland III, Dallas, Texas
Dallas Women's Board

PASTA SALAD

Yield: 8 servings   Pan Size: large salad bowl

1 pound rotini	1 cup cubed Monterey Jack
1 cup Italian salad dressing	cheese
¼ cup chopped green bell	¼ cup chopped parsley
pepper	2 tablespoons chopped basil
1 2-ounce jar pimentos	1 tablespoon chopped
½ cup sliced green onions	oregano
1 cup cubed salami	1 4-ounce can sliced
1 2-ounce can sliced black	mushrooms
olives	1 pint cherry tomatoes

Cook rotini *al dente* according to package directions; drain. Place in bowl. Add salad dressing; mix well. Chill until cool. Add green bell pepper, pimentos, green onions, salami, olives, cheese, parsley, basil, oregano, mushrooms and tomatoes; toss lightly. Chill, tightly covered, for 6 hours or longer. Serve on lettuce-lined salad plates with breadsticks and red wine.

Approx Per Serving: Cal 464; Prot 14 g; Carbo 50 g; T Fat 27 g;
    Chol 22 mg; Potas 314 mg; Sod 490 mg.

Mrs. Chet (Eunice) Bonar, Dallas, Texas
Dallas Women's Board

SUMMER VERMICELLI SALAD

Yield: 18 servings   Pan Size: 3 quart

1 12-ounce package	8 ounces baby Swiss cheese,
vermicelli	shredded
¼ cup olive oil	5 stalks celery, finely chopped
Juice of 1 lemon	⅔ cup finely chopped salad
1 bunch green onions, finely	olives with pimentos
chopped	½ cup mayonnaise
8 ounces sharp Cheddar	Salt and pepper to taste
cheese, shredded	

Break vermicelli into 3 to 4-inch pieces. Cook according to package directions; rinse and drain. Add olive oil and lemon juice; toss lightly. Chill overnight. Combine vermicelli, onions, cheeses, celery and olives in bowl; toss to mix. Stir in mayonnaise and salt and pepper. Chill for several hours before serving.

Approx Per Serving: Cal 202; Prot 9 g; Carbo 16 g; T Fat 11 g;
    Chol 25 mg; Potas 119 mg; Sod 199 mg.

Mrs. Jess R. (Beth) Moore, Houston, Texas
National Director, Northwood Institute National Costume Collection

CURRY RICE SALAD

Yield: 6 servings   *Pan Size: skillet*

1 5-ounce package chicken-flavored Rice-A-Roni	2 9-ounce jars marinated artichokes
1½ teaspoons curry powder	½ cup mayonnaise

Prepare Rice-A-Roni according to package directions adding curry powder. Drain 1 jar artichokes. Combine Rice-A-Roni and drained and undrained artichokes in bowl; mix well. Stir in mayonnaise. Chill until serving time.

Approx Per Serving: Cal 309; Prot 4 g; Carbo 25 g; T Fat 23 g; Chol 11 mg; Potas 226 mg; Sod 863 mg.

Mrs. Nicholas (Doris) Bonvino, Dallas, Texas
Dallas Women's Board

TABOULI SALAD

Yield: 4 servings   *Pan Size: salad bowl*

¾ cup medium cracked wheat	½ cup finely chopped scallions
¼ cup minced onion	2½ cups chopped tomatoes
1 tablespoon allspice	½ cup chopped fresh mint
1 tablespoon salt	½ cup lemon juice
1 tablespoon pepper	½ cup olive oil
2 cups finely chopped parsley	

Soak cracked wheat in cold water in small bowl for 20 minutes; drain well. Combine onion, allspice, salt and pepper in small bowl; mix well. Combine parsley, scallions, tomatoes and mint in large bowl; mix well. Fold in cracked wheat and seasoned onions. Stir in lemon juice and olive oil. Line salad bowl with small romaine lettuce leaves. Spoon cracked wheat mixture into prepared bowl. Use lettuce leaves to "scoop" up salad. This Lebanese salad is the ultimate in taste and nourishment.

Approx Per Serving: Cal 339; Prot 4 g; Carbo 23 g; T Fat 28 g; Chol 0 mg; Potas 540 mg; Sod 1622 mg.

Mrs. Robert (Millie) Hamady, Flint, Michigan
Distinguished Woman

MARINATED ANTIPASTO

Yield: 8 servings   *Pan Size: salad bowl*

1¹/₃ cups white vinegar
1¹/₃ cups oil
¹/₂ cup minced onion
2 teaspoons Italian seasoning
2 teaspoons salt
2 teaspoons sugar
¹/₂ teaspoon minced garlic
¹/₄ teaspoon pepper

2 4-ounce jars mushrooms
2 9-ounce jars artichoke
   hearts
2 16-ounce cans sliced
   carrots
2 tablespoons chopped
   pimentos

Combine vinegar, oil, onion, Italian seasoning, salt, sugar, garlic and pepper in saucepan. Bring to a boil, stirring constantly. Remove from heat; cool slightly. Drain mushrooms, artichoke hearts, carrots and pimentos; place in bowl. Pour vinegar mixture over vegetables; mix well. Chill for 12 hours or longer. A great accompaniment with hot or cold entrées.

Approx Per Serving: Cal 429; Prot 3 g; Carbo 17 g; T Fat 42 g;
    Chol 0 mg; Potas 461 mg; Sod 1265 mg.

Margie August, Dallas, Texas
Dallas Women's Board/Northwood Arts Programs Special Projects Director

SWEET CASHEW SALAD

Yield: 12 servings   *Pan Size: blender*

1 small onion, chopped
²/₃ cup sugar
1 teaspoon celery seed
1 teaspoon salt
¹/₂ teaspoon pepper
2 teaspoons (heaping) dry
   mustard
¹/₄ cup tarragon vinegar

1 cup olive oil
1 head (or more) lettuce
Assorted salad greens
1 pound bacon, crisp-fried,
   crumbled
³/₄ cup sliced mushrooms
12 ounces cashews

Combine onion, sugar, celery seed, salt, pepper, mustard, vinegar and oil in blender container. Process until blended. Tear lettuce and salad greens into bite-sized pieces; place in salad bowl. Add bacon, mushrooms and cashews; toss lightly. Pour dressing over top just before serving.

Approx Per Serving: Cal 590; Prot 17 g; Carbo 21 g; T Fat 50 g;
    Chol 32 mg; Potas 402 mg; Sod 961 mg.

Denise McDonald, Saginaw, Michigan
Saginaw/Bay City Women's Board

CHARLEMAGNE SALAD WITH HOT BRIE DRESSING

Yield: 8 servings   *Pan Size: skillet*

1 medium head curly endive	2 teaspoons minced garlic
1 medium head iceberg	½ cup Sherry vinegar
lettuce	2 tablespoons lemon juice
1 medium head romaine	4 teaspoons Dijon mustard
lettuce	10 ounces ripe Brie, softened,
2 cups garlic croutons	cut into small pieces
½ cup olive oil	Pepper to taste
4 teaspoons minced shallots	

Tear endive, iceberg and romaine lettuce into bite-sized pieces; place in large salad bowl. Toss with desired amount of garlic croutons. Warm olive oil in large heavy skillet over low heat for 10 minutes. Add shallots and garlic. Cook for 5 minutes or until translucent, stirring occasionally. Stir in vinegar, lemon juice and mustard. Add cheese; stir until melted. Season with pepper. Pour hot dressing over lettuce; toss lightly. This delicious salad is served at Charlemagne Restaurant in Aspen, Colorado, and is considered their specialty.

Approx Per Serving: Cal 281; Prot 9 g; Carbo 9 g; T Fat 24 g;
   Chol 35 mg; Potas 257 mg; Sod 362 mg.

Mrs. Don (Carol) Donnally, Dallas, Texas
Dallas Women's Board

JO'S SLAW

Yield: 8 servings   *Pan Size: salad bowl*

1 head cabbage, shredded	1 teaspoon salt
1 green bell pepper, sliced	1 tablespoon sugar
into rings	1½ teaspoons celery seed
1 onion, sliced in rings	1 cup oil
1 cup vinegar	¾ cup sugar

Combine cabbage, green pepper and onion in large bowl; toss lightly. Combine vinegar, salt, 1 tablespoon sugar and celery seed in saucepan. Bring just to the boiling point, stirring constantly; remove from heat. Stir in oil and remaining ¾ cup sugar. Pour over vegetables. Marinate overnight in refrigerator. Drain before serving. May store in refrigerator for up to 1 week. My cousin Jo brought this slaw to a family graveyard cleaning.

Approx Per Serving: Cal 340; Prot 1 g; Carbo 26 g; T Fat 27 g;
   Chol 0 mg; Potas 173 mg; Sod 274 mg.

Mrs. Jack M. (Mary Jane) Sanders, Sr., Marshall, Texas
Friend of Northwood

SUMMER SALAD

Yield: 16 servings	Pan Size: glass bowl

1¹/₂ pounds broccoli, cut into small flowerets
Flowerets of 1 head cauliflower
1 small zucchini, sliced
2 pints cherry tomatoes, trimmed
¹/₂ pound mushrooms, halved
2 bunches green onions, chopped
2 8-ounce cans sliced water chestnuts, drained
1 cup chopped celery
1 6-ounce can pitted black olives, drained
2 cups chopped Swiss cheese
2 cups mayonnaise
2 tablespoons horseradish
2 tablespoons lemon juice
2 tablespoons tarragon vinegar
1 tablespoon dry mustard
2 cloves of garlic, minced
Salt to taste

Combine broccoli, cauliflower, zucchini, cherry tomatoes, mushrooms, onions, water chestnuts, celery, olives and cheese in large bowl. Combine mayonnaise, horseradish, lemon juice, vinegar, mustard, garlic and salt in bowl; mix well. Pour over vegetable mixture; toss lightly. Garnish with sprinkle of chopped parsley just before serving. May substitute Fontina cheese for Swiss cheese.

Approx Per Serving: Cal 317; Prot 7 g; Carbo 12 g; T Fat 24 g; Chol 27 mg; Potas 475 mg; Sod 297 mg.

Mrs. W. W. (Jane H.) Browning, Jr., Dallas, Texas
Dallas Women's Board

GREAT CAESAR SALAD DRESSING

Yield: 32 servings	Pan Size: blender

1 2-ounce can anchovies, drained, rinsed
1 egg
³/₄ cup olive oil
¹/₄ cup red wine vinegar
¹/₂ cup Parmesan cheese
3 cloves of garlic

Combine anchovies, egg, olive oil, vinegar, Parmesan cheese and garlic in blender container. Process until blended. Serve over salad greens. May store in refrigerator for up to 1 week. This recipe comes from my friend's grandmother who lives in Milano, Italy.

Approx Per Serving: Cal 56; Prot 1 g; Carbo 0 g; T Fat 6 g; Chol 9 mg; Potas 13 mg; Sod 28 mg.

Audrey S. Weinberg, Detroit, Michigan
Chairman, Detroit Women's Board

HONEY DRESSING

Yield: 1 recipe   *Pan Size: mixer bowl*

3 to 3½ parts mayonnaise
1 part raw honey
Finely minced fresh garlic to
   taste
Finely chopped fresh shallots
   to taste
Finely chopped fresh onions
   to taste
Finely chopped fresh parsley

Finely chopped fresh scallion
   greens
Apple cider vinegar to taste
Mustard to taste
Dry mustard to taste
Lawry's seasoned salt to taste
White pepper to taste
2½ parts delicate vegetable
   oil

Combine mayonnaise, honey, garlic, shallots, onions, parsley, scallion greens, vinegar, mustard, dry mustard, seasoned salt and pepper in mixer bowl; mix well. Adjust seasonings to taste. Add oil in fine stream, beating constantly until blended. Chill thoroughly before serving.

Nutritional information for this recipe is not available.

Phyllis Diller

Phyllis Diller, Los Angeles, California
Achievement in the Arts Awardee

POPPY SEED DRESSING

Yield: 48 servings   *Pan Size: mixer bowl*

1 cup sugar
2 teaspoons dry mustard
1 teaspoon salt
⅔ cup cider vinegar

2 teaspoons onion juice
2 cups oil
1 tablespoon poppy seed

Combine sugar, mustard, salt, vinegar and onion juice in bowl; mix well. Add oil in fine stream, beating constantly with wire whisk until blended. Stir in poppy seed. Store in airtight container in refrigerator. Serve over fresh fruit or fruit salad.

Approx Per Serving: Cal 97; Prot 0 g; Carbo 4 g; T Fat 9 g;
     Chol 0 mg; Potas 4 mg; Sod 45 mg.

David Wilson, Dallas, Texas
Friend of Northwood, Old Spaghetti Warehouse

Main Dishes,
Soups & Stews

Margaret Chase Smith Library Center
Skowhegan, Maine

MICROWAVE ROAST BEEF WITH PEPPERY GLAZE

Yield: 8 servings   *Pan Size: 8x12 inch*   ≈M≈

2 tablespoons instant beef bouillon	½ teaspoon garlic powder
¼ cup water	Cracked pepper to taste
1 tablespoon Kitchen Bouquet	1 4-pound beef rib roast

Combine instant bouillon, water, Kitchen Bouquet and garlic powder in 1-cup glass measure. Microwave on High for 1 minute. Press cracked pepper over roast. Coat on all sides with bouillon mixture. Place on glass trivet in glass dish. Insert meat thermometer into center of roast. Microwave on High to 140 degrees on meat thermometer. May insert temperature probe and Microwave to desired degree of doneness on Auto Roast if preferred.

Approx Per Serving: Cal 410; Prot 46 g; Carbo 0 g; T Fat 23 g;
     Chol 136 mg; Potas 644 mg; Sod 342 mg.

Northwood Cookbook Committee, Dallas, Texas

STEAK DIANE

Yield: 6 servings   *Pan Size: 10-inch skillet*

3 pounds beef tenderloin	2 tablespoons steak sauce
3 tablespoons butter	Salt and pepper to taste
½ cup minced shallots	¼ cup Brandy
3 tablespoons butter	3 tablespoons minced chives
3 tablespoons Worcestershire sauce	3 tablespoons minced parsley

Trim beef; cut into ¼-inch medallions. Brown on both sides in 3 tablespoons butter in skillet over high heat. Remove beef from skillet. Sauté shallots in 3 tablespoons butter in skillet for 1 minute. Add Worcestershire sauce, steak sauce, salt and pepper; mix well. Add beef and Brandy. Simmer for several minutes. Spoon into large serving dish. Top with chives and parsley. Serve with squash soufflé and buttered asparagus tips. This is my favorite dinner party entrée.

Approx Per Serving: Cal 443; Prot 43 g; Carbo 8 g; T Fat 24 g;
     Chol 159 mg; Potas 534 mg; Sod 242 mg.

Carmalee DeGeorge, Houston, Texas
Houston Women's Board

VICTOR'S STEAK DIVINE

Yield: 1 serving   *Pan Size: 10-inch skillet*

2 tablespoons butter	8 ounces shell filet mignon,
2 ounces Escoffier Diable	sliced
sauce	Salt and pepper to taste
1 tablespoon Worcestershire	1 teaspoon minced chives
sauce	
½ teaspoon spicy brown	
mustard	

Melt butter in skillet over low heat. Blend in Diable sauce, Worcestershire sauce and mustard. Sprinkle steak with salt and pepper. Add to skillet. Add chives. Cook for 3 minutes, stirring and basting constantly. Serve with buttered or unbuttered toast. May increase recipe, reducing Diable sauce to 1 ounce for each additional serving.

Approx Per Serving: Cal 514; Prot 43 g; Carbo 3 g; T Fat 36 g;
    Chol 189 mg; Potas 543 mg; Sod 442 mg.

Victor K. Kiam II, Bridgeport, Connecticut
Honorary Degree Recipient

BEEF STROGANOFF

Yield: 6 servings   *Pan Size: 10-inch skillet*

2 pounds beef	2 teaspoons dry mustard
6 tablespoons flour	1 4-ounce can mushrooms
1 teaspoon salt	1 onion, sliced
¼ teaspoon pepper	2 tablespoons flour
2 tablespoons bacon	2 tablespoons water
drippings	1 cup sour cream
2 cups water	

Cut beef into narrow strips. Coat well with mixture of 6 tablespoons flour, salt and pepper. Brown in bacon drippings in large skillet. Add 2 cups water, dry mustard, mushrooms and onion. Simmer, covered, for 1 hour. Blend 2 tablespoons flour and 2 tablespoons water in cup. Stir gradually into beef mixture. Cook until thickened, stirring constantly. Stir in sour cream. Serve immediately.

Approx Per Serving: Cal 374; Prot 31 g; Carbo 12 g; T Fat 22 g;
    Chol 130 mg; Potas 406 mg; Sod 550 mg.

Mrs. Roy Curry, Dallas, Texas
Dallas Women's Board

OSSO BUCO

Yield: 2 servings   *Pan Size: Dutch oven*   *Preheat: 325 degrees*

2 10-ounce veal shanks	3 sprigs thyme
Salt and pepper to taste	3 sprigs tarragon
Flour	8 cloves of garlic
Olive oil	Cooked baby vegetables
1 teaspoon butter	3 shiitake mushrooms
2 carrots, finely chopped	1 shallot, chopped
1 onion, finely chopped	Fettucini, cooked
Finely chopped celery	Crème fraiche
6 mushrooms, finely chopped	Parmesan cheese
16 ounces red wine	
8 ounces chicken or beef stock	

Sprinkle veal with salt and pepper; coat with flour. Brown in olive oil in Dutch oven for 5 minutes. Add butter and finely chopped vegetables. Cook for 8 minutes, stirring constantly. Add 2 ounces wine, stirring to deglaze pan. Add stock. Bake for 1 hour and 20 minutes. Remove veal with slotted spoon. Add 6 ounces wine, thyme and tarragon to Dutch oven. Simmer until liquid is reduced by 1/2. Strain into saucepan. Cook garlic with 8 ounces wine in small saucepan until wine is absorbed. Crush garlic. Whisk into strained sauce. Add baby vegetables and veal. Heat to serving temperature. Sauté shiitake mushrooms and shallot in olive oil in skillet. Combine hot fettucini with crème fraiche and Parmesan cheese in serving dish; toss to mix well. Top with sautéed vegetables. Serve with Osso Buco. The basis for this dish is a recipe from Montrachet's Restaurant in New York.

Nutritional information for this recipe is not available.

Betsy Hammes, Honolulu, Hawaii/Palm Springs, California
Distinguished Woman

VEAL MARSALA

Yield: 6 servings   *Pan Size: skillet*

1 1/2 pounds veal scallops	1/2 teaspoon salt
1/4 cup flour	1/4 cup butter
1/4 teaspoon garlic powder	1/2 cup Marsala

Pound veal flat. Coat with mixture of flour, garlic powder and salt. Brown in butter in skillet over high heat. Add wine. Cook for 1 minute. Garnish with thin lemon slices and chopped parsley.

Nutritional information for this recipe is not available.

Andrew F. Stasio, Dallas, Texas
Texas Board of Governors, Northwood Institute

VEAL PICANTI

Yield: 4 servings   *Pan Size: 10-inch skillet*

1 pound milk-fed veal, thinly
  sliced
1 cup flour
5 ounces butter
1 ounce olive oil
16 medium mushrooms,
  sliced

12 thin slices lemon
1 cup beef bouillon
¹/₄ cup Sherry
Basil, salt and pepper to taste

Coat veal with flour. Heat butter and olive in skillet over medium heat. Add veal, mushrooms and lemon slices. Cook for 5 minutes, turning frequently. Add bouillon, Sherry, basil, salt and pepper. Simmer for 10 minutes. Serve with vichyssoise and zucchini Parmesan.

Approx Per Serving: Cal 619; Prot 33 g; Carbo 28 g; T Fat 40 g;
    Chol 194 mg; Potas 561 mg; Sod 513 mg.

Carmalee DeGeorge, Houston, Texas
Houston Women's Board

VEAL TONNATO

Yield: 8 servings   *Pan Size: food processor*

3 pounds thinly sliced
  roasted veal
2 7-ounce cans white tuna,
  drained
10 anchovy fillets, chopped
2 cloves of garlic, crushed

1¹/₂ cups mayonnaise
2 tablespoons lemon juice
1 cup oil
Pepper to taste
2 tablespoons capers

Arrange veal on serving platter. Combine tuna, anchovies, garlic, mayonnaise and lemon juice in food processor; process for 30 seconds. Add oil gradually, processing constantly until smooth. Add pepper. Spoon sauce around turkey. Sprinkle with capers. Garnish with parsley and lemon wedges. May substitute turkey for veal if desired.

Approx Per Serving: Cal 600; Prot 58 g; Carbo 2 g; T Fat 39 g;
    Chol 231 mg; Potas 757 mg; Sod 525 mg.

Ann Heavey, Palm Springs, California
Palm Springs Women's Board

HAWAIIAN MEATBALLS

Yield: 6 servings   *Pan Size: 10-inch skillet*

1 13-ounce can pineapple chunks	1 tablespoon chopped pimento
2 tablespoons cornstarch	1½ pounds ground beef
½ cup vinegar	⅔ cup cracker crumbs
½ cup packed brown sugar	½ cup chopped onion
2 tablespoons soy sauce	⅔ cup evaporated milk
2 tablespoons lemon juice	1 teaspoon seasoned salt
1 cup coarsely chopped green bell pepper	⅓ cup flour
	3 tablespoons shortening

Drain pineapple, reserving liquid. Add enough water to reserved syrup to measure 1 cup. Blend with cornstarch in saucepan. Add vinegar, brown sugar, soy sauce and lemon juice. Cook until thickened and clear, stirring constantly. Add pineapple, green pepper and pimento; mix well. Simmer, covered, for 15 minutes. Combine ground beef, cracker crumbs, onion, evaporated milk and seasoned salt in bowl; mix well. Shape into 30 meatballs. Coat with flour. Brown on all sides in shortening in skillet; drain. Add sauce. Simmer, covered, for 15 minutes.

Approx Per Serving: Cal 506; Prot 31 g; Carbo 55 g; T Fat 18 g;
    Chol 89 mg; Potas 604 mg; Sod 863 mg.

Arnold Palmer, Youngstown, Pennsylvania
Outstanding Business Leader

MEAT LOAVES

Yield: 6 servings   *Pan Size: 7x12 inch*   *Preheat: 350 degrees*

1 egg	½ cup seasoned bread crumbs
2 cloves of garlic, minced	1 cup cold water
1 small package Washington broth	1½ pounds chopped meat

Combine egg, garlic, broth, bread crumbs and water in bowl; mix well. Grind meat 3 times. Add to bread crumb mixture; mix well. Shape into 2 loaves. Place in baking pan. Bake for 30 minutes. Turn loaves over. Bake for 30 minutes longer.

Approx Per Serving: Cal 195; Prot 18 g; Carbo 0 g; T Fat 14 g;
    Chol 93 mg; Potas 215 mg; Sod 63 mg.
    Nutritional information does not include Washington broth.

Lillian Vernon Katz, Greenwich, Connecticut
Outstanding Business Leader

STUFFED GREEN BELL PEPPERS

Yield: 4 servings　　　　*Pan Size: 4 quart*

4 green bell peppers
1　16-ounce can tomatoes
1 pound ground round
2 cloves of garlic, minced
3 slices bread, crumbled

3/4 cup Parmesan cheese
1/4 cup chopped parsley
Salt and pepper to taste
8 new potatoes, peeled

Cut slice from top of each green pepper; remove seed. Place undrained tomatoes in food processor container; process until chopped. Brown ground round with garlic in skillet, stirring until crumbly; drain. Add tomatoes, bread crumbs, cheese, parsley, salt and pepper; mix well. Stuff mixture into green peppers. Place in saucepan. Fill with water to half the depth of green peppers. Steam, covered, until green peppers are almost tender. Add new potatoes to top of green peppers; sprinkle with salt and pepper. Cook until potatoes and green peppers are tender.

Approx Per Serving: Cal 463; Prot 32 g; Carbo 35 g; T Fat 22 g;
　　Chol 86 mg; Potas 989 mg; Sod 649 mg.

Mary Brown, Dallas, Texas
Dallas Women's Board

MY OWN FREEZER SPAGHETTI SAUCE

Yield: 20 servings　　　　*Pan Size: 8-quart stockpot*

5 pounds ground chuck
40 ripe tomatoes, cored
3 large onions, chopped
3 large green bell peppers,
　chopped

1 tablespoon garlic powder
1 1/2 tablespoons oregano
1 tablespoon sugar
Salt to taste
1/2 cup dried onion flakes

Brown ground chuck in skillet, stirring until crumbly; drain. Drop tomatoes into boiling water for a short time. Remove and discard skin. Process in food processor fitted with metal blade. Combine with ground chuck in stockpot. Add chopped onions, green peppers, garlic powder, oregano, sugar and salt; mix well. Cook for 3 1/2 hours. Add dried onion flakes. Cook for 30 minutes longer or to desired consistency. Cool. Freeze in convenient-sized portions in airtight plastic bags. This recipe was the result of many trials to find a way to preserve our large crop of tomatoes every summer without canning them.

Approx Per Serving: Cal 298; Prot 24 g; Carbo 15 g; T Fat 17 g;
　　Chol 74 mg; Potas 860 mg; Sod 87 mg.

Mrs. John (Janice) Turner, Orleans, Indiana
Regional Coordinator, External Program of Study

TAGINE OF LAMB WITH PRUNES

Yield: 6 servings   *Pan Size: 5½ quart*

1 pound pitted prunes	3½ pounds lamb shoulder
2 cups cold water	3 tablespoons grated onion
3 tablespoons melted	¼ teaspoon cinnamon
unsalted butter	¼ cup honey
2 tablespoons oil	2 tablespoons sesame seed
Saffron, ginger, coriander,	
salt and pepper to taste	

Soak prunes in 2 cups cold water. Mix melted butter, oil, saffron, ginger, coriander, salt and pepper in bowl. Cut lamb into cubes. Dip in butter mixture, coating well. Brown on all sides in heavy saucepan. Add enough water to almost cover lamb. Bring to a boil; reduce heat. Simmer, covered, for 1 hour. Add onion. Cook for 30 minutes longer. Drain prunes. Add prunes, cinnamon and honey to lamb. Simmer, uncovered, until prunes are plump and sauce is reduced to 1 cup. Spoon lamb onto serving dish. Spoon sauce over lamb. Sprinkle with sesame seed. This is an ethnic Moroccan dish and it smells wonderful!

Approx Per Serving: Cal 1028; Prot 66 g; Carbo 60 g; T Fat 60 g;
    Chol 258 mg; Potas 1207 mg; Sod 150 mg.

Martha Ivey Calcott, Saginaw, Michigan
Chapter Chairman/Distinguished Woman

PLUM-GLAZED HAM

Yield: 16 servings   *Pan Size: roasting pan*   *Preheat: 325 degrees*

¼ cup chutney	1 clove of garlic, minced
¼ cup plum jam	⅛ teaspoon Tabasco sauce
1 teaspoon white wine	1 8-pound precooked ham
vinegar or rice wine vinegar	Whole cloves
1 tablespoon Dijon mustard	½ cup packed brown sugar

Combine chutney, plum jam, vinegar, mustard, garlic and Tabasco sauce in saucepan. Heat until mixture is syrupy. Remove rind and excess fat from ham. Score remaining fat in diamond pattern. Stud with cloves. Place on rack in roasting pan. Roast for 18 to 24 minutes per pound, removing from oven 1 hour before cooking time is complete. Spread chutney mixture evenly over ham. Press brown sugar evenly over surface. Bake until internal temperature registers 125 to 130 degrees on meat thermometer.

Approx Per Serving: Cal 593; Prot 49 g; Carbo 10 g; T Fat 38 g;
    Chol 139 mg; Potas 679 mg; Sod 2708 mg.
    Nutritional information does not include chutney.

Emalie Dodson, Atlantis, Florida
Chapter Chairman/Distinguished Woman

PORC À L'ALBERTO

Yield: 30 servings	Pan Size: roasting pan	Preheat: 400 degrees

1/2 teaspoon saffron
1/4 teaspoon cumin
1 teaspoon salt
1/2 teaspoon pepper
1 teaspoon (about) red wine
   vinegar
1   9-pound pork loin
2 cups boiling water
6 tablespoons mayonnaise

2 tablespoons fine herb
   mustard
2 tablespoons Poupon
   mustard
1/4 cup prepared horseradish
1/4 cup finely chopped
   French pickle
30 small rolls

Mix seasonings in bowl. Add enough vinegar to make a paste. Rub over surface of pork. Chill, wrapped in plastic, overnight. Place pork in roasting pan. Roast for 30 minutes. Reduce temperature to 350 degrees. Add boiling water. Roast for 2 1/2 hours longer or for a total of 20 minutes per pound. Place on platter; cool. Cut into thin slices. Combine mayonnaise, mustard, horseradish and pickle in bowl; mix well. Spread rolls with sauce; place 2 or 3 slices pork on each roll. Serve with remaining sauce for dipping. This recipe was created by Alberto Castre, a native of Peru.

Approx Per Serving: Cal 303; Prot 29 g; Carbo 15 g; T Fat 13 g;
   Chol 85 mg; Potas 403 mg; Sod 335 mg.

Moya Olsen Lear, Reno, Nevada
Distinguished Woman

LOIN OF PORK À LA BOULANGERE

Yield: 8 servings	Pan Size: roasting pan	Preheat: 425 degrees

1   4 1/2-pound pork loin
Salt to taste
1/2 cup water
8 potatoes, peeled, sliced

1 onion, chopped
1 teaspoon chopped parsley
Pepper to taste
2 tablespoons butter

Season pork with salt. Place in roasting pan. Roast for 1 hour, turning several times to brown evenly. Place pork on platter; drain excess fat from pan. Add 1/2 cup water to pan, stirring to deglaze. Add potatoes, onion, parsley, salt and pepper. Dot with butter. Place pork on vegetables. Add enough water to almost cover potatoes. Bring to a boil on top of stove. Reduce oven temperature to 400 degrees. Bake for 1 1/2 hours or until pork is tender.

Approx Per Serving: Cal 617; Prot 56 g; Carbo 53 g; T Fat 20 g;
   Chol 164 mg; Potas 1540 mg; Sod 164 mg.

Mrs. Marshall S. (Frances) Cloyd, Dallas, Texas
Dallas Women's Board

HARRIET'S YUMMY PORK ROAST

Yield: 8 servings	*Pan Size: roaster*	*Preheat: 400 degrees*

1 8-rib (or larger) pork loin	Garlic salt and paprika to
1 large onion	taste
Cracked pepper to taste	1 8-ounce jar apricot
1/4 cup (about) flour	preserves

Have butcher cut through ribs and tie loin. Remove string; score fat. Place bone side down in roaster. Chop onion coarsely; spread around roast. Press cracked pepper generously over top. Mix flour with garlic salt and paprika; pat over pepper. Bake for 1 hour or until roast renders well. Remove roast from pan, drain drippings completely and replace roast in pan. Spread preserves over roast. Reduce oven temperature to 350 degrees. Bake for 45 minutes longer or until nicely glazed.

Approx Per Serving: Cal 692; Prot 44 g; Carbo 24 g; T Fat 45 g;
Chol 181 mg; Potas 539 mg; Sod 143 mg.

Mrs. Arthur (Harriet) Rose, Dallas, Texas
Dallas Women's Board

GLAZED BACON

Yield: 8 servings	*Pan Size: baking sheet*	*Preheat: 350 degrees*

1 pound bacon, at room	1 tablespoon cinnamon
temperature	Nutmeg to taste
1 1/4 cups packed brown	
sugar	

Line baking sheet with foil. Spray with nonstick cooking spray. Arrange bacon in single layer on foil. Mix brown sugar, cinnamon and nutmeg in bowl. Sprinkle on bacon. Bake for 15 to 20 minutes or until crisp. Cover with foil sprayed with nonstick cooking spray to hold until serving time.

Approx Per Serving: Cal 453; Prot 17 g; Carbo 34 g; T Fat 28 g;
Chol 48 mg; Potas 393 mg; Sod 919 mg.

Creative Catering, Cedar Hill, Texas
Friend of Northwood

ALICIA'S CHICKEN AND VEAL LOAF

Yield: 6 servings　　　　*Pan Size: 5x9 inch*　　　　*Preheat: 395 degrees*

8 ounces carrots, peeled, finely chopped	4 cloves of garlic, crushed
8 ounces celery, finely chopped	1/4 cup olive oil
1 large onion, chopped	12 ounces ground veal
	12 ounces ground chicken
	Salt to taste

Sautée carrots, celery, onion and garlic in olive oil in skillet until tender. Cool. Combine with veal, chicken and salt in bowl; mix well. Shape into loaf; place in baking pan. Bake for 1 hour. .

Approx Per Serving: Cal 238; Prot 25 g; Carbo 8 g; T Fat 12 g;
　　Chol 83 mg; Potas 574 mg; Sod 111 mg.

Mrs. William W. (Alicia) Blodgett, Akron, Ohio

Mrs. William (Alicia) Blodgett

ALMOND ORANGE CHICKEN

Yield: 4 servings　　　　*Pan Size: 10-inch skillet*

5 tablespoons lemon juice	2 tablespoons orange marmalade
3 tablespoons Dijon mustard	2 tablespoons butter
2 cloves of garlic, chopped	2 tablespoons chopped fresh parsley
1/4 teaspoon white pepper	1/4 teaspoon red pepper flakes
8 tablespoons olive oil	2 oranges, sliced
8 chicken breasts	
1/2 cup almonds	
2 cups chicken broth	
1 teaspoon cornstarch	

Combine lemon juice, mustard, garlic and white pepper in large bowl. Beat in 5 tablespoons olive oil. Wash chicken and pat dry. Add to marinade. Marinate at room temperature for 1 hour. Sauté almonds in 1 tablespoon olive oil in skillet until golden brown. Remove with slotted spoon. Wipe skillet with paper towel. Drain chicken, reserving marinade. Brown chicken on both sides in remaining 2 tablespoons olive oil in skillet over high heat. Remove chicken and set aside. Add reserved marinade and broth to skillet. Stir in cornstarch blended with a small amount of water. Cook over high heat until thickened and reduced by more than 1/2. Stir in marmalade until melted. Increase heat. Stir in butter, parsley and red pepper flakes. Add chicken, almonds and orange slices. Heat to serving temperature.

Approx Per Serving: Cal 669; Prot 47 g; Carbo 22 g; T Fat 45 g;
　　Chol 114 mg; Potas 899 mg; Sod 698 mg.

Natasha Rawson, Houston, Texas
Houston Women's Board

CHICKEN DIVINE

Yield: 6 servings   *Pan Size: 9x13 inch*   *Preheat: 350 degrees*

8 ounces thinly sliced
   Canadian bacon
6 chicken breast filets
1/4 cup butter
1/4 cup flour
1/2 teaspoon salt

1/4 teaspoon white pepper
1 cup milk
1 cup whipping cream
Oregano to taste
8 ounces Swiss cheese, sliced

Arrange Canadian bacon in 6 portions in baking dish. Wash chicken filets and pat dry. Place on bacon, tucking under edges. Melt butter in saucepan. Blend in flour, salt and pepper. Cook for 1 to 2 minutes, stirring constantly; remove from heat. Stir in milk and cream gradually. Cook until thickened, stirring constantly. Pour over chicken. Sprinkle with oregano. Top servings with cheese. Bake for 50 minutes.

Approx Per Serving: Cal 543; Prot 41 g; Carbo 9 g; T Fat 38 g;
   Chol 183 mg; Potas 479 mg; Sod 957 mg.

Sharon A. Snyder, Grosse Pointe, Michigan
Director of External Affairs, Greater Detroit Area

CHICKEN CACCIATORE

Yield: 4 servings   *Pan Size: 10-inch skillet*

8 chicken breast filets
1/4 cup olive oil
2 medium onions, thinly
   sliced
2 cloves of garlic, minced
1   14-ounce can tomatoes
1   8-ounce can tomato sauce

2 bay leaves
1/4 teaspoon celery seed
1 teaspoon oregano
1 teaspoon salt
1/4 teaspoon pepper
1/4 cup dry white wine

Wash chicken and pat dry. Brown in olive oil in skillet. Remove chicken. Add onions and garlic. Sauté until tender but not brown. Return chicken to skillet. Add tomatoes, tomato sauce, bay leaves, celery seed, oregano, salt and pepper. Simmer, covered, for 30 minutes. Stir in wine. Simmer, uncovered, for 15 minutes longer or until chicken is tender, turning occasionally. Remove bay leaves. Serve over buttered linguine with mixed green salad and garlic toast.

Approx Per Serving: Cal 381; Prot 42 g; Carbo 15 g; T Fat 16 g;
   Chol 98 mg; Potas 1002 mg; Sod 1149 mg.

Mrs. Lawrence R. (Dorothy) Herkimer, Dallas, Texas
Distinguished Woman/Dallas Women's Board

CHICKEN WITH ARTICHOKE HEARTS

Yield: 4 servings   *Pan Size: 9x13 inch*   *Preheat: 350 degrees*

2 or 3 cloves of garlic
3 green onions, chopped
1 tablespoon olive oil
4 chicken breast filets
1/2 can cream of chicken soup

1/2 cup sour cream
1/2 cup dry white wine
1   16-ounce can artichoke
   hearts

Sauté garlic and green onions in olive oil in skillet. Add chicken. Cook over low heat until brown. Place in baking pan. Add soup, sour cream, wine and a small amount of water to skillet; heat until blended, stirring constantly. Cut artichoke hearts into halves; arrange over chicken. Spoon sauce over top. Bake for 30 minutes or until heated through.

Approx Per Serving: Cal 300; Prot 25 g; Carbo 18 g; T Fat 13 g;
   Chol 65 mg; Potas 675 mg; Sod 454 mg.

Mrs. Charles (Pat) Cameron, Cedar Hill, Texas
Cedar Hill Women's Board/Northwood Staff

CHICKEN WITH WHITE WINE AND ARTICHOKE HEARTS

Yield: 6 servings   *Pan Size: 10-inch skillet*

3 pounds chicken pieces
1 teaspoon paprika
1/2 teaspoon ginger
2 teaspoons salt
1/2 teaspoon pepper
9 tablespoons butter
8 ounces mushrooms, sliced
1   7-ounce can sliced water
   chestnuts, drained

4 artichoke hearts, sliced
1/4 cup flour
2 cups chicken stock
1/2 cup sliced black olives
2 1/2 tablespoons chopped
   chives
1 cup frozen peas
5 tablespoons dry white
   wine

Wash chicken and pat dry. Rub with mixture of paprika, ginger, salt and pepper. Cook in 5 tablespoons butter in skillet for 25 minutes or until brown and tender. Remove chicken to serving bowl. Sauté mushrooms in 4 tablespoons butter until almost tender. Add water chestnuts and artichoke hearts. Cook for 3 minutes. Stir in flour. Stir in chicken stock gradually. Cook until thickened, stirring constantly. Add olives, chives and peas. Cook for 5 minutes. Stir in wine. Cook for 1 minute. Pour over chicken. Serve with rice, noodles or potatoes.

Approx Per Serving: Cal 496; Prot 38 g; Carbo 16 g; T Fat 31 g;
   Chol 148 mg; Potas 649 mg; Sod 1794 mg.

Mrs. Kent (Lee) Vennard, Fort Lauderdale, Florida
National Women's Board, Fort Lauderdale Chapter

FAJITAS WITH GUACAMOLE AND PICO DE GALLO

Yield: 6 servings   *Preheat: grill*

½ cup Tamari soy sauce	6 flour tortillas, heated
½ cup fresh lime juice	2 cups shredded Cheddar
Seasoned salt to taste	cheese
6 chicken breast filets	

Combine first 3 ingredients in bowl. Wash chicken and pat dry. Add to marinade. Marinate for 2 to 3 hours; drain. Place chicken on grill over hot mesquite-coal fire. Cook for 5 to 7 minutes on each side; do not overcook. Serve on tortillas with cheese, guacamole and pico de gallo. Use enough charcoal to extend in a single layer 1 inch beyond area of food on grill. Fire is ready when coals have a red-white glow and are about 80% ashed over. For easy lighting, make a pyramid of charcoal in center of grill, add lighter fluid and wait for 1 minute for fluid to soak in before lighting fire.

Approx Per Serving: Cal 430; Prot 35 g; Carbo 35 g; T Fat 18 g;
    Chol 89 mg; Potas 375 mg; Sod 1876 mg.

GUACAMOLE

Yield: 6 servings   *Pan Size: medium bowl*

4 large ripe avocados	½ teaspoon garlic salt
Juice of ½ lemon	Seasoned salt to taste

Mash avocados coarsely in bowl, leaving some chunks. Add lemon juice, garlic salt and seasoned salt; mix well. Serve with chicken fajitas. May serve as dip with chips if preferred.

Approx Per Serving: Cal 217; Prot 3 g; Carbo 10 g; T Fat 21 g;
    Chol 0 mg; Potas 807 mg; Sod 192 mg.

PICO DE GALLO

Yield: 6 servings   *Pan Size: medium bowl*

1 large tomato, chopped	2 tablespoons chopped
3 small green onions,	cilantro
chopped	1 tablespoon vinegar
½ jalapeño pepper, seeded,	Salt and pepper to taste
chopped	

Combine all ingredients in bowl; mix well. Serve with fajitas. Store in covered jar in refrigerator for up to 2 days.

Approx Per Serving: Cal 8; Prot 0 g; Carbo 2 g; T Fat 0 g;
    Chol 0 mg; Potas 79 mg; Sod 72 mg.

Mr. Robert H. (Bob) Holmes, Dallas, Texas
A Favorite Friend of Northwood

CHICKEN OVER FETTUCINI

Yield: 4 servings　　　　*Pan Size: 10-inch skillet*

4 chicken breast filets
2 cloves of garlic, minced
3 tablespoons olive oil
1 cup sliced mushrooms

1 cup cream
1/2 cup Parmesan cheese
8 ounces fettucini noodles,
　cooked

Wash chicken and pat dry; cut into 1-inch strips. Cook with garlic in 2 tablespoons olive oil in skillet over medium-high heat until brown and cooked through. Remove chicken. Add remaining 1 tablespoon oil and mushrooms. Cook for 3 minutes. Add cream. Bring to a boil; reduce heat. Stir in cheese. Simmer for 1 minute. Stir in chicken. Heat to serving temperature. Serve over noodles.

Approx Per Serving: Cal 522; Prot 33 g; Carbo 47 g; T Fat 22 g;
　　Chol 79 mg; Potas 499 mg; Sod 270 mg.

Edgar A. Madden, Hemlock, Michigan
Provost, Michigan Campus

GRILLED SOUTHWESTERN CHICKEN KABOBS

Yield: 6 servings　　　　　　　　　　　　　　　　*Preheat: grill*

1 green bell pepper
1 red bell pepper
1 yellow bell pepper
1　15-ounce can tomato sauce
1 cup Cabernet Sauvignon
1/2 cup red wine vinegar
1/4 cup red pepper sauce
1/4 cup molasses

1/4 teaspoon liquid smoke
4 cloves of garlic, crushed
1 teaspoon cumin
1/2 cup chopped fresh cilantro
Salt and pepper to taste
1/2 cup safflower oil
6 chicken breast filets
12 pearl onions

Soak six 8-inch bamboo skewers in warm water for 30 minutes. Cut each pepper into 6 strips. Combine next 10 ingredients in bowl; mix well. Whisk in oil in thin stream. Pour into shallow dish. Wash chicken and pat dry. Pound flat with meat mallet. Cut each filet into thirds. Thread on skewers alternately with onions and pepper strips. Place in marinade. Marinate for 2 hours, turning every 30 minutes. Place kabobs on grill 6 inches from mesquite-coal fire; reserve marinade. Grill kabobs for 15 minutes or until chicken is tender, basting with marinade. Serve on steamed rice with salad, sourdough baguettes and a chilled California Chardonnay such as 1988 Kendall-Jackson.

Approx Per Serving: Cal 362; Prot 22 g; Carbo 20 g; T Fat 20 g;
　　Chol 49 mg; Potas 872 mg; Sod 536 mg.

Debbi Fields, Park City, Utah
Distinguished Woman/President, Mrs. Fields Cookies

CHICKEN CURRY

Yield: 6 servings   *Pan Size: 10-inch skillet*

1 3-pound fryer	2 tablespoons curry powder
2 medium apples, chopped	1/2 teaspoon ginger
2 medium onions, chopped	Cayenne pepper and salt to
2 green bell peppers,	taste
chopped	1 16-ounce can tomatoes,
2 stalks celery, chopped	drained, chopped
1/4 cup butter	1/2 cup chutney
1 teaspoon chopped garlic	

Wash chicken and pat dry. Cook in water to cover in saucepan until tender. Remove and chop chicken; reserve broth. Sauté apples, onions, green peppers and celery in butter until tender. Add garlic, curry powder, ginger, cayenne pepper, salt and 1 cup reserved broth. Simmer, covered, for 30 minutes. Add tomatoes, chutney and 3/4 to 1 cup chicken broth. Simmer for 15 minutes. May thicken with 1 tablespoon cornstarch blended with a small amount of broth if desired. Serve over rice with dishes of raisins, cashews and coconut for toppings.

Approx Per Serving: Cal 367; Prot 36 g; Carbo 17 g; T Fat 17 g;
    Chol 122 mg; Potas 755 mg; Sod 558 mg.
    Nutritional information does not include chutney.

Leslie A. Gowan, Dallas, Texas
Director of External Affairs, Dallas

PARMESAN CHICKEN

Yield: 4 servings   *Pan Size: skillet*

3 eggs	1/2 cup olive oil
2 tablespoons milk	2 cups spaghetti sauce
1 cup Italian bread crumbs	1 cup shredded mozzarella
1/2 cup Parmesan cheese	cheese
4 chicken breast filets	

Beat eggs with milk in bowl. Combine bread crumbs with Parmesan cheese in bowl. Wash chicken and pat dry. Dip in eggs; coat well with crumb mixture. Fry in olive oil in skillet until brown. Add spaghetti sauce. Simmer, covered, for 2 to 3 minutes or until heated through. Sprinkle chicken with mozzarella cheese. May sprinkle chicken with additional Parmesan cheese while browning if desired.

Approx Per Serving: Cal 755; Prot 42 g; Carbo 40 g; T Fat 47 g;
    Chol 234 mg; Potas 830 mg; Sod 1250 mg.

Melinda Garcia, Waxahachie, Texas
Friend of Northwood

CHICKEN ENCHILADAS

Yield: 8 servings   *Pan Size: 9x13 inch*   *Preheat: 325 degrees*

1 16-ounce can tomatoes
1 clove of garlic, crushed
1 large onion, chopped
3/4 teaspoon coriander or
   fresh cilantro
1 teaspoon salt
2 cups sour cream

16 soft corn tortillas
Vegetable oil
3 cups chopped cooked
   chicken
1 pound sharp cheese,
   shredded

Purée tomatoes, garlic, onion, coriander and salt in blender. Pour into saucepan. Simmer for 30 minutes. Cool slightly. Stir in sour cream. Soften tortillas in hot oil in skillet. Dip into tomato sauce. Spoon chicken and cheese onto tortillas; roll to enclose filling. Place in baking dish. Pour remaining sauce over top. Sprinkle with remaining cheese. Bake for 30 minutes. Serve with pico de gallo and tortilla chips.

Nutritional information for this recipe is not available.

Barbara Nichols, Dallas, Texas
Dallas Women's Board/Director, National Arts Programs Development

CHICKEN ROSEMARY

Yield: 4 servings   *Pan Size: 9x13 inch*   *Preheat: 350 degrees*

4 chicken breasts, skinned
2 tablespoons olive oil
1/4 cup chopped fresh
   rosemary
1/2 cup chopped fresh basil

2 tablespoons chopped fresh
   thyme
8 cloves of garlic
2 cups cooked rice
1 cup dry vermouth

Wash chicken and pat dry. Place in baking pan. Drizzle with olive oil; sprinkle with chopped rosemary, basil and thyme. Place garlic around chicken. Bake, loosely covered with foil, for 30 to 40 minutes or until juices run clear when chicken is pierced with fork. Baste with pan juices. Broil for 5 to 10 minutes or until brown. Arrange chicken on rice on serving plate. Drain fat from pan. Add wine to pan, stirring to deglaze. Serve over chicken. Garnish with rosemary sprigs.

Approx Per Serving: Cal 438; Prot 42 g; Carbo 30 g; T Fat 9 g;
   Chol 98 mg; Potas 511 mg; Sod 121 mg.

Julia Sweeney, Dallas, Texas
Dallas Women's Board

CHICKEN BREASTS IN SHERRY AND SOUR CREAM

Yield: 4 servings   *Pan Size: 9x9 inch*   *Preheat: 350 degrees*

4 chicken breasts, skinned
Salt and pepper to taste
1 3-ounce can mushrooms, drained
1/2 soup can Sherry

3/4 cup sour cream
1 can cream of mushroom soup
1/3 teaspoon Italian seasoning
Paprika to taste

Wash chicken and pat dry. Sprinkle with salt and pepper. Arrange in single layer in baking pan. Top with mushrooms. Combine wine, sour cream, mushroom soup and Italian seasoning in bowl; mix well. Pour over chicken, covering completely. Sprinkle with paprika. Bake, covered, for 30 minutes. Bake, uncovered, for 30 to 40 minutes longer or until tender. Garnish with green grapes.

Approx Per Serving: Cal 538; Prot 52 g; Carbo 9 g; T Fat 28 g; Chol 172 mg; Potas 578 mg; Sod 879 mg.

Lenore S. Forti, Sun City West, Arizona
Distinguished Woman
Second President Detroit Women's Board

SEASONED TURKEY PATTIES WITH SAUCE

Yield: 4 servings   *Pan Size: medium skillet*

1 1/4 pounds ground fresh turkey
1 cup cracker crumbs
1 teaspoon onion juice
1 egg
1 1/4 teaspoons Worcestershire sauce
1/2 teaspoon poultry seasoning

1/2 teaspoon garlic salt
1/2 teaspoon seasoned salt
2 teaspoons margarine
1 16-ounce can jellied cranberry sauce
1/2 cup water
2 teaspoons low-sodium instant chicken bouillon

Combine turkey, cracker crumbs, onion juice, egg, Worcestershire sauce, poultry seasoning, garlic salt and seasoned salt in bowl; mix well. Shape into 4 patties. Brown on both sides in margarine in skillet. Combine cranberry sauce, water and chicken bouillon in saucepan. Cook over medium heat until cranberry sauce is melted. Pour over turkey patties. Simmer, covered, for 15 minutes. Spoon into serving bowl.

Nutritional information for this recipe is not available.

Vada B. Dow, Midland, Michigan
Distinguished Woman
Founding Chairman, Library League of Northwood

FISH STUFFED WITH LEMON RICE STUFFING

Yield: 6 servings *Pan Size: 10x16 inch* *Preheat: 350 degrees*

3/4 cup chopped celery
1/2 cup chopped onion
1/4 cup oil
1 1/3 cups water
2 tablespoons grated lemon
   rind
1 teaspoon paprika
Thyme to taste

1 teaspoon salt
1 1/2 cups cooked rice
1/3 cup sour cream
1/2 cup chopped onion
3 pounds fish
1 1/2 teaspoons salt
2 tablespoons melted butter

Sauté celery and 1/2 cup onion in oil in skillet until tender. Add water, lemon rind, paprika, thyme and 1 teaspoon salt. Bring to a boil. Stir in rice. Let stand, covered, for 5 to 10 minutes or until liquid is absorbed. Stir in sour cream and 1/2 cup onion. Clean, wash and pat fish dry. Sprinkle with 1 1/2 teaspoons salt inside and out. Stuff with rice mixture; close openings with skewers. Place in greased baking dish. Brush with butter. Bake for 40 to 60 minutes or until fish flakes easily. Remove skewers; place fish on serving plate. Garnish with lemon wedges.

Approx Per Serving: Cal 570; Prot 61 g; Carbo 16 g; T Fat 27 g;
    Chol 159 mg; Potas 1203 mg; Sod 1116 mg.

Mrs. Charles V. (Judy) Shepard, Dallas, Texas
Dallas Women's Board

SAVORY SALMON STEAKS

Yield: 4 servings *Preheat: grill*

3 tablespoons Dijon mustard
3 tablespoon low-sodium
   soy sauce
3 tablespoons dark brown
   sugar

3 tablespoons safflower oil
1 teaspoon prepared
   horseradish
4 8-ounce salmon steaks

Combine mustard, soy sauce, brown sugar, oil and horseradish in small bowl. Brush over fish. Marinate in refrigerator for up to 6 hours if desired. Place on grill. Grill for 5 minutes. Brush with remaining glaze. Grill until fish flakes easily. Serve hot or at room temperature.

Approx Per Serving: Cal 460; Prot 46 g; Carbo 11 g; T Fat 25 g;
    Chol 125 mg; Potas 1166 mg; Sod 252 mg.
    Nutritional information does not include low-sodium soy sauce.

Debra Littlefield Blauwiekel, Geneva, Illinois
Midland, Michigan Women's Board

Debra Littlefield Blauwiekel

SOLE OF DECEPTION

Yield: 1 serving   *Pan Size: small baking dish*   *Preheat: 350 degrees*

1 8-ounce sole fillet	1/2 cup sour cream
3 mushroom caps, sliced	1/4 cup mayonnaise
24 green grapes	1 tablespoon lemon juice
1 teaspoon butter	

Place fish in individual baking dish. Sauté mushrooms and grapes in butter in skillet. Add sour cream, mayonnaise and lemon juice; mix well. Spoon over fish. Bake for 20 minutes.

Approx Per Serving: Cal 972; Prot 48 g; Carbo 30 g; T Fat 75 g; Chol 203 mg; Potas 1293 mg; Sod 593 mg.

Mrs. Robert (Genie) Parker, Phoenix, Arizona
Chairman 1985-1988, Valley of the Sun Chapter

CEVICHE

Yield: 6 servings   *Pan Size: medium bowl*

1 1/2 pounds trout or redfish	1 large tomato, peeled,
1 cup fresh lime juice	chopped
4 cups water	3 medium jalapeño peppers,
1 medium purple onion,	seeded, finely chopped
thinly sliced	1/4 teaspoon salt
1/4 cup finely chopped	1/4 cup olive oil
cilantro	

Cut fish into 1/2-inch cubes. Combine with lime juice in bowl; toss with wooden spoon. Marinate, covered, in refrigerator for 4 hours, stirring with wooden spoon after 2 hours. Bring water to a boil in saucepan. Add onion. Cook for 2 minutes. Rinse with cold water in strainer; drain well. Combine with fish, cilantro, tomato, jalapeño peppers, salt and olive oil in bowl; mix well. Chill, covered, for 4 hours to overnight.

Approx Per Serving: Cal 281; Prot 31 g; Carbo 8 g; T Fat 14 g; Chol 83 mg; Potas 896 mg; Sod 298 mg.

David Wilson, Dallas, Texas
Friend of Northwood, Old Spaghetti Warehouse

DEVILED CRAB

Yield: 6 servings	Pan Size: 2 quart	Preheat: 350 degrees

1/4 cup butter
6 tablespoons flour
2 tablespoons catsup
1 tablespoon salt
1 teaspoon pepper
2 cups milk
2/3 cup chopped onion
2/3 cup chopped green bell
  pepper
1 1/2 cups chopped celery

1 cup chopped fresh
  tomatoes
3 cloves of garlic, minced
1 teaspoon Worcestershire
  sauce
1 pound crab meat
4 hard-boiled eggs, chopped
1 cup cracker crumbs
2 tablespoons butter

Melt 1/4 cup butter in large skillet. Blend in flour, catsup, salt and pepper. Cook until flour is light brown. Add milk gradually. Cook until thickened and smooth, stirring constantly. Combine with next 8 ingredients in bowl; mix gently. Spoon into baking dish. Top with cracker crumbs; dot with 2 tablespoons butter. Bake until bubbly.

Approx Per Serving: Cal 440; Prot 27 g; Carbo 36 g; T Fat 21 g;
  Chol 251 mg; Potas 778 mg; Sod 1717 mg.

Mrs. Edward B. (Virginia) Linthicum, Dallas, Texas
Distinguished Woman/Dallas Women's Board

MARYLAND CRAB CAKES

Yield: 8 servings	Pan Size: large skillet

1 pound fresh crab meat
3 eggs, beaten
1/2 teaspoon salt
Pepper to taste
1/2 cup mayonnaise
1 teaspoon vinegar
1/2 teaspoon dry mustard
3 slices white bread,
  crumbled

1 teaspoon Worcestershire
  sauce
Dry onion soup mix to taste
2 tablespoons melted butter
  or margarine
Chopped parsley
Paprika to taste
Butter cracker crumbs
Shortening for frying

Combine crab meat, eggs, salt and pepper in bowl; mix well. Add mayonnaise, vinegar and dry mustard. Mix bread, Worcestershire sauce, onion soup mix and butter in small bowl. Fold into crab mixture. Add parsley and paprika. Add a small amount of milk if needed for desired consistency. Let stand for several hours. Shape into 8 patties. Coat with cracker crumbs. Brown on both sides in shortening in skillet.

Nutritional information for this recipe is not available.

Mrs. Charles V. (Judy) Shepard, Dallas, Texas
Dallas Women's Board

OYSTERS CASINO

Yield: 4 servings   *Pan Size: 9x13 inch*   *Preheat: broiler*

18 oyster shells
1 cup thawed frozen
  chopped spinach
1 pint fresh oysters

1/2 cup Romano cheese
1/3 cup toasted seasoned
  bread crumbs
18 1-inch squares bacon

Arrange oyster shells in baking dish. Press excess moisture out of spinach. Spoon into oyster shells. Layer oysters, cheese and bread crumbs over spinach. Top with bacon. Broil for 3 to 4 minutes or until bacon is crisp. Serve hot.

Approx Per Serving: Cal 267; Prot 20 g; Carbo 14 g; T Fat 14 g;
    Chol 95 mg; Potas 520 mg; Sod 637 mg.

Ellen Weinstein, Dallas, Texas
Dallas Women's Board

LANGOUSTINES DE BRETAGNE

Yield: 6 servings   *Pan Size: 10-inch skillet*

2 pounds rock shrimp tails
2 large shallots, finely
  chopped
1 tablespoon unsalted butter
1 tablespoon oil
Cayenne pepper, salt and
  pepper to taste

1 tablespoon flour
3 tablespoons Cognac
1/4 cup dry vermouth
1/4 cup clam juice
1 teaspoon curry powder
1 cup heavy cream

Peel and devein shrimp; pat dry. Sauté shallots in butter and oil in skillet until transparent; do not brown. Add shrimp. Sauté for 3 minutes. Sprinkle with cayenne pepper, salt, pepper and flour. Cook for 2 minutes. Add Cognac. Ignite; let flame for 1 minute. Add wine and clam juice. Remove shrimp with slotted spoon. Stir mixture of curry powder and cream into skillet. Bring to a boil. Cook until mixture is thickened, stirring constantly. Season to taste. Add shrimp. Heat to serving temperature. Serve over hot cooked rice. I do it right half the time—but then it is heaven. Serve with your best white wine.

Approx Per Serving: Cal 383; Prot 33 g; Carbo 10 g; T Fat 21 g;
    Chol 354 mg; Potas 400 mg; Sod 359 mg.

Dr. David E. Fry, Midland, Michigan
President, Northwood Institute

SEAFOOD CASSEROLE IN PASTRY SHELLS

Yield: 8 servings   *Pan Size: 2 quart*

¼ cup flour	1 cup sliced fresh
¼ cup butter	mushrooms
1 cup whipping cream	8 ounces crab meat
1 cup half and half	8 ounces shrimp
2 egg yolks, beaten	3 tablespoons chopped
½ teaspoon Worcestershire	parsley
sauce	¼ cup vermouth
Salt to taste	8 pastry shells, baked

Brown flour lightly in butter in saucepan. Add whipping cream and half and half. Cook until thickened and smooth, stirring constantly. Cool. Stir in egg yolks. Add Worcestershire sauce and salt; mix well. Add mushrooms, crab meat, shrimp and parsley; mix well. Stir in wine. Serve in pastry shells. May place in baking dish, sprinkle with bread crumbs and bake at 350 degrees for 30 minutes if preferred. This recipe is from East Feliciana Parish in Louisiana.

Approx Per Serving: Cal 516; Prot 17 g; Carbo 26 g; T Fat 37 g; Chol 201 mg; Potas 297 mg; Sod 512 mg.

Mrs. Lee D. (Susan Cross) Cornell, Cedar Hill, Texas
Cedar Hill Women's Board

COCONUT SHRIMP

Yield: 8 servings   *Pan Size: large skillet*   *Preheat: 375 degrees*

1½ cups coconut	½ teaspoon salt
35 extra-large shrimp, peeled	2 cups flour
¼ cup fresh lemon juice	2 teaspoons baking powder
1½ teaspoons curry powder	1⅓ cups cold milk
½ teaspoon ginger	Oil for frying

Sprinkle coconut on baking sheet. Bake until lightly toasted. Butterfly shrimp lengthwise with sharp knife. Combine lemon juice, curry powder, ginger and salt in bowl. Add shrimp. Marinate in refrigerator for 2 to 6 hours. Mix flour, baking powder and milk in bowl. Drain shrimp, reserving marinade. Add marinade to batter; mix well. Heat oil to 375 degrees in skillet. Dip shrimp into batter. Fry in oil for 3 to 5 minutes or until golden brown. Dip into coconut, coating well. Serve warm.

Approx Per Serving: Cal 240; Prot 11 g; Carbo 33 g; T Fat 7 g; Chol 53 mg; Potas 195 mg; Sod 314 mg.
Nutritional information does not include oil for frying.

Ms. Gail Kershner, Dallas, Texas
Dallas Women's Board

EAST INDIAN SHRIMP CURRY

Yield: 4 servings　　　　　*Pan Size: 4 quart*

2 pounds fresh shrimp	Thyme, marjoram and dried
1 clove of garlic, crushed	mint to taste
1 large onion, finely chopped	2 cloves
3 stalks celery, chopped	1/4 teaspoon basil
1 green bell pepper, chopped	1/2 teaspoon each salt, pepper
1 apple, peeled, chopped	1/4 teaspoon cayenne pepper
1 carrot, chopped	1/4 teaspoon nutmeg
2 tomatoes, peeled, chopped	2 tablespoons flour
1/2 cup butter	2 tablespoons curry powder
1 tablespoon chopped parsley	2 cups consommé
1 bay leaf, crumbled	1 cup dry white wine

Cook shrimp partially in water to cover in saucepan. Drain and set aside. Add next 7 ingredients to butter in saucepan. Sprinkle with next 5 ingredients. Sauté until vegetables are tender. Sprinkle with salt, pepper, cayenne pepper, nutmeg and mixture of flour and curry powder. Cook for 5 minutes, stirring constantly. Add consommé gradually. Cook until mixture begins to thicken. Stir in wine. Cook over low heat for 30 minutes. Add shrimp. Cook until shrimp are tender and heated through. Serve over rice with dishes of chutney, chopped peanuts, coconut, chopped olives, sieved egg yokes, India relish, chopped bacon or slivered almonds for toppings.

Approx Per Serving: Cal 564; Prot 52 g; Carbo 19 g; T Fat 27 g;
　　Chol 505 mg; Potas 992 mg; Sod 1398 mg.

Mrs. Robert H. (Sunny) Miller, West Palm Beach, Florida
West Palm Beach Women's Board

SHRIMP NEW ORLEANS

Yield: 8 servings　　　*Pan Size: broiler pan*　　　*Preheat: broiler*

4 pounds jumbo shrimp	1 pound margarine, melted
1 can pepper	Juice of 2 lemons
1 16-ounce bottle of Italian	3 dashes Worcestershire sauce
salad dressing	

Coat unshelled shrimp with pepper. Place in broiler pan. Do not shake salad dressing. Discard some of the oil from dressing. Heat salad dressing with remaining ingredients in saucepan until blended. Pour over shrimp. Broil for 10 minutes on each side or until shrimp are pink.

Approx Per Serving: Cal 899; Prot 48 g; Carbo 8 g; T Fat 82 g;
　　Chol 442 mg; Potas 460 mg; Sod 1321 mg.

Mrs. R.E.L. (Ann) Gowan, Jr., Houston, Texas
Friend of Northwood

SHRIMP AND EGGPLANT CASSEROLE

Yield: 8 servings   Pan Size: 2 quart   Preheat: 350 degrees

2 eggplants, peeled, chopped
1 green bell pepper, chopped
1 large onion, chopped
2 tablespoons butter
1 quart tomatoes
1 teaspoon (heaping) oregano
1 teaspoon salt

2 tablespoons butter
1 cup coarsely crushed
   seasoned croutons
1 cup shredded Swiss cheese
2 cups cooked angel shrimp
1 cup shredded mozzarella
   cheese

Cook eggplant in small amount of water in saucepan for 5 minutes; drain. Sauté green pepper and onion in 2 tablespoons butter in heavy saucepan until tender. Add eggplant, tomatoes, oregano and salt. Cook over low heat for 10 minutes or to desired consistency. Add 2 tablespoons butter, croutons, Swiss cheese and shrimp; mix well. Spoon into greased baking dish. Top with mozzarella cheese. Bake for 15 minutes or until cheese is melted.

Approx Per Serving: Cal 252; Prot 22 g; Carbo 12 g; T Fat 13 g;
   Chol 147 mg; Potas 472 mg; Sod 614 mg.

Mrs. Jack M. (Mary Jane) Sanders, Sr., Marshall, Texas
Friend of Northwood

SCAMPI FLAMBÉED WITH BRANDY AND CALVADOS

Yield: 8 servings   Pan Size: deep saucepan

2 shallots
1 carrot
1 teaspoon each thyme,
   tarragon and parsley
1/4 cup butter
1 bay leaf
48 medium peeled shrimp

1/4 cup Brandy
1/4 cup Calvados
1/4 cup dry white wine
2 tablespoons butter
2 tablespoons flour
1 tomato, peeled, seeded
1/2 cup cream

Process shallots, carrot, thyme, tarragon and parsley in food processor until chopped. Sauté in 1/4 cup butter in saucepan until tender. Add bay leaf and shrimp. Cook until shrimp are pink, stirring constantly. Add Brandy. Ignite; let flame subside. Add Calvados. Ignite; let flame subside. Stir in white wine. Simmer for 5 minutes. Remove shrimp with slotted spoon. Strain cooking liquid into blender container. Add 2 tablespoons butter, flour and tomato. Blend until smooth. Pour into saucepan. Cook until thickened and smooth. Add cream. Cook until reduced to desired consistency. Add shrimp. Heat to serving temperature over low heat. Remove bay leaf.

Approx Per Serving: Cal 254; Prot 10 g; Carbo 13 g; T Fat 15 g;
   Chol 109 mg; Potas 228 mg; Sod 149 mg.

Mrs. Robert (Genie) Parker, Phoenix, Arizona
Founding Member and Chairman 1985-1988, Valley of the Sun Chapter

MEDALLIONS OF VENISON

Yield: 4 servings	Pan Size: 2 quart	Preheat: 250 degrees

3 or 4 cloves of garlic,
  minced
2 tablespoons oil
1 pound backstrap venison,
  sliced 1/4 inch thick
5 juniper berries, crushed
1/2 cup cooking Sherry

2/3 cup coffee
1 cup water
1/2 teaspoon garlic salt or salt
1/4 teaspoon pepper
2 tablespoons flour
Salt and pepper to taste
1/2 cup water

Sauté garlic in oil in skillet for 1 minute. Add venison. Cook until brown on both sides. Combine with juniper berries, Sherry, coffee, 1 cup water, garlic salt, and pepper in baking dish. Bake, covered, for 1 hour. Blend flour with salt and pepper to taste and 1/2 cup water in bowl. Stir into venison. Bake for 10 minutes or until thickened. Serve with rice pilaf or noodles.

Approx Per Serving: Cal 239; Prot 26 g; Carbo 5 g; T Fat 9 g;
  Chol 55 mg; Potas 345 mg; Sod 330 mg.

Frances Freeman, Dallas, Texas
Dallas Women's Board

DUCK CASSEROLE

Yield: 4 servings	Pan Size: two 1 quart	Preheat: 350 degrees

2 ducks
3 stalks celery, chopped
1/2 onion, chopped
1 1/2 teaspoons salt
1 8-ounce package wild rice
1/2 cup chopped onion
1/2 cup butter
1/4 cup flour

1 4-ounce can sliced
  mushrooms
1 1/4 cups half and half
1/4 cup wine
1/4 teaspoon parsley
1/4 teaspoon pepper
1/2 cup sliced almonds

Combine ducks, celery, 1/2 onion and salt in saucepan. Add water to cover. Bring to a boil; reduce heat. Simmer for 1 hour. Cool. Remove ducks, reserving broth; chop into bite-sized pieces. Cook rice using package directions. Sauté 1/2 cup onion in butter in skillet. Add flour. Cook until smooth, stirring constantly. Drain mushrooms, reserving broth. Add mushrooms to skillet. Cook for 10 minutes. Combine mushroom liquid with enough reserved duck broth to measure 1 1/2 cups. Add to skillet. Cook until thickened, stirring constantly. Add chopped duck, rice, half and half, wine, parsley and pepper . Spoon into 2 baking dishes. Top with almonds. Bake, covered, for 20 minutes. Bake, uncovered, for 5 to 10 minutes.

Approx Per Serving: Cal 927; Prot 42 g; Carbo 64 g; T Fat 55 g;
  Chol 204 mg; Potas 811 mg; Sod 1259 mg.

Ms. Kristin S. Kaufman, Dallas, Texas
Dallas Women's Board

QUICK AND EASY COUNTRY QUAIL

Yield: 4 servings　　*Pan Size: baking sheet*　　*Preheat: 425 degrees*

4 bobwhite quail	4 tablespoons butter
4 slices bacon	4 tablespoons
4 small onions	Worcestershire
4 small carrots	

Clean, wash and dry quail. Wrap each quail with slice of bacon; place each on square of heavy-duty foil. Place 1 onion, 1 carrot, 1 tablespoon butter and 1 tablespoon Worcestershire sauce on each quail. Seal foil tightly; place on baking sheet. Bake for 1 hour.

Approx Per Serving: Cal 422; Prot 41 g; Carbo 13 g; T Fat 23 g;
Chol 36 mg; Potas 852 mg; Sod 457 mg.

Northwood Cookbook Committee, Dallas, Texas

CROCK•POT BLACK-EYED PEA SOUP

Yield: 8 servings　　*Pan Size: Crock•Pot*

3　23-ounce cans black-eyed pea soup, or frozen peas	1 cup chopped onion
1　10-ounce can Ro-Tel tomatoes	1 cup chopped celery
1　10-ounce package frozen cut okra	1 cup chopped green bell pepper
	3 tablespoons margarine

Combine pea soup, tomatoes and okra in Crock•Pot. Sauté onion, celery and green pepper in margarine in skillet. Add to soup. Cook on Low for 6 to 8 hours. May substitute 1 can black-eyed pea soup with jalapeño peppers if desired. This recipe is great for winter parties to warm up guests Texas style.

Approx Per Serving: Cal 375; Prot 18 g; Carbo 57 g; T Fat 10 g;
Chol 0 mg; Potas 615 mg; Sod 1961 mg.

Mrs. Ronald (Linda) Hopton-Jones, Cedar Hill, Texas
Founding Chairman, Cedar Hill Chapter

Linda Hopton-Jones

SOPA DE ELOTE (CORN SOUP)

Yield: 6 servings	Pan Size: large saucepan

³/4 cup whole kernel corn	3 small tomatoes, peeled,
1 clove of garlic	chopped
¹/2 teaspoon salt	4 cups beef broth
1 small onion, chopped	¹/2 teaspoon oregano
1 tablespoon butter	¹/4 cup whipping cream

Purée corn in blender or food processor. Crush garlic with salt to form paste in small bowl. Sauté garlic and onion in butter in saucepan until tender but not brown. Add tomatoes. Cook over low heat for 10 minutes, mashing tomatoes with spoon. Add beef broth, oregano and corn purée. Bring to a boil; reduce heat. Simmer, covered, for 30 minutes. Stir in cream. Cook just until heated through. May thicken with a small amount of cornstarch blended with water if desired. Ladle into soup bowls. Garnish with cilantro or parsley leaves.

Approx Per Serving: Cal 98; Prot 3 g; Carbo 8 g; T Fat 6 g; Chol 19 mg; Potas 287 mg; Sod 772 mg.

John E. Washburn, Lewisville, Texas
Chairman of Computer Science Department, Cedar Hill Campus

BEBE'S TORTILLA SOUP

Yield: 8 servings	Pan Size: 4 quart

1 small onion, chopped	2 teaspoons chili powder
1 4-ounce can green chilies, drained	2 teaspoons Worcestershire sauce
3 cloves of garlic, crushed	1 tablespoon steak sauce
2 tablespoons olive oil	1 teaspoon salt
1 cup chopped peeled tomatoes	¹/2 teaspoon white or cayenne pepper
1 14-ounce can beef bouillon	6 flour tortillas, cut into ¹/2-inch strips
1 14-ounce can chicken broth	¹/4 cup shredded Cheddar cheese
1¹/2 cups water	1 avocado, thinly sliced
1¹/2 cups tomato juice	
2 teaspoons cumin	

Sauté onion, chilies and garlic in oil in saucepan until tender. Add tomatoes and next 10 ingredients; mix well. Bring to a boil; reduce heat. Simmer for 1 hour. Place tortilla strips, cheese and avocados in soup bowls. Ladle soup into bowls. Serve with tortilla chips.

Approx Per Serving: Cal 249; Prot 7 g; Carbo 32 g; T Fat 12 g; Chol 4 mg; Potas 499 mg; Sod 952 mg.

Mrs. R. H. (Beverly) Holmes, Dallas, Texas
Dallas Women's Board Chairman

BEER BEEF STEW

Yield: 4 servings   *Pan Size: large saucepan*

2 pounds round steak cubes	1 medium bay leaf
1/3 cup flour	1/8 teaspoon thyme
Salt and pepper to taste	1 1/2 cups flour
2 tablespoons shortening	2 1/4 teaspoons baking powder
1/4 cup wine vinegar	1/4 teaspoon salt
1 14-ounce can beef broth	1/4 cup shortening
1 12-ounce can beer	1/2 cup milk

Coat steak well with mixture of 1/3 cup flour and salt and pepper to taste. Brown on all sides in 2 tablespoons shortening in saucepan. Add vinegar, beef broth, beer, bay leaf and thyme. Simmer, covered, for 2 hours or until steak is tender. Mix 1 1/2 cups flour, baking powder and 1/4 teaspoon salt in bowl. Cut in 1/4 cup shortening. Add milk; mix well. Drop by spoonfuls into simmering stew. Simmer, covered, for 20 minutes; do not remove cover. Cook for several minutes longer if necessary after testing dumplings for doneness. Remove bay leaf.

Approx Per Serving: Cal 1065; Prot 66 g; Carbo 50 g; T Fat 62 g; Chol 194 mg; Potas 1018 mg; Sod 796 mg.

June Braun, Saginaw, Michigan
Distinguished Woman

FRENCH SEAFOOD STEW

Yield: 6 servings   *Pan Size: 4-quart enamel*

1 cup chopped onion	1 cup dry white wine
3 cloves of garlic, minced	Saffron to taste
1/2 cup canola oil	1/2 teaspoon thyme
2 16-ounce packages frozen	1 teaspoon seasoned salt
haddock	1/2 teaspoon white pepper
2 cups boiling water	1 6-ounce package frozen
1 pound carrots, parboiled	shrimp
1 16-ounce can tomatoes	

Sauté onion and garlic in oil in saucepan for 10 minutes. Add frozen fish and next 8 ingredients. Bring to a boil over low heat. Simmer, covered, for 10 minutes, breaking up fish as it thaws. Add shrimp. Cook just until shrimp are pink; do not overcook. Ladle into soup bowls. Garnish with parsley.

Approx Per Serving: Cal 393; Prot 36 g; Carbo 14 g; T Fat 20 g; Chol 141 mg; Potas 1005 mg; Sod 673 mg.

Celeste Holm, New York, New York
Distinguished Woman/Honorary Degree Recipient
Achievement in the Arts Recipient

GRANDMA'S STEW IN THE OVEN

Yield: 6 servings   *Pan Size: 3 quart*   *Preheat: 250 degrees*

2 pounds stew beef	1 tablespoon sugar
6 carrots, chopped	2 teaspoons salt
3 large potatoes, cut into	2 tablespoons tapioca
quarters	1 12-ounce can vegetable
1 small onion, chopped	juice cocktail
1 stalk celery, chopped	

Combine stew beef, carrots, potatoes, onion, celery, sugar, salt, tapioca and vegetable juice in order listed in greased baking dish. Bake, covered, for 4 to 5 hours or to desired consistency. Do not brown beef first.

Nutritional information for this recipe is not available.

Mrs. Jack (Linda) King, Cedar Hill, Texas
Evaluator/Administrative Coordinator Northwood External Plan of Study

HAM AND SAUSAGE JAMBALAYA

Yield: 12 servings   *Pan Size: heavy 5 quart*

1 pound hard Italian	2 cups canned tomatoes
sausage, thinly sliced	2 bay leaves, crumbled
1¹/₂ cups chopped onion	¹/₂ teaspoon thyme
¹/₂ cup chopped celery	2 teaspoons salt
¹/₂ cup chopped green bell	2 cups chopped cooked ham
pepper	2 tablespoons chopped
8 scallions, chopped	parsley
2 cloves of garlic, crushed	3 cups uncooked rice
2 tablespoons oil	4 cups water

Sauté sausage with onion, celery, green pepper, scallions and garlic in oil in large saucepan until light brown. Add tomatoes, bay leaves, thyme and salt. Simmer for 10 to 15 minutes. Add ham, parsley, rice and water. Simmer, tightly covered, for 30 minutes or until liquid is absorbed and flavors are well blended.

Approx Per Serving: Cal 316; Prot 11 g; Carbo 43 g; T Fat 11 g;
   Chol 23 mg; Potas 336 mg; Sod 851 mg.

Mrs. Jess R. (Beth) Moore, Houston, Texas
Senior Officer - Development and External Affairs

Casseroles

Johann M. & Arthur E. Turner Education Center
West Palm Beach, Florida

ARTICHOKE AND MUSHROOM CASSEROLE

Yield: 6 servings   *Pan Size: 1¹/₂ quart*   *Preheat: 350 degrees*

2 9-ounce packages frozen
   artichoke hearts
1 pound mushrooms,
   sliced
¹/₄ cup butter

1 can cream of mushroom
   soup
3 tablespoons dry Sherry
Salt and pepper to taste
¹/₂ cup Parmesan cheese

Cook artichoke hearts using package directions. Drain; chop coarsely. Sauté mushrooms in butter in skillet for 5 minutes or until tender; drain. Combine artichoke hearts, mushrooms, soup, Sherry, salt and pepper in bowl; mix well. Spoon into casserole. Sprinkle with Parmesan cheese. Bake for 20 minutes or until bubbly. May substitute two 8-ounce cans artichoke hearts for frozen artichokes.

Approx Per Serving: Cal 217; Prot 8 g; Carbo 15 g; T Fat 14 g;
    Chol 27 mg; Potas 554 mg; Sod 650 mg.

Jean Donner Grove, A.N.A., West Palm Beach, Florida
Northwood Women's Board, Committee Member

LASAGNA

Yield: 10 servings   *Pan Size: 9x13 inch*   *Preheat: 325 degrees*

1¹/₂ pounds ground round
1 16-ounce package lasagna
   noodles
2 30-ounce jars spaghetti
   sauce
5 cups shredded mozzarella
   cheese

2 cups shredded provolone
   cheese
1¹/₂ cups Parmesan cheese
24 ounces cottage cheese
¹/₂ cup shredded Romano
   cheese

Brown ground beef in large skillet, stirring until crumbly; drain. Cook noodles using package directions; drain. Alternate layers of spaghetti sauce, noodles, ground beef, mozzarella cheese, provolone cheese, Parmesan cheese and cottage cheese in baking dish, ending with spaghetti sauce. Top with Romano cheese. Bake for 1 to 1¹/₂ hours or until bubbly.

Approx Per Serving: Cal 753; Prot 63 g; Carbo 44 g; T Fat 34 g;
    Chol 135 mg; Potas 771 mg; Sod 1514 mg.

Donna Curry Miller, Waxahachie, Texas
External Affairs Assistant, Dallas, Texas

DINING WITH THE MURCHESONS

Yield: 12 servings   *Pan Size: 9x13 inch*   *Preheat: 375 degrees*

1¹/4 cups chopped canned
  tomatoes
1 12-ounce can whole kernel
  corn
1 4-ounce can chopped
  black olives
1 4-ounce can jalapeño
  peppers

1 cup chili con carne
4 teaspoons olive oil
1 tablespoon sugar
1 tablespoon (scant) salt
24 tamales
2 cups shredded Cheddar
  cheese

Combine tomatoes, corn, olives, jalapeño peppers, chili, olive oil, sugar and salt in bowl; mix well. Alternate layers of tamales, tomato mixture and cheese in greased casserole until all ingredients are used. Bake for 45 minutes or until firm.

Approx Per Serving: Cal 166; Prot 7 g; Carbo 12 g; T Fat 12 g;
  Chol 23 mg; Potas 229 mg; Sod 1284 mg.
  Nutritional information for this recipe does not include tamales.

Mrs. George (Jodie) Biddle, Dallas, Texas
Distinguished Women's Group/Dallas Women's Board

EASY TAMALE PIE

Yield: 12 servings   *Pan Size: 9x13 inch*   *Preheat: 350 degrees*

1¹/2 pounds ground beef
2 Spanish onions, chopped
¹/2 cup oil
1 20-ounce can cream-style
  corn
1 20-ounce can tomato purée
1 tablespoon Worcestershire
  sauce

1 tablespoon chili powder
Salt and pepper to taste
1 cup cornmeal
1 cup cold water
3 eggs, well beaten
1 4-ounce can chopped
  olives

Sauté ground beef and onions in oil in skillet, stirring until ground beef is crumbly; drain. Add cream-style corn, tomato purée, Worcestershire sauce, chili powder, salt and pepper; mix well. Combine cornmeal and water in bowl; mix to make paste. Stir into ground beef mixture. Remove from heat; cool. Fold in eggs and olives. Spoon into casserole. Bake for 1 hour or until hot and bubbly.

Approx Per Serving: Cal 291; Prot 15 g; Carbo 25 g; T Fat 16 g;
  Chol 85 mg; Potas 452 mg; Sod 418 mg.

Mrs. George Randolph (Rosalie) Hearst, Sr., Palm Springs, California
Distinguished Woman

Rosalie Hearst

CHICKEN ASPARAGUS CASSEROLE

Yield: 6 servings   *Pan Size: 2 quart*   *Preheat: 350 degrees*

3/4 cup chopped onion
1 tablespoon butter
4 chicken breast filets, cooked
1 16-ounce can asparagus, drained
1 can chicken and mushroom soup
1 5-ounce can evaporated milk

1 4-ounce jar sliced mushrooms, drained
3 dashes of Tabasco sauce
1 teaspoon soy sauce
Salt and pepper to taste
1 cup shredded Cheddar cheese

Sauté onion in butter in skillet until tender. Chop chicken and asparagus coarsely. Combine onion, chicken, asparagus, soup, evaporated milk, mushrooms, Tabasco sauce, soy sauce and 3/4 cup cheese in bowl; mix well. Spoon into buttered casserole. Sprinkle with remaining 1/4 cup cheese. Bake for 25 to 30 minutes or until hot and bubbly. Serve with rice, fruit and green salad if desired.

Approx Per Serving: Cal 227; Prot 23 g; Carbo 7 g; T Fat 13 g;
Chol 67 mg; Potas 408 mg; Sod 598 mg.

Ms. Lane L. Sadler, Philadelphia, Pennsylvania
Friend of Northwood

CHICKEN CASSEROLE

Yield: 10 servings   *Pan Size: 9x13 inch*   *Preheat: 350 degrees*

16 chicken breast filets
1 large red onion, sliced
1 large green bell pepper, coarsely chopped
4 stalks celery, coarsely chopped

4 medium red potatoes, cut into quarters
2 cans golden mushroom soup
1/4 cup water
1 cup sliced fresh mushrooms

Brown chicken lightly in skillet. Place onion, green pepper, celery and potatoes in casserole. Arrange chicken over vegetables. Mix soup and water in bowl; pour over chicken. Top with mushroom slices. Bake for 1 hour and 20 minutes or until chicken is tender.

Approx Per Serving: Cal 311; Prot 35 g; Carbo 28 g; T Fat 7 g;
Chol 79 mg; Potas 841 mg; Sod 602 mg.

Nell M. H. Smith, Palm Desert, California
Palm Springs Chapter

CHICKEN CHOW MEIN

Yield: 12 servings	Pan Size: 9x13 inch	Preheat: 350 degrees

4 cups chopped cooked
  chicken breast
1 can mushroom soup
1 can cheese soup
1 5-ounce can evaporated
  milk
1 16-ounce can green beans
1 2-ounce jar chopped
  pimento
1 tablespoon chopped onion

1 cup chopped celery
1/2 cup sliced almonds
1 8-ounce can sliced water
  chestnuts
1 3-ounce can chow mein
  noodles
1 teaspoon salt
1 31/2-ounce can French-fried
  onion rings

Combine chicken, soups, milk, vegetables, almonds, water chestnuts, chow mein noodles and salt in bowl; mix well. Spoon into casserole. Bake for 45 minutes or until hot and bubbly. Top with onion rings. Bake for several minutes longer. May boil chicken in water seasoned with bay leaf and celery tops if desired.

Approx Per Serving: Cal 266; Prot 19 g; Carbo 18 g; T Fat 14 g;
  Chol 55 mg; Potas 323 mg; Sod 816 mg.

Mrs. Jack (Dianne) Adleta, Dallas, Texas
Dallas Women's Board

CHICKEN AND GREEN CHILI CASSEROLE

Yield: 6 servings	Pan Size: 9x13 inch	Preheat: 350 degrees

1 cup cottage cheese
8 ounces cream cheese
1 cup sour cream
1 cup thin cream sauce
1 teaspoon salt

1 clove of garlic, minced
4 chicken breast filets, cooked
8 ounces Monterey Jack cheese
1 4-ounce can green chilies
12 thin crêpes

Combine cottage cheese, cream cheese, sour cream, cream sauce, salt and garlic in bowl; mix well. Cut chicken into twelve 1/2x3-inch strips. Cut Monterey Jack cheese and green chilies into 12 strips each. Place 1 strip each chicken, Monterey Jack cheese and green chili in center of each crêpe. Add 1 tablespoon cottage cheese mixture. Roll to enclose filling; place seam side down in casserole. Cover with remaining cottage cheese mixture. Bake for 30 to 45 minutes or until hot and bubbly.

Approx Per Serving: Cal 461; Prot 31 g; Carbo 6 g; T Fat 35 g;
  Chol 131 mg; Potas 371 mg; Sod 869 mg.
  Nutritional information for this recipe does not include
  cream sauce and crêpes.

Mrs. Jack (Dianne) Adleta, Dallas, Texas
Dallas Women's Board

GREEN NOODLE CHICKEN CASSEROLES

Yield: 20 servings   *Pan Size: two 9x13 inch*   *Preheat: 350 degrees*

1 12-ounce package green
   noodles
2 3-pound chickens, cooked
1 pound mushrooms, sliced
5 cans cream of mushroom
   soup
2 pounds shredded Cheddar
   cheese

1 soup can milk
1 4-ounce can pimentos,
   drained
2 cans sliced water chestnuts,
   drained
2 cups sliced almonds

Cook noodles using package directions; drain. Bone and chop chicken. Sauté mushrooms in large saucepan until tender. Add chicken, soup, cheese, milk, pimentos, water chestnuts and 1 cup almonds. Cook over low heat until cheese melts, stirring constantly. Add noodles; mix well. Spoon into casseroles. Sprinkle with remaining 1 cup almonds. Bake for 1 hour or until hot and bubbly.

Nutritional information for this recipe is not available.

Northwood Cookbook Committee, Dallas, Texas

HOT CHICKEN SALAD

Yield: 10 servings   *Pan Size: 2 quart*   *Preheat: 375 degrees*

2 cups chopped cooked
   chicken
2 cups chopped celery
1 cup sliced almonds
1/2 teaspoon salt
1/8 teaspoon pepper
2 tablespoons grated onion

2 tablespoons lemon juice
1 cup mayonnaise
Tabasco sauce to taste
1 cup shredded Cheddar
   cheese
1 1/2 cups crushed potato chips

Combine chicken, celery, almonds, salt, pepper, onion, lemon juice, mayonnaise and Tabasco sauce in bowl; mix well. Spoon into greased casserole. Sprinkle with cheese and potato chips. Bake for 20 to 25 minutes or until hot and bubbly. May substitute 1/2 cup low-fat yogurt for half the mayonnaise.

Approx Per Serving: Cal 465; Prot 15 g; Carbo 19 g; T Fat 38 g;
   Chol 50 mg; Potas 599 mg; Sod 481 mg.

Northwood Cookbook Committee, Dallas, Texas

KING RANCH CHICKEN

Yield: 10 servings   *Pan Size: 3 quart*   *Preheat: 350 degrees*

1 3-pound chicken, cooked, boned
1 large onion, chopped
1 large green bell pepper, chopped
12 corn tortillas, cut into bite-sized pieces
8 ounces shredded Cheddar cheese

1 teaspoon chili powder
Garlic salt to taste
1 can cream of chicken soup
1 can cream of mushroom soup
1 10-ounce can Ro-Tel tomatoes, chopped

Cut chicken into bite-sized pieces. Combine with onion and green pepper in bowl; mix well. Alternate layers of chicken mixture and tortilla pieces in greased casserole. Sprinkle with cheese, chili powder and garlic salt. Add layers of soups and Ro-Tel. Bake for 30 to 45 minutes or until hot and bubbly. Serve with chips, guacamole and chili con queso.

Approx Per Serving: Cal 371; Prot 30 g; Carbo 23 g; T Fat 18 g;
    Chol 87 mg; Potas 387 mg; Sod 733 mg.

Northwood Cookbook Committee, Dallas, Texas

CHICKEN AND RICE CASSEROLE

Yield: 6 servings   *Pan Size: large stockpot*

4 chicken breasts
8 chicken legs
1 tablespoon salt
2 quarts water

2 cups rice
1 can cream of mushroom soup
1/2 cup water

Combine chicken, salt and 2 quarts water in stockpot. Bring to a boil over high heat; reduce heat. Simmer for 1 hour or until chicken is tender, stirring occasionally. Remove chicken. Bring broth to a boil. Add rice; reduce heat. Simmer, covered, for 15 minutes or until rice is tender. Bone and chop chicken. Add chicken, soup and remaining 1/2 cup water to rice; mix well. Simmer, covered, for 5 minutes; remove from heat. Let stand, covered, for 5 minutes. Spoon into serving dish.

Approx Per Serving: Cal 420; Prot 35 g; Carbo 53 g; T Fat 6 g;
    Chol 77 mg; Potas 428 mg; Sod 1565 mg.

Mrs. Herman (Barbara) Wilkerson, Duncanville, Texas
Cedar Hill Women's Board

CHICKEN SPAGHETTI

Yield: 20 servings   *Pan Size: roaster*   *Preheat: 350 degrees*

2 16-ounce packages
   spaghetti
3 large white onions, chopped
1 cup olive oil
2 28-ounce cans tomatoes,
   chopped
1 large green bell pepper,
   finely chopped
1 stalk celery, finely chopped
2 tablespoons salt

1 20-ounce can small
   English peas
1 6-ounce can sliced
   mushrooms
2 8-ounce cans bamboo
   shoots, finely chopped
7 pounds chicken, cooked,
   chopped
16 ounces American cheese,
   shredded

Cook spaghetti using package directions; drain and blanch. Sauté onions in olive oil in large saucepan until tender. Add tomatoes, green pepper, celery and salt; mix well. Simmer over very low heat for 1 hour, stirring occasionally. Add peas, mushrooms and bamboo shoots; mix well. Alternate layers of spaghetti, cheese, chicken and tomato sauce in roaster. Bake for 20 to 30 minutes or until hot and bubbly. Invert onto serving platter.

Approx Per Serving: Cal 696; Prot 59 g; Carbo 44 g; T Fat 31 g;
    Chol 163 mg; Potas 818 mg; Sod 1320 mg.

Lorraine B. Bland

Mrs. William W. (Lorraine) Bland, Houston, Texas
Houston Women's Board/Distinguished Woman

SHRIMP AND CHEESE CASSEROLE

Yield: 4 servings   *Pan Size: 1¹/₂ quart*   *Preheat: 350 degrees*

4 ounces mushrooms, sliced
2 tablespoons butter
1 pound shrimp, cooked,
   shelled
1¹/₂ cups cooked rice
1¹/₂ cups shredded Cheddar
   cheese

¹/₂ cup cream
¹/₂ teaspoon salt
¹/₄ cup catsup
1 teaspoon Worcestershire
   sauce

Sauté mushrooms in butter in skillet until tender. Combine with shrimp, rice, cheese, cream, salt, catsup and Worcestershire sauce in bowl; toss gently. Spoon into lightly greased casserole. Bake for 35 minutes or until heated through. Serve with green salad and garlic bread.

Approx Per Serving: Cal 483; Prot 37 g; Carbo 293 g; T Fat 30 g;
    Chol 292 mg; Potas 499 mg; Sod 1035 mg.

Leslie A. Gowan, Dallas, Texas
Director of External Affairs, Dallas

SHRIMP CASSEROLE HARPIN

Yield: 6 servings *Pan Size: 2 quart* *Preheat: 350 degrees*

2¹/₂ pounds large shrimp,
  shelled, deveined
1 tablespoon lemon juice
3 tablespoons oil
¹/₄ cup finely chopped green
  bell pepper
¹/₄ cup finely chopped onion
2 tablespoons butter
³/₄ cup rice, cooked, chilled

1 teaspoon salt
¹/₈ teaspoon pepper
¹/₈ teaspoon mace
Dash of cayenne pepper
1 can tomato soup
¹/₂ cup Sherry
1 cup whipping cream
³/₄ cup slivered blanched
  almonds

Cook shrimp in boiling salted water in saucepan for 5 minutes; drain. Place in casserole; sprinkle with lemon juice and oil. Chill for several hours. Reserve 8 shrimp for garnish. Sauté vegetables in butter in skillet for 5 minutes. Add with rice, seasonings, soup, Sherry, whipping cream and ¹/₂ cup almonds to shrimp; toss to mix. Bake for 35 minutes. Top with reserved shrimp and remaining almonds. Bake for 20 minutes longer or until mixture is bubbly and shrimp are slightly browned.

Approx Per Serving: Cal 670; Prot 47 g; Carbo 31 g; T Fat 38 g;
  Chol 433 mg; Potas 676 mg; Sod 1184 mg.

Mrs. Robert H. (Sunny) Miller, West Palm Beach, Florida
West Palm Beach Women's Board

SHRIMP AND EGGPLANT

Yield: 6 servings *Pan Size: 2 quart* *Preheat: 350 degrees*

1 large green bell pepper
¹/₂ bunch green onions
¹/₂ stalk celery
1 tablespoon butter
1 pound shrimp, cooked
1 large eggplant, cooked

¹/₄ cup bread crumbs
¹/₂ cup cream
Salt and pepper to taste
¹/₂ bunch parsley, chopped
1 tablespoon butter
¹/₄ cup bread crumbs

Mince vegetables. Sauté in 1 tablespoon butter in skillet until tender. Add minced shrimp, mashed eggplant, ¹/₄ cup bread crumbs, cream, salt, pepper and parsley. Spoon into greased casserole; dot with remaining butter. Top with ¹/₄ cup bread crumbs. Bake for 20 minutes or until bubbly.

Approx Per Serving: Cal 196; Prot 18 g; Carbo 11 g; T Fat 8 g;
  Chol 171 mg; Potas 347 mg; Sod 262 mg.

Mrs. Maurice (Winifred) Hirsch, Houston, Texas
Founding Chairman, Houston Women's Board
Distinguished Woman/Honorary Degree Recipient

SEAFOOD CASSEROLES

Yield: 6 servings   *Pan Size: 6 individual casseroles*   *Preheat: broiler*

¹/₂ cup chopped lobster	¹/₂ cup butter
¹/₂ cup chopped shrimp	1 cup flour
¹/₂ cup chopped oysters	1 quart milk
¹/₂ cup chopped snapper	2 tablespoons Parmesan
¹/₂ cup chopped mushrooms	cheese
¹/₄ cup chopped onion	1 egg, beaten
1 teaspoon salt	6 medium potatoes, cooked,
¹/₂ teaspoon pepper	mashed
¹/₂ teaspoon red pepper sauce	2 tablespoons Parmesan
1 cup Sherry	cheese

Combine first 10 ingredients in large saucepan. Bring to a boil; reduce heat. Simmer for 10 minutes, stirring occasionally. Drain; keep warm. Melt butter in skillet over low heat; blend in flour. Add milk gradually, mixing well after each addition. Simmer until sauce thickens, stirring constantly. Add seafood and 2 tablespoons Parmesan cheese; mix well. Spoon into individual casseroles. Combine egg and potatoes in bowl; mix well. Force through pastry tube around edge of each casserole. Sprinkle with remaining Parmesan cheese. Place casseroles on baking sheet. Broil until lightly browned.

Approx Per Serving: Cal 575; Prot 21 g; Carbo 59 g; T Fat 24 g; Chol 138 mg; Potas 1048 mg; Sod 711 mg.

Mrs. Charles (Laude Cleary) Bowman, Dallas Texas
Dallas Women's Board/Library League

EGG AND CHEESE CASSEROLE OLÉ

Yield: 10 servings   *Pan Size: 9x13 inch*   *Preheat: 350 degrees*

12 eggs, beaten	1 pound Monterey Jack
¹/₂ cup flour	cheese, shredded
1 teaspoon baking powder	2 4-ounce cans green chilies,
¹/₂ cup melted butter	finely chopped

Combine eggs, flour, baking powder, butter, cheese and chilies in bowl; mix well. Pour into buttered casserole. Bake for 35 minutes or until eggs are set. Serve immediately. This is a great brunch casserole and is always a hit at Northwood functions.

Approx Per Serving: Cal 378; Prot 20 g; Carbo 8 g; T Fat 30 g; Chol 322 mg; Potas 201 mg; Sod 438 mg.

Creative Catering, Cedar Hill, Texas
Friend of Northwood

MAKE-AHEAD BREAKFAST CASSEROLE

Yield: 8 servings   *Pan Size: 9x13 inch*   *Preheat: 350 degrees*

1 pound bulk sausage	6 eggs, beaten
¼ cup butter	2 cups half and half
6 slices bread, crusts trimmed	1 teaspoon salt
1½ cups shredded Cheddar cheese	

Brown sausage in skillet, stirring until crumbly; drain. Butter bread slices. Place in greased casserole. Spoon sausage over bread. Sprinkle with cheese. Combine eggs, half and half and salt in bowl; mix well. Pour over cheese. Chill, covered, overnight. Let stand at room temperature for 15 minutes before baking. Bake, uncovered, for 45 minutes or until eggs are set.

Approx Per Serving: Cal 441; Prot 16 g; Carbo 14 g; T Fat 36 g; Chol 240 mg; Potas 226 mg; Sod 820 mg.

Mrs. Leonard (Mary Tullie) Critcher, Dallas, Texas
Dallas Women's Board

JALAPEÑO CHEESE QUICHE

Yield: 6 servings   *Pan Size: 9-inch pie plate*   *Preheat: 350 degrees*

4 eggs	1 4-ounce can jalapeño
1 cup milk	peppers, drained, chopped
8 ounces Monterey Jack cheese, chopped	

Combine eggs and milk in blender container. Process until well mixed. Add cheese gradually, processing on Low. Spread jalapeño peppers in pie plate. Pour egg mixture over peppers. Bake for 25 minutes or until eggs are set. This recipe was given to me by a good friend in San Antonio while my husband was in law school. Serve with chips, salsa and Border Buttermilk, alias Margaritas.

Approx Per Serving: Cal 231; Prot 14 g; Carbo 5 g; T Fat 17 g; Chol 183 mg; Potas 223 mg; Sod 1295 mg.

Mrs. R. H. (Beverly) Holmes, Dallas, Texas
Chairman, Dallas Women's Board

KAPPA ALPHA EGG CASSEROLE

Yield: 10 servings   Pan Size: 9x13 inch   Preheat: 350 degrees

1 pound bulk sausage	6 eggs, beaten
1/2 cup butter, softened	3 cups milk
8 slices white bread, crusts	Tabasco sauce to taste
trimmed	3/4 teaspoon dry mustard
3/4 cup shredded sharp	3/4 teaspoon salt
Cheddar cheese	1 tablespoon grated onion

Brown sausage in skillet, stirring until crumbly; drain. Butter bread slices; cut into 1/2-inch squares. Reserve 1/4 cup cheese for topping. Layer bread, remaining cheese and sausage in buttered casserole. Combine eggs, milk, seasonings and onion in bowl; mix well. Pour over layers. Sprinkle with reserved cheese. Chill, covered, overnight. Let stand at room temperature for 30 minutes. Bake, uncovered, for 40 minutes or until eggs are set. This is a traditional breakfast served for the Kappa Alpha Fraternity at the University of Texas before the Texas-O.U. game for the last 10 years. Serve with hot rolls, miniature Danish and cinnamon rolls.

Approx Per Serving: Cal 357; Prot 13 g; Carbo 15 g; T Fat 27 g;
    Chol 186 mg; Potas 218 mg; Sod 619 mg.

Mrs. R. H. (Beverly) Holmes, Dallas, Texas
Chairman, Dallas Women's Board

CHEESE STRATA

Yield: 6 servings   Pan Size: 2 quart   Preheat: 350 degrees

1/3 cup butter, softened	3 cups milk
10 slices white bread, crusts	1 1/2 teaspoons salt
trimmed	1 teaspoon dry mustard
3 cups shredded sharp	Pinch of cayenne pepper
Cheddar cheese	Chopped parsley to taste
4 eggs, slightly beaten	Paprika to taste

Butter bread slices; cut each slice into 4 strips. Alternate layers of bread strips and cheese in buttered casserole, ending with cheese. Beat eggs with milk, salt, mustard and cayenne pepper. Pour over layers. Chill for 24 hours. Let stand at room temperature for 1 hour. Sprinkle with parsley and paprika. Bake for 40 to 50 minutes or until puffed and brown. This is a great "do-ahead" recipe for brunch. Serve with fresh fruit salad and chicken or seafood salad.

Approx Per Serving: Cal 570; Prot 26 g; Carbo 30 g; T Fat 39 g;
    Chol 245 mg; Potas 318 mg; Sod 1306 mg.

Mrs. Charles (Louise) Rounsaville, Jr., Dallas, Texas
Dallas Women's Board

Vegetables
& Side Dishes

The Chapel, c. early 1900's
Cedar Hill, Texas

CHILLED TARRAGON ASPARAGUS

Yield: 4 servings   *Pan Size: shallow dish*

1 pound fresh asparagus	1/2 teaspoon freshly ground
1/3 cup Italian salad dressing	pepper
1/3 cup tarragon vinegar	1/2 teaspoon garlic powder
1/2 teaspoon tarragon	Leaf lettuce

Trim asparagus. Cook in a small amount of water in covered saucepan for 6 to 8 minutes or until tender-crisp; drain. Arrange in shallow dish. Combine salad dressing, vinegar, tarragon, pepper and garlic powder in small jar. Cover jar; shake until well mixed. Pour over asparagus. Chill, covered, for 6 hours to overnight. Drain just before serving. Serve on lettuce-lined plates. May substitute one 15-ounce can asparagus spears, drained, for fresh asparagus.

Approx Per Serving: Cal 118; Prot 4 g; Carbo 7 g; T Fat 12 g;
    Chol 0 mg; Potas 365 mg; Sod 97 mg.

Mrs. Jim (Barbara) Lake, Dallas, Texas
Dallas Women's Board

BAKED BEANS

Yield: 16 servings   *Pan Size: Dutch oven*   *Preheat: 325 degrees*

1 quart dry beans	1/2 teaspoon ginger
1/4 teaspoon soda	1 tablespoon molasses
2 teaspoons salt	1 onion
3 tablespoons olive oil	Dry mustard and red pepper
2 ounces salt pork	to taste

Soak beans in water to cover in Dutch oven overnight; drain. Add soda and cold water to cover. Bring to a boil; reduce heat. Simmer until bean skins break; remove from heat. Let stand for several minutes; drain. Rinse with cold water. Add salt, olive oil, salt pork, ginger, molasses, onion, mustard and red pepper. Add hot water to cover. Let stand for several minutes. Bake for 8 hours, adding additional water as needed.

Approx Per Serving: Cal 218; Prot 12 g; Carbo 35 g; T Fat 4 g;
    Chol 2 mg; Potas 891 mg; Sod 329 mg.

Former Senator Margaret Chase Smith, Skowhegan, Maine
Distinguished Woman

BEAN CASSEROLE

Yield: 15 servings	Pan Size: 3 quart	Preheat: 350 degrees

1/2 pound bacon
1/2 pound ground beef
1 medium onion, chopped
Salt and pepper to taste
1/2 cup catsup
2/3 cup packed brown sugar
1 tablespoon cider vinegar
1 teaspoon dry mustard

1 15-ounce can lima beans, drained
1 15-ounce can kidney beans
1 16-ounce can pork and beans
1 15-ounce can butter beans, drained

Chop bacon into bite-sized pieces. Brown ground beef with bacon and onion in skillet, stirring until ground beef is crumbly; drain. Season with salt and pepper. Add mixture of catsup, brown sugar, vinegar and mustard; mix well. Spoon into casserole. Stir in lima beans, kidney beans, pork and beans and butter beans. Bake for 1 hour.

Approx Per Serving: Cal 278; Prot 14 g; Carbo 34 g; T Fat 10 g;
   Chol 25 mg; Potas 471 mg; Sod 683 mg.

Mrs. Charles V. (Judy) Shepard, Dallas, Texas
Dallas Women's Board

CROCK-O-BEANS

Yield: 72 servings	Pan Size: 4 quart	Preheat: 325 degrees

2 pounds dry navy beans
3 smoked ham hocks
1/2 pound salt pork, finely chopped
1 teaspoon dry mustard

1/2 cup packed brown sugar
1 small onion, chopped
Salt and pepper to taste
1 1/4 cups tomato juice
Bacon

Sort beans. Soak in water to cover in saucepan overnight; drain. Add water just to cover. Bring to a boil; reduce heat. Simmer for 10 minutes or until bean skins break; remove from heat. Let stand, covered, for 30 minutes. Place ham hocks in casserole. Drain beans, reserving liquid. Layer beans, salt pork, mustard, brown sugar, onion, salt and pepper and tomato juice over ham hocks. Pour bean liquid over layers. Arrange bacon over top. Bake, covered, for 5 to 6 hours, adding hot water as necessary. This dish is especially good served with chili sauce, corn bread and coleslaw. This "secret" recipe was perfected by Donald T. Baumann, Ph.D., after years of experimentation and refinement.

Approx Per Serving: Cal 60; Prot 4 g; Carbo 10 g; T Fat 1 g;
   Chol 4 mg; Potas 227 mg; Sod 43 mg.
   Nutritional information for this recipe does not include bacon.

Paul J. Strawhecker, Midland, Michigan
Vice President, Development of Northwood Institute

MOM'S ITALIAN BROCCOLI

Yield: 4 servings   *Pan Size: 10-inch skillet*

1 bunch broccoli	1 cup Italian-seasoned bread
Salt and pepper to taste	crumbs
Garlic powder to taste	1/4 cup olive oil

Separate broccoli into stalks. Season with salt and pepper. Cook in steamer over boiling water until tender-crisp; drain. Coat with mixture of garlic powder and seasoned bread crumbs. Sauté in olive oil in skillet until browned. Serve immediately.

Approx Per Serving: Cal 229; Prot 5 g; Carbo 21 g; T Fat 15 g; Chol 1 mg; Potas 181 mg; Sod 196 mg.

Mrs. A. Baron (Darlene) Cass III, Dallas, Texas
Dallas Women's Board

BROCCOLI AND RICE CASSEROLE

Yield: 20 servings   *Pan Size: 4 quart*   *Preheat: 350 degrees*

2 cups uncooked rice	1 can cream of mushroom soup
4 10-ounce packages frozen	1 pound Velveeta cheese,
chopped broccoli	chopped

Cook rice using package directions. Cook broccoli using package directions; drain well. Combine rice, broccoli, soup and cheese in bowl; mix well. Spoon into greased casserole. Bake until hot and bubbly.

Approx Per Serving: Cal 172; Prot 7 g; Carbo 16 g; T Fat 8 g; Chol 22 mg; Potas 155 mg; Sod 576 mg.

Ms. Denise Ward, Dallas, Texas
Director of Annual Giving, Texas Campus

FLAN DE CAROTTES

Yield: 10 servings   *Pan Size: 12-inch pie plate*   *Preheat: 425 degrees*

1 recipe 1-crust pie pastry	1/4 teaspoon salt
1 3/4 pounds carrots, thinly sliced	1/2 cup margarine
1/2 cup margarine	1/2 cup cream
1 tablespoon sugar	1/2 cup sautéed chopped onion
	1/2 teaspoon dillweed

Roll pastry into 12-inch circle. Press into pie plate; crimp edge. Prick in several places with fork. Line with waxed paper; top with pie weights. Bake until light golden brown. Remove waxed paper and pie weights. Reserve 1 1/4 cups carrots for garnish. Combine remaining carrots, 1/2 cup margarine, sugar and salt in saucepan. Add water just to cover. Cook until carrots are tender and liquid is absorbed. Purée in food processor until smooth. Add remaining 1/2 cup margarine 1 tablespoon at a time, mixing until well blended after each addition. Add cream; mix well. Stir in sautéed onion and dillweed. Return mixture to saucepan. Cook until heated through, stirring constantly. Spoon into pie shell. Bake for 20 minutes or until set. Garnish with reserved carrots.

Approx Per Serving: Cal 333; Prot 2 g; Carbo 18 g; T Fat 29 g;
Chol 16 mg; Potas 284 mg; Sod 409 mg.

Mary Jane Bostick, Birmingham, Michigan
Detroit Chapter National Chair 1983-1985/Distinguished Woman

MARINATED CARROTS

Yield: 12 servings   *Pan Size: 2-quart bowl*

2 pounds carrots, thinly sliced	1 teaspoon dry mustard
1 cup sugar	1 teaspoon salt
1 cup tomato soup	1/2 teaspoon pepper
1 cup oil	1 large onion, thinly sliced
3/4 cup vinegar	1 large green bell pepper, thinly sliced

Cook carrots in water to cover in saucepan for 10 minutes; drain well. Combine sugar, tomato soup, oil, vinegar, mustard, salt and pepper in small bowl; mix well. Spoon hot carrots into bowl. Arrange onion and green pepper over top. Pour marinade over vegetables immediately. Chill in refrigerator until serving time.

Approx Per Serving: Cal 273; Prot 1 g; Carbo 28 g; T Fat 19 g;
Chol 0 mg; Potas 320 mg; Sod 278 mg.

Henrietta L. McInally

Henrietta McInally, Grosse Pointe, Michigan
Distinguished Woman, Detroit Chapter

CORN CASSEROLE

Yield: 12 servings	Pan Size: 9x13 inch	Preheat: 350 degrees

1/2 cup butter	2 eggs, slightly beaten
1 17-ounce can cream-style corn	2 tablespoons milk
	2 tablespoons flour
1 16-ounce can whole kernel corn, drained	2 tablespoons sugar

Melt butter in baking dish; tilt to coat evenly. Combine cream-style corn, whole kernel corn, eggs, milk, flour and sugar in bowl; mix well. Spoon into baking dish. Bake for 45 minutes.

Approx Per Serving: Cal 155; Prot 3 g; Carbo 18 g; T Fat 9 g;
    Chol 57 mg; Potas 130 mg; Sod 279 mg.

Mrs. James I. (Monta) Dunn, Jewett, Texas
Friend of Northwood

CORN PUDDING

Yield: 8 servings	Pan Size: 1 quart	Preheat: 400 degrees

7 ears fresh corn	1 tablespoon sugar
3 tablespoons melted butter	1 teaspoon salt
3 eggs, slightly beaten	Red pepper to taste
2 cups milk	

Grate enough corn from cobs to measure 1 cup. Combine butter, eggs, milk, corn, sugar, salt and red pepper in bowl; mix well. Spoon into lightly greased baking dish. Bake for 10 minutes. Reduce temperature to 325 degrees. Bake for 30 to 35 minutes longer or until pudding is set.

Approx Per Serving: Cal 184; Prot 7 g; Carbo 22 g; T Fat 9 g;
    Chol 100 mg; Potas 276 mg; Sod 366 mg.

Mrs. Edward B. (Virginia) Linthicum, Dallas, Texas
Distinguished Woman/Dallas Women's Board

CREOLE OKRA

Yield: 6 servings   *Pan Size: large skillet*

¹/₂ **pound bacon, chopped**
1 large green bell pepper,
  chopped
1 large onion, chopped
	1¹/₂ pounds small okra, sliced
	  ¹/₂ inch thick
	6 ounces chili sauce

Cook bacon in skillet until crisp. Remove to paper towels to drain. Sauté green pepper and onion in pan drippings until tender. Add okra. Sauté over low heat for 5 to 10 minutes longer. Drizzle chili sauce over vegetables. Simmer, covered, for 10 to 20 minutes or to desired consistency. Sprinkle with bacon just before serving. Do not add water at any point during cooking process.

Approx Per Serving: Cal 300; Prot 16 g; Carbo 17 g; T Fat 19 g;
    Chol 32 mg; Potas 644 mg; Sod 983 mg.

Mrs. Chet (Eunice) Bonar, Dallas, Texas
Dallas Women's Board

POTATO CASSEROLE

Yield: 8 servings   *Pan Size: 2 quart*   *Preheat: 350 degrees*

³/₄ **cup melted margarine**
1 32-ounce package frozen
  hashed brown potatoes
1 cup chopped onion
2 cups sour cream
	8 ounces Cheddar cheese,
	  shredded
	1 can cream of chicken soup
	1 teaspoon garlic salt
	1 cup cornflake crumbs

Combine margarine, potatoes, onion, sour cream, cheese, soup and garlic salt in bowl; mix well. Spoon half the mixture into baking dish sprayed with nonstick cooking spray. Combine remaining mixture with cornflake crumbs. Spoon over top. Bake for 1 hour and 15 minutes. This dish can be frozen before baking.

Approx Per Serving: Cal 710; Prot 15 g; Carbo 46 g; T Fat 54 g;
    Chol 58 mg; Potas 677 mg; Sod 1097 mg.

Mrs. Mary Lou Harvey, Dallas, Texas
Dallas Women's Board

POTATOES SUPREME

Yield: 8 servings   *Pan Size: 9x13 inch*   *Preheat: 350 degrees*

1 can cream of chicken-
  mushroom soup
1 can milk
1 cup sour cream
2 pounds frozen hashed
  brown potatoes

3 green onions, chopped
Salt and pepper to taste
Shredded Cheddar cheese

Combine soup, milk and sour cream in bowl; mix well. Layer potatoes, green onions and soup mixture 1/2 at a time in greased baking dish. Sprinkle cheese over top. Bake for 1 hour.

Nutritional information for this recipe is not available.

Sy Clark, Dallas, Texas
Dallas Women's Board

SPINACH PIE

Yield: 6 servings   *Pan Size: 9-inch pie plate*   *Preheat: 350 degrees*

2 1/2 cups cooked spinach
8 ounces shredded
  mozzarella cheese
3 tablespoons melted butter

1/2 cup whipping cream
Salt to taste
1 9-inch baked pie shell

Squeeze spinach dry. Reserve 1/3 of the cheese for topping. Combine spinach, remaining cheese, butter, cream and salt in bowl; mix well. Spoon into pie shell. Sprinkle reserved cheese over top. Bake for 15 minutes or until cheese melts and pie is heated through.

Approx Per Serving: Cal 398; Prot 15 g; Carbo 19 g; T Fat 30 g;
  Chol 63 mg; Potas 304 mg; Sod 507 mg.

Carolyn A. Rabidoux, Palm Beach, Florida
Chair of Palm Beach Chapter

TEXAS CRABGRASS

Yield: 6 servings   *Pan Size: chafing dish*

1 10-ounce package frozen
   chopped spinach
1 medium onion, finely
   chopped
1/2 cup margarine

1/4 cup dry Sherry
1/2 pound cooked crab meat,
   flaked
3/4 cup Parmesan cheese

Cook spinach using package directions; drain. Sauté onion in margarine in skillet until tender. Add spinach, Sherry, crab meat and Parmesan cheese; mix well. Spoon into chafing dish. Serve as vegetable or as appetizer dip.

Approx Per Serving: Cal 253; Prot 14 g; Carbo 5 g; T Fat 19 g;
    Chol 42 mg; Potas 350 mg; Sod 535 mg.

Ms. Ellen Weinstein, Dallas, Texas
Dallas Women's Board

CROOKNECK CHIFFON PIE

Yield: 8 servings   *Pan Size: 9-inch pie plate*   *Preheat: 350 degrees*

2 cups whole wheat bread
   crumbs
6 cups coarsely chopped
   crookneck squash
1/3 cup chopped onion
1/2 cup chopped red bell
   pepper
1 1/2 tablespoons oil

2 eggs, beaten
1/2 cup cottage cheese
2 tablespoons cornmeal
2 tablespoons Parmesan
   cheese
4 basil leaves
1/2 teaspoon salt
1/3 cup chopped walnuts

Press bread crumbs over bottom and side of pie plate. Steam squash until tender-crisp. Place in blender container; process until smooth. Sauté onion and bell pepper in oil in skillet until tender. Add squash; mix well. Combine eggs, cottage cheese, cornmeal, Parmesan cheese, basil and salt in blender container; process until smooth. Add to squash mixture; mix well. Spoon into prepared pie plate. Sprinkle with walnuts. Bake for 40 to 45 minutes or until set. May substitute zucchini for crookneck squash.

Approx Per Serving: Cal 160; Prot 7 g; Carbo 16 g; T Fat 9 g;
    Chol 55 mg; Potas 315 mg; Sod 317 mg.

Margaret Long Arnold, Washington, D. C.
Distinguished Woman

SQUASH SOUFFLÉ

Yield: 8 servings   *Pan Size: 2 quart*   *Preheat: 350 degrees*

¼ cup finely chopped onion	¼ cup chopped pimentos
¼ cup butter	1 tablespoon salt
4 pounds yellow squash	¼ teaspoon pepper
1½ cups fine bread crumbs	2 eggs, beaten

Sauté onion in butter in skillet until tender. Cook squash in boiling salted water to cover for 20 minutes or until very tender; drain. Mash squash in bowl. Add onion; mix well. Stir in bread crumbs, pimentos, salt and pepper. Beat in eggs. Spoon into greased casserole. Bake for 30 minutes.

Approx Per Serving: Cal 194; Prot 7 g; Carbo 24 g; T Fat 8 g;
    Chol 86 mg; Potas 480 mg; Sod 991 mg.

Mrs. Randy (Merle) Roten, Cedar Hill, Texas
Cedar Hill Women's Board

SWEET POTATOES LUCILE

Yield: 4 servings   *Pan Size: baking sheet*   *Preheat: 450 degrees*

4 medium sweet potatoes	2 tablespoons whipping
Mace to taste	cream
Salt and pepper to taste	4 teaspoons Sherry
2 tablespoons butter	

Bake sweet potatoes for 1 hour or until tender. Cut sweet potatoes into halves; remove pulp carefully, leaving skins intact. Combine pulp, mace, salt and pepper in mixer bowl; beat until light and fluffy. Add butter and cream; beat until well blended. Add Sherry; mix well. Spoon into potato skins. Place on baking sheet. Broil until lightly browned.

Approx Per Serving: Cal 212; Prot 2 g; Carbo 28 g; T Fat 9 g;
    Chol 26 mg; Potas 416 mg; Sod 65 mg.

Mrs. William (Lucile) Doheny, Fort Lauderdale, Florida
Fort Lauderdale Women's Board

HARRIET'S SWEET POTATO FRIES

Yield: 6 servings   *Pan Size: deep skillet*

3 large sweet potatoes   1 cup sugar
Shortening for frying

Peel potatoes; cut into strips as for French fries. Fry in hot 1½-inch deep shortening in skillet until tender, turning to brown on all sides. Drain on paper towels. Coat with sugar. Serve warm with pork roast or ham.

Approx Per Serving: Cal 187; Prot 1 g; Carbo 47 g; T Fat 0 g;
    Chol 0 mg; Potas 200 mg; Sod 7 mg.
    Nutritional information for this recipe does not include
    shortening for frying.

Mrs. Arthur (Harriet) Rose, Dallas, Texas
Dallas Women's Board

BOURBON SWEET POTATOES IN ORANGE CUPS

Yield: 10 servings   *Pan Size: glass pie plate*   ≈M≈

5 large oranges   ¼ cup orange juice
1   16-ounce can sweet   ¼ cup Bourbon
    potatoes   2 tablespoons melted butter
2 apples, peeled, finely   Cinnamon, nutmeg, cloves,
    chopped   and salt to taste
¼ cup packed brown sugar

Cut oranges into halves. Remove pulp, leaving skins intact. Reserve pulp for another purpose. Combine sweet potatoes, apples, brown sugar, orange juice, Bourbon, butter, cinnamon, nutmeg, cloves and salt in blender container; process until smooth. Spoon into orange cups. Arrange in ring around outside edge of pie plate. Microwave on High for 5 to 8 minutes or until heated through.

Approx Per Serving: Cal 117; Prot 1 g; Carbo 22 g; T Fat 3 g;
    Chol 6 mg; Potas 185 mg; Sod 57 mg.

Mrs. Robert (Genie) Parker, Phoenix, Arizona
Founding Member and Chapter Chair 1985-1988, Valley of the Sun Chapter

SWEET POTATO PIE

Yield: 8 servings   *Pan Size: 8-inch pie plate*   *Preheat: 450 degrees*

3 medium sweet potatoes	1 8-ounce can pineapple
1 cup sugar	chunks
2 tablespoons butter	1½ ounces Drambuie
2 tablespoons flour	20 large marshmallows
2 teaspoons vanilla extract	

Cook unpeeled sweet potatoes in water to cover in saucepan until tender; drain. Peel and mash sweet potatoes. Combine with sugar, butter, flour, vanilla, pineapple and Drambuie in bowl; mix well. Adjust sugar and Drambuie as necessary. Spoon into pie plate. Bake for 30 minutes or until set. Cool; top with marshmallows. Bake until marshmallows are golden brown.

Approx Per Serving: Cal 263; Prot 1 g; Carbo 137 g; T Fat 3 g;
    Chol 8 mg; Potas 182 mg; Sod 30 mg.

Maureen Smith, Fort Lauderdale, Florida
Chairperson, Fort Lauderdale Women's Chapter

MICROWAVE TOMATO HALVES AU GRATIN

Yield: 12 servings   *Pan Size: two 8x12 inch*   ≈M≈

6 medium tomatoes	1 tablespoon shredded
½ teaspoon onion flakes	Cheddar cheese
½ teaspoon sugar	½ teaspoon basil
1 tablespoon crushed potato	¼ teaspoon salt
chips	Pepper to taste

Cut tomatoes into halves. Place cut side up in glass baking dishes. Combine onion flakes, sugar, potato chips, cheese, basil, salt and pepper in bowl; mix well. Sprinkle on tomatoe halves. Microwave, covered lightly with waxed paper, on High for 11 to 12 minutes.

Approx Per Serving: Cal 28; Prot 1 g; Carbo 4 g; T Fat 1 g;
    Chol 1 mg; Potas 160 mg; Sod 64 mg.

Northwood Cookbook Committee, Dallas, Texas

TOMATO CHEESE PIE

Yield: 6 servings   *Pan Size: 10-inch pie plate*   *Preheat: 350 degrees*

8 ounces Gruyère cheese, shredded
3 large tomatoes, sliced, drained
1 cup (about) Parmesan cheese

1 10-inch baked pie shell
Fresh basil leaves, chopped
Salt and pepper to taste
¼ cup melted butter

Layer Gruyère cheese, tomatoes and Parmesan cheese in cooled pie shell. Sprinkle with basil, salt and pepper. Drizzle with butter. Bake for 25 minutes. This is a good brunch dish or vegetarian main dish.

Approx Per Serving: Cal 447; Prot 19 g; Carbo 17 g; T Fat 34 g; Chol 72 mg; Potas 190 mg; Sod 631 mg.

Ms. Lynn O'Brien, Dallas, Texas
Dallas Women's Board

M.S. TOMATOES

Yield: 6 servings   *Pan Size: salad bowl*

6 medium firm ripe tomatoes
1 small onion, grated
3 tablespoons mayonnaise

Salt, curry powder and white pepper to taste

Peel and seed tomatoes. Cut tomatoes into bite-sized pieces. Combine tomatoes, onion, mayonnaise, salt, curry powder and white pepper in salad bowl; mix gently. Chill in freezer for 10 minutes or until tomatoes become crispy-cold. Garnish with chopped fresh parsley or basil. Serve immediately.

Approx Per Serving: Cal 80; Prot 1 g; Carbo 7 g; T Fat 6 g; Chol 4 mg; Potas 288 mg; Sod 50 mg.

Mrs. Kenneth D. Owen, New Harmony, Indiana
Outstanding Business Leader
Red Geranium Restaurant, Historic New Harmony

TURNIPS AND PEAS À LA CRÈME

Yield: 6 servings   *Pan Size: 2 quart*

4 cups chopped peeled turnips .	1 cup cream
1 cup finely chopped onion	1 tablespoon sugar
1/4 cup butter	1 teaspoon garlic salt
1 teaspoon flour	Red pepper to taste
	1 16-ounce can peas

Cook turnips in lightly salted water to cover in saucepan until tender; drain. Sauté onion in butter in skillet until tender. Add flour. Cook until brown, stirring constantly. Stir in cream, sugar, garlic salt and red pepper. Bring to a boil, stirring constantly. Add peas and turnips; mix well. Simmer for 2 minutes, stirring occasionally. Garnish with parsley. Low-fat milk and frozen peas may be substituted for cream and canned peas.

Approx Per Serving: Cal 304; Prot 6 g; Carbo 21 g; T Fat 23 g; Chol 75 mg; Potas 370 mg; Sod 720 mg.

Mrs. Kathleen Johnson, DeSoto, Texas
Cedar Hill Women's Board

RATATOUILLE CASSEROLE

Yield: 4 servings   *Pan Size: 2 quart*   *Preheat: 375 degrees*

4 slices bacon, chopped	2 medium tomatoes, sliced
1/2 medium eggplant, cut into 1/2-inch cubes	1 8-ounce can tomato sauce
1 medium onion, cut into wedges	1/4 cup water
1 medium zucchini, sliced	1/2 teaspoon oregano
2/3 cup wheat germ	1/2 teaspoon marjoram
2 cups shredded Monterey Jack cheese	1/2 teaspoon rosemary
	1/4 teaspoon salt

Cook bacon in skillet until almost crisp. Add eggplant, onion and zucchini. Sauté for 10 minutes or until eggplant is tender. Layer half the eggplant mixture, wheat germ and half the cheese in baking dish. Arrange tomato slices over cheese. Top with remaining eggplant mixture. Combine tomato sauce, water, oregano, marjoram, rosemary and salt in small bowl; mix well. Pour over layers. Sprinkle with remaining cheese. Bake for 20 minutes. May substitute Grape Nuts for wheat germ.

Approx Per Serving: Cal 346; Prot 22 g; Carbo 18 g; T Fat 22 g; Chol 57 mg; Potas 704 mg; Sod 888 mg.

Dr. Kathleen Day Feisel, Cedar Hill, Texas
Cedar Hill Women's Board

ZUCCHINI PARMESAN

Yield: 6 servings   *Pan Size: 2 quart*   *Preheat: 375 degrees*

6 medium zucchini
1/4 cup thinly sliced onion
1/4 cup olive oil
2 tomatoes, peeled, sliced

Salt and pepper to taste
1/2 cup freshly grated
  Parmesan cheese

Slice zucchini 1/2 inch thick. Cook in boiling water to cover in saucepan until tender; drain. Sauté onion in olive oil in skillet until tender. Layer zucchini, tomatoes and onion in greased baking dish. Season with salt and pepper. Sprinkle with Parmesan cheese. Bake for 30 minutes.

Approx Per Serving: Cal 140; Prot 5 g; Carbo 6 g; T Fat 11 g;
    Chol 5 mg; Potas 424 mg; Sod 132 mg.

Carmalee DeGeorge, Houston, Texas
Houston Women's Board

VEGETABLES MARANGO

Yield: 8 servings   *Pan Size: 2 quart*   *Preheat: 350 degrees*

3 tomatoes
1 zucchini
2 potatoes
1 large onion
1 green bell pepper
1 cup melted margarine
Basil, oregano, salt and
  pepper to taste

1/4 cup uncooked rice
1/4 cup water
1/2 cup milk
3/4 cup shredded Cheddar
  cheese
1/2 cup bread crumbs

Slice vegetables. Layer 1/3 of the tomatoes in casserole. Add layers of half the zucchini, potatoes, onion and green pepper, drizzling each layer with 1 tablespoon margarine and sprinkling with seasonings. Add layers of rice, half the remaining tomatoes and all the remaining zucchini, potatoes, onion and green pepper, drizzling each layer with 1 tablespoon margarine and sprinkling with seasonings. Top with remaining tomatoes. Sprinkle with 1/4 cup water. Bake, covered with foil, for 45 minutes. Remove foil; pour milk over top. Bake, uncovered, for 30 minutes longer. Sprinkle with mixture of cheese and bread crumbs. Drizzle with remaining margarine. Increase oven temperature to 450 degrees. Bake for 10 minutes or until brown.

Approx Per Serving: Cal 377; Prot 7 g; Carbo 28 g; T Fat 27 g;
    Chol 14 mg; Potas 460 mg; Sod 395 mg.

Feather Buchanan, Orchard Lake, Michigan
Detroit Women's Board/Graduate Northwood Institute

CURRIED BAKED FRUIT

Yield: 10 servings   *Pan Size: 3 quart*   *Preheat: 325 degrees*

1 16-ounce can pear halves, cut into halves
1 16-ounce can cling peaches, cut into halves
1 16-ounce can pineapple chunks
1 16-ounce can apricot halves, cut into halves
1 16-ounce can pitted Bing cherries

1 tablespoon cornstarch
3/4 cup packed light brown sugar
2 teaspoons curry powder
1/2 cup melted butter
1 large banana, sliced
2/3 cup slivered blanched almonds

Drain canned fruit, reserving 1 cup juice. Combine juice with cornstarch in saucepan. Bring to a boil, stirring constantly. Cook until thickened, stirring constantly. Add brown sugar, curry powder and butter. Heat until butter melts, stirring constantly. Layer fruit and almonds in baking dish. Spoon butter mixture over top. Bake for 1 hour.

Approx Per Serving: Cal 390; Prot 3 g; Carbo 67 g; T Fat 15 g;
Chol 25 mg; Potas 424 mg; Sod 94 mg.

Mrs. Jim (Barbara) Lake, Dallas, Texas
Dallas Women's Board

BACKYARD GRITS

Yield: 8 servings   *Pan Size: 9x13 inch*   *Preheat: 350 degrees*

3 cups water
1/2 teaspoon salt
1 cup grits
1 cup milk
2 eggs, beaten
1/4 cup butter

1 cup shredded Cheddar cheese
1 teaspoon salt
1/2 teaspoon pepper
Cayenne pepper to taste

Bring water to a boil in saucepan. Add 1/2 teaspoon salt, grits and milk; stir until well mixed. Reduce heat. Simmer, covered, for 10 minutes; remove from heat. Add eggs, butter, cheese, 1 teaspoon salt, pepper and cayenne pepper; mix well. Pour into greased baking dish. Sprinkle with additional cheese if desired. Bake for 45 minutes. Do not use quick-cooking grits in this dish. This family favorite is great for brunch accompanied by an egg casserole and fresh fruit.

Approx Per Serving: Cal 219; Prot 8 g; Carbo 17 g; T Fat 13 g;
Chol 88 mg; Potas 100 mg; Sod 566 mg.

Mrs. W. S. (Anne) Permenter, Cedar Hill, Texas
Cedar Hill Women's Board

MACARONI AND CHEESE

Yield: 6 servings	Pan Size: 2 quart	Preheat: 350 degrees

1 8-ounce package elbow
   macaroni
2 tablespoons butter
2 tablespoons flour
1/4 teaspoon Worcestershire
   sauce
1/2 teaspoon onion salt

1 teaspoon salt
Pepper to taste
2 1/2 cups milk
2 cups shredded sharp
   Cheddar cheese
1/4 teaspoon paprika

Cook macaroni using package directions; drain well. Spoon into greased baking dish. Melt butter in small saucepan over low heat. Add flour, Worcestershire sauce, onion salt, salt and pepper; stir until well blended. Add milk gradually. Cook just until mixture starts to thicken, stirring constantly; remove from heat. Stir in cheese until melted. Pour over macaroni; mix well. Sprinkle with paprika. Bake for 45 to 50 minutes or until hot and bubbly.

Approx Per Serving: Cal 397; Prot 18 g; Carbo 36 g; T Fat 20 g;
   Chol 64 mg; Potas 262 mg; Sod 844 mg.

Ms. Gwen Pharo, Dallas, Texas
Dallas Women's Board

PASTA ALFREDO

Yield: 6 servings	Pan Size: 12-inch skillet

24 ounces favorite pasta
4 egg yolks
2 cups whipping cream
3 tablespoons ricotta cheese
2 ounces cooked ham,
   chopped

2 ounces canned mushrooms
2 tablespoons butter
1/3 cup frozen peas
Salt and pepper to taste
1 tablespoon Parmesan cheese

Cook pasta using package directions; drain. Combine egg yolks, cream and ricotta cheese in small bowl; mix well. Sauté ham and mushrooms in butter in skillet until lightly browned. Add peas; stir until peas are thawed. Add pasta; mix well. Season with salt and pepper. Stir in egg mixture gradually. Add Parmesan cheese; mix well. Serve immediately.

Approx Per Serving: Cal 813; Prot 21 g; Carbo 89 g; T Fat 41 g;
   Chol 270 mg; Potas 253 mg; Sod 250 mg.

Penny Valko, Fort Lauderdale, Florida
Fort Lauderdale Women's Board

PASTA À LA POMPEII

Yield: 6 servings *Pan Size: skillet*

1 large onion, chopped
1 stalk celery with leaves,
  chopped
1 clove of garlic, chopped
¼ cup butter
⅓ cup olive oil
1 16-ounce can tomatoes,
  chopped

3 envelopes chicken bouillon
1 clove of garlic, crushed
2 tablespoons basil
¼ cup chopped parsley
Pepper to taste
1 12-ounce package fresh
  pasta
½ cup Parmesan cheese

Sauté onion, celery and chopped garlic in butter and oil in skillet until tender. Add tomatoes, bouillon, crushed garlic, basil, parsley and pepper; mix well. Simmer for 30 minutes or until sauce thickens, stirring frequently. Cook pasta using package directions; drain. Rinse with cold water. Place pasta in warm serving dish. Pour a small amount of sauce over pasta; toss lightly. Spoon into individual bowls. Ladle additional sauce over each serving. Sprinkle with Parmesan cheese. This recipe can be doubled or tripled, and is excellent for other pasta-based dishes.

Approx Per Serving: Cal 447; Prot 12 g; Carbo 49 g; T Fat 23 g;
  Chol 26 mg; Potas 375 mg; Sod 878 mg.

Mrs. Terry Costa Weathers, Dallas, Texas
Dallas Women's Board

PASTA PRIMAVERA

Yield: 12 servings *Pan Size: large skillet*

1 16-ounce package shell
  macaroni
2 cloves of garlic, crushed
½ cup margarine
Flowerets of 1 head
  cauliflower
Flowerets of 1 bunch broccoli

3 zucchini, sliced
8 ounces snow peas
3 almost ripe tomatoes,
  chopped
1 cup half and half
1 cup grated Parmesan cheese

Cook macaroni using package directions; drain. Sauté garlic in margarine in skillet for 1 minute. Discard garlic. Sauté cauliflower, broccoli, zucchini, snow peas and tomatoes in order given in margarine in skillet. Cook, covered, over low heat for 2 to 3 minutes. Combine with macaroni, half and half and cheese in serving bowl; toss well. This makes a wonderful light lunch for the ladies.

Approx Per Serving: Cal 292; Prot 10 g; Carbo 35 g; T Fat 13 g;
  Chol 13 mg; Potas 412 mg; Sod 234 mg.

Mrs. Robert H. (Beverly) Holmes, Dallas, Texas
Chairman, Dallas Women's Board

PEANUT CRUNCH LOAF

Yield: 8 servings   *Pan Size: tube pan*   *Preheat: 350 degrees*

1¹/₂ cups shredded carrots
2 cups cooked rice
2 eggs, slightly beaten
6 tablespoons crumbled
  crisp-fried bacon
1 cup crunchy peanut butter
2 tablespoons chopped green
  bell pepper

2 tablespoons grated onion
1 teaspoon dry mustard
Salt and pepper to taste
1 can tomato soup
1 can cream of mushroom
  soup
1 4-ounce can mushrooms

Combine carrots, rice, eggs, bacon, peanut butter, green pepper, onion, mustard and salt and pepper in bowl; mix well. Pack into greased tube pan. Place in baking dish half-filled with hot water. Bake for 1 hour. Invert onto serving plate. Combine tomato soup, mushroom soup and mushrooms in small saucepan. Heat to serving temperature. Spoon over warm loaf.

Approx Per Serving: Cal 360; Prot 14 g; Carbo 30 g; T Fat 23 g;
    Chol 54 mg; Potas 441 mg; Sod 872 mg.

Mrs. William W. (Lorraine) Bland, Houston, Texas
Houston Women's Board/Distinguished Woman

Lorraine B. Bland

APRICOT RICE BAKE

Yield: 8 servings   *Pan Size: 1¹/₂ quart*   *Preheat: 350 degrees*

2 teaspoons margarine
1 cup cooked, long grain rice
¹/₂ cup chopped onion
¹/₄ cup finely chopped, dried
  apricots
¹/₄ cup finely chopped prunes

2 cups water
2 teaspoons chicken bouillon
  granules
¹/₄ teaspoon thyme
2 tablespoons slivered
  blanched almonds, toasted

Spray skillet with nonstick cooking spray. Add margarine. Sauté rice and onion in margarine over medium-high heat until rice is browned and onion is tender. Spoon mixture into baking dish sprayed with nonstick cooking spray. Add apricots and prunes; mix well. Combine water, bouillon and thyme in small saucepan. Bring to a boil. Pour over rice mixture. Bake, covered, for 20 minutes or until heated through. Sprinkle with almonds.

Approx Per Serving: Cal 99; Prot 2 g; Carbo 15 g; T Fat 4 g;
    Chol 0 mg; Potas 197 mg; Sod 322 mg.

Mrs. Norman (Nancy) Brinker, Dallas, Texas
Distinguished Woman/Dallas Women's Board

RICE CHILE VERDE

Yield: 6 servings   *Pan Size: 2 quart*   *Preheat: 350 degrees*

2 cups sour cream
1 4-ounce can chopped
   green chilies
3 cups cooked minute rice

8 ounces Monterey Jack
   cheese, cut into strips
¼ cup grated Parmesan
   cheese

Combine sour cream and green chilies in bowl; mix well. Layer ⅓ of the rice, half the sour cream mixture and half the cheese in baking dish. Repeat layers, ending with rice. Bake for 25 minutes. Sprinkle with Parmesan cheese. Bake for 5 minutes longer or until cheese melts.

Approx Per Serving: Cal 440; Prot 16 g; Carbo 30 g; T Fat 29 g;
   Chol 71 mg; Potas 237 mg; Sod 307 mg.

Mrs. Bill (Pat) Burford, Dallas, Texas
Dallas Women's Board

SAVORY FRIED RICE

Yield: 8 servings   *Pan Size: skillet*

2 onions, chopped
3 tablespoons butter
1 cup rice

1 teaspoon rosemary
1 teaspoon summer savory
3 cups chicken broth

Sauté onions in butter in skillet for 5 minutes. Add rice and seasonings. Sauté until rice is light brown. Stir in broth. Simmer, covered, until rice is tender and broth is absorbed.

Approx Per Serving: Cal 150; Prot 4 g; Carbo 22 g; T Fat 5 g;
   Chol 12 mg; Potas 163 mg; Sod 329 mg.

Ms. Lynn O'Brien, Dallas, Texas
Dallas Women's Board

Breads

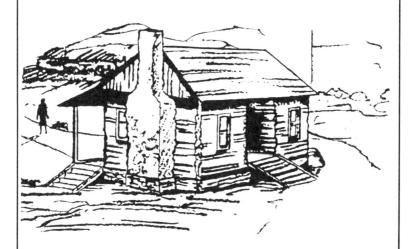

Historic Sloan Cabin, c. mid 1840's
Cedar Hill, Texas

ROMAN BISCUITS

Yield: 60 servings   *Pan Size: 10x15 inch*   *Preheat: 375 degrees*

1 cup butter, softened	4 to 5 cups Pillsbury Best
4 eggs	flour
1¹/₂ cups sugar	2¹/₂ teaspoons baking powder
4¹/₂ teaspoons anise extract	¹/₂ teaspoon salt
4 teaspoons aniseed	1 egg yolk, beaten

Cream butter and eggs in bowl until well blended. Add sugar, anise extract and aniseed; mix well. Add mixture of 4 cups flour, baking powder and salt gradually, mixing well after each addition. Turn onto floured board. Knead until smooth, adding enough remaining 1 cup flour to make of consistency of sugar cookie dough. Divide into small portions. Roll into logs; shape into S shapes. Place on baking sheet. Brush with beaten egg yolk for glaze. Bake for 15 minutes or until light brown. May be stored, tightly wrapped, for several weeks. Experiment with different flavors, such as almond, lemon, orange, nutmeg or cinnamon.

Approx Per Serving: Cal 101; Prot 2 g; Carbo 13 g; T Fat 2 g;
Chol 22 mg; Potas 15 mg; Sod 49 mg.

Rose Totino, Fridley, Minnesota
Vice-President, The Pillsbury Company
Outstanding Business Leader

ELLIS FAMILY SWEET POTATO BISCUITS

Yield: 18 servings   *Pan Size: 10x15 inch*   *Preheat: 450 degrees*

4 medium sweet potatoes,	1 teaspoon salt
baked, mashed	¹/₂ cup sugar
2 tablespoons shortening	2¹/₂ cups flour
2 teaspoons baking powder	3 tablespoons milk

Blend sweet potatoes and shortening in bowl. Add mixture of baking powder, salt, sugar and 2 cups flour gradually, mixing well after each addition. Add milk; mix well. Roll to ¹/₂-inch thickness on board sprinkled with remaining ¹/₂ cup flour. Cut with biscuit cutter; place on ungreased baking sheet. Bake for 10 to 12 minutes or until golden brown. This recipe came to Texas from Tennessee right after the Civil War.

Approx Per Serving: Cal 126; Prot 2 g; Carbo 25 g; T Fat 2 g;
Chol 0 mg; Potas 109 mg; Sod 159 mg.

Dr. James I. Dunn, Jewett, Texas
Friend of Northwood

THE LADY PRIMROSE'S SCONES

Yield: 6 servings   *Pan Size: 10x15 inch*   *Preheat: 475 degrees*

2 cups flour
1/2 teaspoon baking powder
1 teaspoon cream of tartar
1 teaspoon sugar

Pinch of salt
3 tablespoons butter
1/2 cup (about) buttermilk

Mix flour with baking powder, cream of tartar, sugar and salt in bowl. Cut in butter until crumbly. Add enough buttermilk to make soft dough. Roll to 1/2-inch thickness on floured surface. Cut into rounds with edge of teacup. Place on baking sheet. Bake for 5 to 10 minutes or until golden brown. Serve with jam and clotted or whipped cream.

Approx Per Serving: Cal 214; Prot 5 g; Carbo 34 g; T Fat 6 g;
    Chol 16 mg; Potas 73 mg; Sod 142 mg.

Caroline Rose Hunt, Dallas, Texas
Distinguished Woman/Dallas Women's Board

JALAPEÑO CORN BREAD

Yield: 9 servings   *Pan Size: 8 inch square*   *Preheat: 450 degrees*

2 cups cornmeal
3/4 cup flour
1 tablespoon baking powder
1 teaspoon sugar
1 teaspoon salt
2/3 cup oil
3 eggs, beaten

1   17-ounce can cream-style
    corn
1 cup sour cream
3 jalapeño peppers, chopped
2 cups shredded Cheddar
    cheese

Sift cornmeal, flour, baking powder, sugar and salt together 2 times; place in bowl. Add oil, eggs, corn, sour cream and jalapeño peppers; mix well. Layer batter and cheese 1/2 at a time in greased baking pan. Bake for 25 to 30 minutes or until brown and crispy. This is great served with chili on a winter day.

Approx Per Serving: Cal 517; Prot 14 g; Carbo 44 g; T Fat 32 g;
    Chol 109 mg; Potas 214 mg; Sod 803 mg.

Dr. James I. Dunn, Jewett, Texas
Friend of Northwood

NORTH CAROLINA CORN BREAD

Yield: 6 servings   *Pan Size: 2 quart*   *Preheat: 350 degrees*

1 cup yellow cornmeal	1 cup sour cream
1¹/₂ teaspoons salt	¹/₄ cup (scant) oil
1 tablespoon baking powder	1 17-ounce can cream-style
2 eggs, beaten	corn

Combine cornmeal, salt and baking powder in bowl; mix well. Beat eggs with sour cream, oil and corn. Add to cornmeal mixture; mix well. Pour into preheated greased baking pan. Bake for 25 minutes or until golden brown.

Approx Per Serving: Cal 333; Prot 6 g; Carbo 35 g; T Fat 20 g;
    Chol 88 mg; Potas 215 mg; Sod 970 mg.

Lois Cannady, Cedar Hill, Texas
Cedar Hill Women's Board

SPOON BREAD

Yield: 6 servings   *Pan Size: 2 quart*   *Preheat: 375 degrees*

1 cup cornmeal	1 teaspoon salt
3 tablespoons butter	2 teaspoons baking powder
1¹/₂ cups boiling water	3 eggs, beaten
1 tablespoon sugar	1 cup milk

Combine cornmeal and butter in bowl. Add boiling water; mix well. Cool. Add mixture of sugar, salt and baking powder; mix well. Beat eggs with milk. Add to cornmeal mixture; mix well. Pour into buttered deep casserole. Bake for 30 to 40 minutes or until brown and fairly firm. This is an old family favorite from an old Episcopal Church Cookbook.

Approx Per Serving: Cal 209; Prot 6 g; Carbo 23 g; T Fat 10 g;
    Chol 128 mg; Potas 118 mg; Sod 565 mg.

Mrs. Jack M. (Mary Jane) Sanders, Sr., Marshall, Texas
Friend of Northwood

VEGGIE CORN MUFFINS WITH CHEESE

Yield: 60 servings   *Pan Size: muffin cups*   *Preheat: 400 degrees*

5 cups flour
2 teaspoons salt
1/4 cup baking powder
1/2 cup (scant) sugar
1/2 cup (scant) cornmeal
1 large green bell pepper, chopped
1 small onion, chopped
1/4 cup (or more) chopped pimentos
11/2 cups shredded sharp Cheddar cheese
4 eggs, beaten
3 cups milk
11/2 cups melted margarine

Combine flour, salt, baking powder, sugar and cornmeal in bowl. Add green pepper, onion, pimentos and cheese; mix well. Beat eggs with milk and margarine. Add to flour mixture; stir just until moistened. Spoon into paper-lined muffin cups. Bake for 20 to 30 minutes or until muffins test done.

Approx Per Serving: Cal 116; Prot 3 g; Carbo 12 g; T Fat 6 g;
     Chol 19 mg; Potas 45 mg; Sod 218 mg.

Northwood Cookbook Committee, Dallas, Texas

BROWN BREAD

Yield: 12 servings   *Pan Size: 1 quart*

1 slice dry bread, cubed
11/2 cups buttermilk
1/2 cup molasses
1 teaspoon salt
1 teaspoon (heaping) soda
2 cups graham flour

Combine bread, buttermilk and molasses in bowl; mix well. Add mixture of salt, soda and flour; mix well. Spoon into buttered pudding mold. Steam over medium heat for 1 hour. Reduce heat. Steam over low heat for 3 hours. May substitute cornmeal or all-purpose flour for graham flour or doughnut or cake for bread. May add nuts and raisins.

Approx Per Serving: Cal 123; Prot 3 g; Carbo 26 g; T Fat 1 g;
     Chol 1 mg; Potas 459 mg; Sod 303 mg.

Former Senator Margaret Chase Smith, Skowhegan, Maine
Distinguished Woman

CPC BREAD (CRANBERRY, PUMPKIN, COCONUT BREAD)

Yield: 24 servings　　*Pan Size: two 5x9 inch*　　*Preheat: 350 degrees*

2 tablespoons sugar	1 4-ounce package vanilla
1/2 teaspoon cinnamon	instant pudding mix
2 eggs, beaten	1/2 teaspoon nutmeg
1 cup sugar	1/2 teaspoon ginger
3/4 cup oil	1 cup canned pumpkin
1 1/2 cups flour	1/2 cup chopped pecans
1 teaspoon baking powder	1 cup shredded coconut
1 teaspoon soda	1 1/2 cups cranberries
1/2 teaspoon salt	2 teaspoons vanilla extract

Spray loaf pans with nonstick cooking spray; coat bottoms and sides with mixture of sugar and cinnamon. Combine eggs, sugar and oil in bowl; mix well. Add mixture of flour, baking powder, soda, salt, dry pudding mix, nutmeg and ginger to egg mixture alternately with pumpkin, beginning and ending with flour mixture and mixing well after each addition. Stir in pecans, coconut and cranberries. Spoon into prepared loaf pans. Bake for 1 hour or until loaves test done. Cool in pans for 10 minutes. Remove to wire rack to cool completely. Loaves slice best when chilled.

Approx Per Serving: Cal 217; Prot 2 g; Carbo 30 g; T Fat 11 g;
　　Chol 18 mg; Potas 99 mg; Sod 141 mg.

Gretchen L. Kaufman, North Little Rock, Arkansas
Friend of Northwood

HEALTH BREAD

Yield: 12 servings　　*Pan Size: 5x9 inch*　　*Preheat: 350 degrees*

4 cups nutty wheat flour	1/2 teaspoon salt
2 tablespoons wheat germ	8 ounces plain yogurt
1 teaspoon (heaping) soda	1 tablespoon honey

Combine flour, wheat germ, soda and salt in bowl; mix well. Add yogurt and honey; mix well. Spoon into greased loaf pan. Bake for 1 hour. Turn off oven. Let bread stand in closed oven for 15 minutes longer. Nutty wheat flour is available in health food stores or whole food markets.

Approx Per Serving: Cal 154; Prot 7 g; Carbo 32 g; T Fat 1 g;
　　Chol 1 mg; Potas 200 mg; Sod 172 mg.

Karen Stoel, Dallas, Texas
Friend of Northwood

GREAT-GRANDMOTHER'S GINGERBREAD

Yield: 15 servings   *Pan Size: 9x13 inch*   *Preheat: 350 degrees*

1/2 cup sugar
1/2 cup margarine, softened
1 egg, beaten
1 cup molasses
2 1/2 cups sifted flour
1 teaspoon ginger

1 teaspoon cinnamon
1/2 teaspoon cloves
1/2 teaspoon salt
1 teaspoon soda
1 cup hot water

Grease baking pan; line with waxed paper. Cream sugar and margarine in bowl until light and fluffy. Add egg and molasses; mix well. Sift flour, ginger, cinnamon, cloves, salt and soda together. Add to creamed mixture; mix well. Add hot water; beat until smooth. Spoon into prepared pan. Bake for 35 minutes or until gingerbread tests done. This recipe is over 150 years old and originally used a mixture of butter and lard for margarine.

Approx Per Serving: Cal 206; Prot 3 g; Carbo 34 g; T Fat 7 g;
    Chol 14 mg; Potas 652 mg; Sod 223 mg.

Mrs. Walter T. (Betty E.) Gray, Dallas, Texas
Dallas Women's Board

ONION CHEESE BREAD

Yield: 8 servings   *Pan Size: 1 quart*   *Preheat: 400 degrees*

1/2 cup chopped onion
1 tablespoon butter
1 egg, slightly beaten
1/2 cup milk
1 1/2 cups buttermilk
    baking mix

1 cup shredded sharp
    Cheddar cheese
1 tablespoon poppy seed
2 tablespoons melted butter

Sauté onion in 1 tablespoon butter in skillet until tender. Beat egg with milk in bowl. Mix in baking mix. Add sautéed onion and half the cheese; mix well. Spoon into greased casserole. Sprinkle with remaining cheese and poppy seed. Drizzle with 2 tablespoons melted butter. Bake for 25 to 30 minutes or until bread tests done. Serve piping hot with lots of butter. This is very light and fluffy and a terrific substitute for potatoes or other bread, especially with grilled steak.

Approx Per Serving: Cal 220; Prot 7 g; Carbo 17 g; T Fat 14 g;
    Chol 55 mg; Potas 93 mg; Sod 437 mg.

Mrs. Robert Parker, Phoenix, Arizona
Founding Member and Chapter Chair, 1985-1988, Valley of the Sun Chapter

PEAR BREAD

Yield: 12 servings   *Pan Size: 5x9 inch*   *Preheat: 325 degrees*

3 cups flour
1 teaspoon soda
1/4 teaspoon baking powder
1 teaspoon salt
1 tablespoon cinnamon
3 eggs, beaten

2 cups sugar
3/4 cup oil
2 teaspoons vanilla extract
2 cups grated pears
1 cup chopped pecans

Combine flour, soda, baking powder, salt and cinnamon in bowl; mix well. Make well in center. Beat eggs with sugar, oil and vanilla. Pour into well; mix well. Stir in pears and pecans. Spoon into greased loaf pan. Bake for 1 hour and 15 minutes or until bread tests done. Bread is delicious when frozen and served with cream cheese.

Approx Per Serving: Cal 465; Prot 6 g; Carbo 63 g; T Fat 22 g;
Chol 53 mg; Potas 121 mg; Sod 272 mg.

Mrs. Oliver (Faye) Gould, Dallas, Texas
Dallas Women's Board

CHRISTMAS PLUM BREAD

Yield: 24 servings   *Pan Size: two 5x9 inch*   *Preheat: 350 degrees*

2 2/3 cups sugar
2 2/3 cups flour
1 1/4 teaspoons cinnamon
1 1/4 teaspoons cloves
1/4 teaspoon salt
3/4 teaspoon soda
3/4 teaspoon baking powder
4 eggs, beaten

1 1/4 teaspoons vanilla extract
1 1/3 cups oil
3 4-ounce jars strained baby
food plums
1/4 teaspoon red food coloring
2/3 cup sugar
1/2 cup lemon juice

Combine 2 2/3 cups sugar, flour, cinnamon, cloves, salt, soda and baking powder in bowl; mix well. Beat eggs with vanilla, oil and plums. Add to flour mixture; mix well. Stir in food coloring. Spoon into greased and floured loaf pans. Bake for 50 to 60 minutes or until loaves test done. Combine remaining 2/3 cup sugar and lemon juice in saucepan. Bring to a boil, stirring constantly. Spoon over hot bread. Cool in pan for 10 minutes. Remove to wire rack to cool completely.

Approx Per Serving: Cal 287; Prot 3 g; Carbo 41 g; T Fat 13 g;
Chol 36 mg; Potas 54 mg; Sod 71 mg.

Northwood Cookbook Committee, Dallas, Texas

STRAWBERRY BREAD

Yield: 24 servings	Pan Size: two 5x9 inch	Preheat: 350 degrees

2 10-ounce packages frozen
strawberries
3 cups flour
1 teaspoon soda
1 teaspoon salt

2 teaspoons cinnamon
2 cups sugar
4 eggs, beaten
1¹/2 cups oil
1¹/2 cups chopped pecans

Thaw and partially drain strawberries. Combine flour, soda, salt, cinnamon and sugar in large bowl; mix well. Add strawberries; mix well. Make well in center. Add eggs, oil and pecans; stir just until moistened. Spoon into greased loaf pans. Bake for 1 hour or until loaves test done. May sprinkle hot loaves with mixture of 2 tablespoons sugar and 2 tablespoons cinnamon. Remove to wire rack to cool. May serve with meal or as dessert.

Approx Per Serving: Cal 313; Prot 3 g; Carbo 32 g; T Fat 20 g;
  Chol 36 mg; Potas 91 mg; Sod 136 mg.

Susan Garnett, Dallas, Texas
Director Of Public Relations/Dallas Women's Board

ZUCCHINI BREAD

Yield: 24 servings	Pan Size: two 5x9 inch	Preheat: 350 degrees

3 eggs, beaten
1 cup oil
2 cups sugar
4 medium zucchini, grated
1 tablespoon vanilla extract
3 cups sifted flour

¹/2 teaspoon baking powder
1 teaspoon soda
2 teaspoons cinnamon
1 teaspoon salt
¹/2 cup chopped pecans

Combine eggs, oil, sugar, zucchini and vanilla in bowl; mix well. Sift flour, baking powder, soda, cinnamon and salt together. Add to zucchini mixture; mix well. Stir in pecans. Spoon into greased and floured loaf pans. Bake for 1 hour or until loaves test done. Cool in pans on wire rack for 10 minutes. Remove to wire rack to cool completely. Makes a great hostess gift.

Approx Per Serving: Cal 231; Prot 3 g; Carbo 30 g; T Fat 12 g;
  Chol 27 mg; Potas 87 mg; Sod 140 mg.

Northwood Cookbook Committee, Dallas, Texas

REFRIGERATOR BRAN MUFFINS

Yield: 48 servings   *Pan Size: muffin cups*   *Preheat: 400 degrees*

2 cups shredded bran cereal
1 cup boiling water
4 eggs, beaten
2 cups sugar
1 cup oil
1 quart buttermilk

4 cups quick-cooking oats
5 teaspoons soda
1½ teaspoons salt
5 cups flour
1 cup coarse bran

Combine cereal and boiling water in bowl; mix well. Cool. Beat eggs with sugar, oil and buttermilk in large bowl. Add oats, soda, salt, flour and coarse bran; stir just until moistened. Fold in cereal. Fill greased or paper-lined muffin cups ⅔ full. Bake for 18 to 20 minutes or until muffins test done. May store batter, covered, in refrigerator for up to 1 month. May add raisins or chopped fresh fruit just before baking.

Approx Per Serving: Cal 171; Prot 4 g; Carbo 27 g; T Fat 6 g;
    Chol 21 mg; Potas 123 mg; Sod 218 mg.

Mrs. Robert H. (Penny) Holmes, II, Dallas, Texas
Dallas Women's Board

BRAZILIAN CHEESE MUFFINS

Yield: 8 servings   *Pan Size: muffin cups*   *Preheat: 350 degrees*

1   14-ounce can sweetened
    condensed milk
3 eggs, beaten

1 cup coconut
3 tablespoons Parmesan
    cheese

Combine condensed milk, eggs, coconut and cheese in bowl; mix well. Spoon into paper-lined muffin cups. Bake for 35 minutes. The title of this recipe in Portuguese is Quejadinnas which means little cheese things. Serve as luncheon muffin with chicken salad.

Approx Per Serving: Cal 256; Prot 7 g; Carbo 33 g; T Fat 11 g;
    Chol 98 mg; Potas 250 mg; Sod 155 mg.

Faye Lynn King, DeSoto, Texas
Cedar Hill Women's Board

PINEHURST MUFFINS

Yield: 36 servings   Pan Size: miniature muffin cups   Preheat: 350 degrees

1 cup sugar	6 tablespoons melted butter
1¹/₂ cups flour	¹/₂ cup chopped pecans
1¹/₂ teaspoons soda	¹/₂ cup coconut
1¹/₂ teaspoons cinnamon	¹/₂ cup raisins
¹/₂ teaspoon salt	1 small apple, peeled, grated
2 eggs, slightly beaten	2 cups grated carrots
6 tablespoons oil	

Combine sugar, flour, soda, cinnamon and salt in large bowl; mix well. Beat eggs with oil and butter. Stir into dry ingredients; mix well. Add pecans, coconut and raisins. Fold in apple and carrots gradually. Spoon into paper-lined muffin cups. Bake for 20 minutes or until muffins test done. This recipe was adapted from one of executive chef Paul DeGroot of the 2001 Club in Dallas.

Approx Per Serving: Cal 109; Prot 1 g; Carbo 13 g; T Fat 6 g;
    Chol 17 mg; Potas 61 mg; Sod 89 mg.

Robert H. Dedman, Dallas, Texas
Outstanding Business Leader

POPOVERS

Yield: 5 servings   Pan Size: five 6-ounce custard cups   Preheat: 450 degrees

2 eggs	1 cup milk
1 cup flour	1 tablespoon melted
¹/₄ teaspoon salt	margarine

Spray custard cups with nonstick cooking spray. Beat eggs in mixer bowl until light and fluffy. Add mixture of flour and salt alternately with milk ¹/₂ at a time, beating well after each addition. Add butter. Beat at highest speed for 3 minutes or until batter is bubbly. Pour ¹/₃ cup batter into each custard cup. Bake for 25 minutes or until popovers are brown and show no moisture on top. Do not open oven while baking. Reduce temperature to 350 degrees. Bake for 20 minutes longer or until popovers are dry. Popovers bake in all sorts of intriguing shapes. Serve with a bowl of soup, a glass of white wine and some fresh fruit to make a wonderful light luncheon. They are so easy to make.

Approx Per Serving: Cal 173; Prot 7 g; Carbo 22 g; T Fat 6 g;
    Chol 92 mg; Potas 116 mg; Sod 182 mg.

Helen Dow Whiting, Sun Valley, Idaho
Distinguished Woman

BED AND BREAKFAST CINNAMON ROLLS

Yield: 40 servings	*Pan Size: 10x15 inch*	*Preheat: 325 degrees*

12 ounces cream cheese,
   softened
1 tablespoon mayonnaise
1/4 cup (about) milk
1 loaf sliced white bread,
   crusts trimmed

1/2 cup melted margarine
1 cup sugar
1 to 2 tablespoons cinnamon

Combine cream cheese, mayonnaise and enough milk to make of spreading consistency in bowl; beat until creamy. Spread on bread slices. Roll each slice as for jelly roll. Place seam side down on baking sheet. Chill in refrigerator overnight. Roll in melted margarine; coat with mixture of sugar and cinnamon. Cut each into 4 pieces. Return to baking sheet. Bake for 15 minutes. Place under hot broiler for several seconds until bubbly. This recipe is from a bed and breakfast in east Texas.

Approx Per Serving: Cal 104; Prot 0 g; Carbo 12 g; T Fat 8 g;
   Chol 8 mg; Potas 28 mg; Sod 116 mg.

Ann Dowdy, Dallas, Texas
Friend of Northwood

QUICK AND YUMMY YEAST ROLLS

Yield: 12 servings	*Pan Size: muffin cups*	*Preheat: 375 degrees*

1 package dry yeast
1 cup warm water
1 egg, beaten
1/4 cup melted butter

1/4 cup sugar
2 1/2 cups whole wheat flour
1/2 cup melted butter

Dissolve yeast in warm water in bowl. Add egg and 1/4 cup melted butter; mix well. Add sugar and flour; mix well. Let rise, covered with plastic wrap, in warm place for 45 minutes. Shape into small balls. Brush with melted butter. Place 3 balls in each greased muffin cup. Bake for 10 to 15 minutes or until light brown. Brush with melted butter.

Approx Per Serving: Cal 209; Prot 4 g; Carbo 22 g; T Fat 13 g;
   Chol 49 mg; Potas 113 mg; Sod 104 mg.

Mrs. Bud (Jane) Smith, Dallas, Texas
Dallas Women's Board

Cakes, Candies, Cookies & Pies

Edwin and Amy Hopkins Academic Building
Cedar Hill, Texas

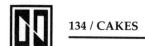

ANGEL FOOD WITH MOCHA SAUCE

Yield: 12 servings   *Pan Size: double boiler*

1 cup confectioners' sugar	3 tablespoons strong coffee
2 tablespoons (heaping) baking cocoa	1 cup whipping cream
	1 angel food cake

Combine confectioners' sugar, cocoa and coffee in top of double boiler; mix well. Cook until sugar and cocoa are dissolved, stirring constantly; remove from heat. Cool completely. Beat whipping cream in mixer bowl until soft peaks form. Fold in coffee mixture. Spoon over sliced angel food cake.

Approx Per Serving: Cal 234; Prot 4 g; Carbo 39 g; T Fat 8 g;
Chol 27 mg; Potas 99 mg; Sod 277 mg.

Mrs. James H. (Rose May) Curts, Saginaw, Michigan
Midland Women's Board

CHRISTMAS CAKE

Yield: 12 servings   *Pan Size: double boiler*

1 package angel food cake mix	1½ cups half and half
5 egg yolks	2 teaspoons unflavored gelatin
¾ cup sugar	2 cups whipping cream
1 teaspoon cornstarch	1 teaspoon vanilla extract

Prepare and bake cake mix according to package directions using tube pan. Invert on funnel to cool completely. Loosen cake from side of pan. Beat egg yolks, sugar and cornstarch in mixer bowl until light. Pour half and half in top of double boiler. Stir in egg mixture. Cook until thickened, stirring constantly. Remove from heat. Dissolve gelatin in a small amount of cold water. Add to hot egg mixture; stir until dissolved. Cool custard in refrigerator just until chilled. Beat whipping cream in mixer bowl until soft peaks form. Stir in vanilla. Add chilled custard. Beat at low speed until blended. Cut cake into 2 layers. Spread custard mixture between layers and over top and side of cake. Chill until serving time. This is our annual family Christmas Eve treat.

Approx Per Serving: Cal 378; Prot 7 g; Carbo 44 g; T Fat 21 g;
Chol 154 mg; Potas 147 mg; Sod 300 mg.

Nancy Barker, Midland, Michigan
Vice President, Northwood Institute/Distinguished Woman

APPLE CAKE

Yield: 12 servings   *Pan Size: 8 inch*   *Preheat: 375 degrees*

1 egg	1 pound Granny Smith
1 cup milk	apples, peeled, sliced
1 cup flour	1 tablespoon sugar
2 teaspoons baking powder	1/2 teaspoon cinnamon
1 cup sugar	1/2 cup margarine
2 tablespoons oil	

Beat egg and 1/2 cup milk in small mixer bowl until light. Sift flour, baking powder and 1/2 cup sugar into medium mixer bowl. Add egg mixture; beat until smooth. Add oil; mix well. Fold in apples. Spoon into greased pie plate. Sprinkle with 1 tablespoon sugar and cinnamon. Reduce oven temperature to 350 degrees. Bake for 30 minutes. Pierce with fork. Combine remaining 1/2 cup milk, remaining 1/2 cup sugar and margarine in saucepan. Bring to a boil, stirring constantly. Pour boiling sauce over hot cake. Bake for 30 minutes longer. Sauce should be prepared 5 minutes prior to end of first baking time.

Approx Per Serving: Cal 236; Prot 2 g; Carbo 32 g; T Fat 11 g;
    Chol 21 mg; Potas 91 mg; Sod 159 mg.

Karen Stoel, Dallas, Texas
Friend of Northwood

MARGARET CHASE SMITH'S BLUEBERRY CAKE

Yield: 12 servings   *Pan Size: two 9 inch round*   *Preheat: 350 degrees*

1/2 cup shortening	1/2 teaspoon salt
3/4 cup sugar	1 teaspoon nutmeg
2 eggs	1 cup milk
2 cups sifted cake flour	2 cups fresh blueberries
4 teaspoons baking powder	

Cream shortening and sugar in mixer bowl until light. Add eggs; beat until fluffy. Sift flour, baking powder, salt and nutmeg together. Add to creamed mixture alternately with milk, beating well after each addition. Fold in blueberries. Spoon into greased and floured cake pans. Bake for 25 to 30 minutes or until cakes test done. Remove to wire rack. Cool in pans for 10 minutes; remove to wire rack to cool completely. Frost between layers and over top and side of cake with favorite cream cheese icing if desired. May substitute frozen blueberries for fresh.

Approx Per Serving: Cal 223; Prot 3 g; Carbo 30 g; T Fat 10 g;
    Chol 38 mg; Potas 77 mg; Sod 221 mg.

Former Senator Margaret Chase Smith, Skowhegan, Maine
Distinguished Woman

CARROT AND PINEAPPLE CAKE

Yield: 16 servings   *Pan Size: bundt*   *Preheat: 350 degrees*

2 cups flour
2 teaspoons baking powder
1½ teaspoons soda
1 teaspoon salt
2 cups sugar
1½ cups oil
4 eggs
2 cups grated carrots

1 8-ounce can crushed
  pineapple, drained
½ cup chopped walnuts
1 pound confectioners' sugar
8 ounces cream cheese,
  softened
¼ cup margarine, softened
1 teaspoon lemon extract

Sift first 4 ingredients together. Combine sugar, oil and eggs in large bowl; mix well. Add flour mixture; mix well. Stir in carrots, pineapple and walnuts. Spoon into greased and floured bundt pan. Bake for 50 minutes. Cool in pan for 15 minutes. Remove to wire rack to cool completely. Cream remaining ingredients in mixer bowl until smooth. Add enough hot water to make of desired consistency. Spread over cooled cake.

Approx Per Serving: Cal 597; Prot 5 g; Carbo 75 g; T Fat 32 g;
   Chol 69 mg; Potas 131 mg; Sod 350 mg.

Mrs. Lawrence H. Short, Midland, Michigan
Distinguished Woman

THE BEST CHOCOLATE CAKE

Yield: 15 servings   *Pan Size: 9x13 inch*   *Preheat: 350 degrees*

1 cup butter
1 cup strong coffee
3 tablespoons baking cocoa
2 cups sugar
2 cups flour
⅛ teaspoon salt
2 eggs
½ cup buttermilk

1 teaspoon soda
½ cup butter, softened
3 tablespoons baking cocoa
6 tablespoons boiling water
2 teaspoons vanilla extract
1 pound confectioners' sugar
1 cup chopped pecans

Combine first 3 ingredients in saucepan; mix well. Bring to a boil, stirring constantly. Add sugar, flour and salt; mix well. Add eggs 1 at a time, beating well after each addition. Stir in buttermilk and soda. Pour into ungreased cake pan. Bake for 35 to 45 minutes or until cake tests done. Beat remaining ½ cup butter, remaining 3 tablespoons cocoa, boiling water, vanilla and confectioners' sugar in mixer bowl until smooth. Fold in pecans. Spread over warm cake. May substitute sour cream for buttermilk.

Approx Per Serving: Cal 538; Prot 4 g; Carbo 78 g; T Fat 25 g;
   Chol 78 mg; Potas 110 mg; Sod 247 mg.

Rosemary Haggar Vaughan, Dallas, Texas
Dallas Women's Board

CHARLIE'S COCA-COLA CAKE

Yield: 15 servings　　　　*Pan Size: 9x13 inch*　　　　*Preheat: 350 degrees*

2 cups flour
2 cups sugar
1 cup butter
1 cup Coca-Cola
3 tablespoons baking cocoa
1/2 cup buttermilk
2 eggs, beaten
1 teaspoon soda
1 teaspoon vanilla extract
2 cups miniature
　　marshmallows

1/2 cup butter
2 cups sugar
1　5-ounce can evaporated
　　milk
1 cup semisweet chocolate
　　chips
12 marshmallows
1 teaspoon vanilla extract

Combine flour and 2 cups sugar in large bowl; mix well. Combine 1 cup butter, Coca-Cola and cocoa in saucepan. Bring just to the boiling point, stirring constantly. Pour over flour mixture. Add buttermilk, eggs, soda and vanilla; mix well. Stir in miniature marshmallows. Spoon into greased cake pan. Bake for 30 minutes. Combine remaining 1/2 cup butter, 2 cups sugar and evaporated milk in saucepan. Bring to a boil, stirring constantly. Cook for 5 minutes, stirring constantly; remove from heat. Add chocolate chips, 12 marshmallows and vanilla; beat until of desired consistency. Spread over cooled cake.

Approx Per Serving: Cal 564; Prot 5 g; Carbo 87 g; T Fat 24 g;
　　Chol 81 mg; Potas 126 mg; Sod 253 mg.

Marla Zion, Dallas, Texas
Dallas Women's Board

MICROWAVE CHOCOLATE FUDGE CAKE

Yield: 16 servings　　　　*Pan Size: glass bundt*　　　　≈M≈

1　2-layer package chocolate
　　fudge cake mix
3 eggs
1/3 cup oil

2 cups semisweet chocolate
　　chips
1 cup water

Combine cake mix, eggs, oil, chocolate chips and water in bowl; beat with spoon until well mixed. Spoon into pan sprayed with nonstick cooking spray. Microwave on Medium for 12 minutes. Microwave on High for 6 minutes. Let stand for 5 minutes before serving. Serve warm with vanilla ice cream if desired.

Approx Per Serving: Cal 253; Prot 3 g; Carbo 30 g; T Fat 15 g;
　　Chol 40 mg; Potas 86 mg; Sod 147 mg.

Karen Wilson, Dallas, Texas
Public Relations Assistant/Texas Campus

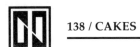

CHOCOLATE MOUSSE CAKE

Yield: 12 servings	*Pan Size: 8 inch*	*Preheat: 350 degrees*

2 egg whites
1/2 cup sugar
1 1/4 cups flour
1 cup sugar
1/2 cup baking cocoa
3/4 teaspoon soda
1/2 teaspoon salt
1/2 cup oil
1 cup buttermilk
2 egg yolks

1 cup whipping cream
2 tablespoons sugar
1 teaspoon vanilla extract
1/2 cup sugar
1/2 cup baking cocoa
1 cup whipping cream
1 teaspoon vanilla extract
1   21-ounce can cherry pie
    filling

Beat egg whites in mixer bowl until foamy. Add 1/2 cup sugar gradually, beating constantly until stiff peaks form. Combine flour, 1 cup sugar, 1/2 cup cocoa, soda and salt in large bowl; mix well. Add oil, buttermilk and egg yolks; beat until smooth. Fold in stiffly beaten egg whites gently. Pour into 2 greased and floured layer cake pans. Bake for 18 to 20 minutes or until cakes test done. Cool. Whip 1 cup whipping cream with 2 tablespoons sugar and 1 teaspoon vanilla. Combine 1/2 cup sugar, 1/2 cup cocoa, 1 cup whipping cream and 1 teaspoon vanilla in mixer bowl; beat at low speed until blended. Beat at high speed until whipped. Spread 1 cake layer with half the plain whipped cream; add half the pie filling. Top with remaining cake layer, plain whipped cream and pie filling. Frost top and side of cake with chocolate whipped cream. Store in refrigerator.

Approx Per Serving: Cal 488; Prot 5 g; Carbo 63 g; T Fat 26 g;
    Chol 91 mg; Potas 207 mg; Sod 203 mg.

Mrs. R. H. (Beverly) Holmes, Dallas, Texas
Chairman, Dallas Women's Board

ROSE'S CHOCOLATE AMARETTO TORTE

Yield: 9 servings	*Pan Size: 8x8 inch*

1 pound cake
Amaretto

Pudding
Whipping cream, whipped

Cut pound cake into 1/4 to 1/2-inch thick slices. Line bottom of cake pan with cake slices. Sprinkle with Amaretto; spread with layer of pudding. Repeat layers. Chill for 24 hours or longer. Serve with whipped cream. Garnish with colorful candy confection sprinkles.

Nutritional information for this recipe is not available.

Rose Totino, Fridley, Minnesota
Vice President, The Pillsbury Company
Outstanding Business Leader

GENIE'S MISSISSIPPI MUD CAKE

Yield: 15 servings   *Pan Size: 9x13 inch*   *Preheat: 350 degrees*

4 eggs
2 cups sugar
1 cup melted margarine
1½ cups flour
⅓ cup baking cocoa
1 teaspoon vanilla extract
1 cup coconut
1 cup chopped pecans

1 13-ounce jar marshmallow creme
½ cup margarine, softened
6 tablespoons milk
⅓ cup baking cocoa
1 pound confectioners' sugar
1 teaspoon vanilla extract
1 cup chopped pecans

Beat eggs and sugar in mixer bowl until thick. Add mixture of next 6 ingredients; mix well. Spoon into greased cake pan. Bake for 30 minutes. Spread with marshmallow creme. Cool for several minutes. Melt remaining ½ cup margarine in saucepan; remove from heat. Add milk, remaining ⅓ cup cocoa, confectioners' sugar and remaining 1 teaspoon vanilla; mix well. Spread gently over marshmallow creme layer. Sprinkle with remaining 1 cup pecans. Do not refrigerate.

Approx Per Serving: Cal 700; Prot 6 g; Carbo 100 g; T Fat 34 g;
    Chol 58 mg; Potas 184 mg; Sod 268 mg.

Mrs. Robert Parker, Phoenix, Arizona
Founding Member and Chapter Chairman, 1985-1988, Valley of the Sun Chapter

ORANGE FRUITCAKE

Yield: 10 servings   *Pan Size: springform tube*   *Preheat: 300 degrees*

¾ cup butter, softened
1 cup sugar
3 eggs
1 teaspoon vanilla extract
2½ cups flour
1½ teaspoons soda
1 cup sour milk

1 cup grated fresh coconut
1 cup chopped pecans
1½ cups chopped dates
Grated rind of 1 orange
Juice and grated rind of 1 orange
½ cup sugar

Cream butter and sugar in mixer bowl until light and fluffy. Add eggs 1 at a time, beating well after each addition. Stir in vanilla. Combine flour and soda. Add to creamed mixture alternately with milk, mixing well after each addition. Stir in coconut, pecans, dates and grated rind of 1 orange. Spoon into greased and floured pan. Bake for 1 hour. Combine juice and grated rind of remaining 1 orange and remaining ½ cup sugar in bowl; mix until sugar is dissolved. Pour over hot cake. Cool in pan.

Approx Per Serving: Cal 575; Prot 8 g; Carbo 79 g; T Fat 28 g;
    Chol 104 mg; Potas 350 mg; Sod 274 mg.

Rosalie T. Carstens, Fort Lauderdale, Florida
Fort Lauderdale Women's Board

CALIFORNIA FRUITCAKE

Yield: 12 servings	Pan Size: 5x9 inch	Preheat: 300 degrees

3/4 cup sifted flour
1/4 teaspoon baking powder
1/4 teaspoon soda
1/2 teaspoon salt
3/4 cup packed brown sugar

2 cups pitted whole dates
1 1/2 cups dried apricot halves
3 cups walnut halves
3 eggs
1 teaspoon vanilla extract

Sift flour, baking powder, soda and salt into bowl. Stir in brown sugar. Add dates, apricots and walnuts; stir to coat well. Beat eggs in mixer bowl until foamy; add vanilla. Add to flour mixture; stir just until moistened. Spoon into greased and waxed paper-lined loaf pan. Bake for 1 1/2 hours. Remove from pan. Cool on wire rack.

Nutritional information for this recipe is not included.

Mrs. Robert H. (Sunny) Miller, West Palm Beach, Florida
West Palm Beach Women's Board

EVERYBODY'S FAVORITE CAKE

Yield: 15 servings	Pan Size: 9x13 inch	Preheat: 350 degrees

1 cup butter
3 tablespoons baking cocoa
1 cup water
1 teaspoon vanilla extract
2 cups flour
2 cups sugar
1/4 teaspoon salt
1 teaspoon cinnamon
2 eggs

1 cup buttermilk
1 teaspoon soda
1/2 cup butter
3 tablespoons baking cocoa
6 tablespoons milk
1 1/2 teaspoons vanilla extract
1 cup chopped pecans
1 pound confectioners' sugar

Combine 1 cup butter, 3 tablespoons cocoa, water and 1 teaspoon vanilla in saucepan; mix well. Cook until butter is melted, stirring constantly. Bring just to the boiling point, stirring constantly; remove from heat. Cool. Combine flour, sugar, salt and cinnamon in large bowl; mix well. Stir in butter mixture. Add eggs; beat well. Add mixture of buttermilk and soda; stir until well mixed. Spoon into greased and floured cake pan. Bake for 30 to 45 minutes or until cake tests done. Cool in pan. Pierce with fork. Combine remaining 1/2 cup butter, 3 tablespoons cocoa and milk in saucepan. Bring to a low boil, stirring constantly; remove from heat. Beat in remaining 1 1/2 teaspoons vanilla, pecans and confectioners' sugar. Pour over warm cake.

Approx Per Serving: Cal 545; Prot 4 g; Carbo 79 g; T Fat 25 g;
Chol 80 mg; Potas 122 mg; Sod 276 mg.

Leslie A. Gowan, Dallas, Texas
Director of External Affairs, Dallas

LEMON PUDDING CAKE

Yield: 18 servings	Pan Size: two 8x8 inch	Preheat: 325 degrees

1 2-layer package white
  cake mix
1 4-ounce package lemon
  instant pudding mix
3/4 cup water

3/4 cup oil
4 eggs
1/2 cup lemon juice
2 cups confectioners' sugar

Combine cake mix, pudding mix, water, oil and eggs in mixer bowl. Beat at low speed for 2 minutes. Pour into buttered cake pans. Bake for 45 minutes. Pierce holes 1 inch apart in top of cake with toothpick. Combine lemon juice and confectioners' sugar in bowl; stir until confectioners' sugar is dissolved. Pour over warm cake. Cool in pans.

Approx Per Serving: Cal 255; Prot 2 g; Carbo 36 g; T Fat 12 g;
  Chol 47 mg; Potas 24 mg; Sod 174 mg.

Dr. Mildred R. Larson, Phoenix, Arizona
Phoenix Women's Board

MEXICAN WEDDING CAKE

Yield: 15 servings	Pan Size: 9x13 inch	Preheat: 350 degrees

2 cups flour
2 cups sugar
1 cup chopped pecans
2 teaspoons soda
2 eggs, beaten
1 20-ounce can crushed
  pineapple

3/4 cup butter, softened
8 ounces cream cheese,
  softened
1 cup super-fine sugar
1 teaspoon vanilla extract
1 cup roasted pecans

Combine flour, 2 cups sugar, 1 cup pecans and soda in bowl; mix well. Add eggs and pineapple; mix well. Pour into greased and floured cake pan. Bake for 30 minutes. Cool completely. Combine butter, cream cheese, super-fine sugar and vanilla in mixer bowl; beat until creamy. Stir in roasted pecans. Spread over cake. Store in refrigerator or freezer.

Approx Per Serving: Cal 495; Prot 5 g; Carbo 64 g; T Fat 26 g;
  Chol 70 mg; Potas 148 mg; Sod 243 mg.

Mrs. John (Gini) Marston, Jr., Dallas, Texas
Dallas Women's Board

MISS JEWEL'S POUND CAKE L'ORANGE

Yield: 16 servings   *Pan Size: bundt*   *Preheat: 325 degrees*

1 cup butter, softened	1/2 teaspoon baking powder
2 cups sugar	1/2 teaspoon vanilla extract
6 eggs	1/2 teaspoon orange extract
2 cups sifted flour	5 tablespoons Grand Marnier
1/2 teaspoon salt	

Cream butter and sugar in mixer bowl until light and fluffy. Add eggs 1 at a time, beating well after each addition. Combine flour, salt and baking powder in bowl; mix well. Combine vanilla, orange extract and Grand Marnier in small bowl; mix well. Add dry ingredients to creamed mixture alternately with Grand Marnier mixture, mixing well after each addition. Pour into lightly greased and floured pan. Bake for 45 minutes. May substitute fresh orange juice for liqueur.

Approx Per Serving: Cal 298; Prot 4 g; Carbo 39 g; T Fat 14 g;
    Chol 111 mg; Potas 44 mg; Sod 201 mg.

Mrs. Jess R. (Beth) Moore, Houston, Texas
National Director, National Costume Collection

PRUNE CAKE

Yield: 10 servings   *Pan Size: two 8 inch*   *Preheat: 275 degrees*

1 cup oil	1 cup (or more) chopped,
3 eggs	cooked prunes
2 cups sugar	1 cup chopped pecans
2 1/2 cups flour	6 tablespoons melted butter
1 teaspoon soda	1 cup sugar
1 teaspoon cinnamon	1/8 teaspoon salt
1/2 teaspoon allspice	1/2 cup buttermilk
1 cup buttermilk	1/4 teaspoon soda

Beat oil and eggs in large mixer bowl until fluffy. Combine 2 cups sugar, flour, 1 teaspoon soda, cinnamon and allspice in bowl; mix well. Add to egg mixture alternately with 1 cup buttermilk, mixing well after each addition. Stir in prunes and pecans. Spoon into greased cake pans. Bake for 1 hour or until cakes test done. Cool for several minutes. Pierce with toothpick. Combine butter, remaining 1 cup sugar, salt, remaining 1/2 cup buttermilk and remaining 1/4 teaspoon soda in small saucepan. Heat until butter is melted and sugar is dissolved, stirring constantly; do not boil. Pour over cakes. Cool in pans.

Approx Per Serving: Cal 739; Prot 8 g; Carbo 94 g; T Fat 39 g;
    Chol 84 mg; Potas 227 mg; Sod 249 mg.

Mrs. Edith Lycke, Dallas, Texas
Dallas Women's Board

ORANGE BLOSSOM CUPCAKES

Yield: 60 servings   *Pan Size: miniature muffin cups*   *Preheat: 375 degrees*

1/2 cup butter, softened
1 cup sugar
2 eggs
1 teaspoon soda
2 cups flour

1/4 teaspoon salt
2/3 cup buttermilk
Juice of 2 oranges
Grated rind of 1 orange
1 cup sugar

Cream butter and 1 cup sugar in mixer bowl until light and fluffy. Beat in eggs 1 at a time. Add sifted dry ingredients alternately with buttermilk, mixing well after each addition. Fill greased muffin cups less than half full. Bake for 12 minutes. Combine orange juice, rind and 1 cup sugar in saucepan. Cook until sugar dissolves, stirring constantly. Spoon 1 teaspoonful over each warm cupcake in pan. Cool in pans. Serve warm or cold.

Nutritional information for this recipe is not available.

Mrs. R. Thomas (Helen) Wolfe, Dallas, Texas
Friend of Northwood

FRESH SWEET POTATO CAKE

Yield: 12 servings   *Pan Size: three 8 inch*   *Preheat: 350 degrees*

1 1/2 cups oil
2 cups sugar
4 egg yolks
1/4 cup hot water
2 1/2 cups sifted cake flour
1 tablespoon baking powder
1/4 teaspoon salt
1 teaspoon cinnamon
1 teaspoon nutmeg
1 1/2 cups shredded sweet
  potatoes

1 cup chopped walnuts
1 teaspoon vanilla extract
4 egg whites, stiffly beaten
1   12-ounce can evaporated
  milk
1 cup sugar
1/2 cup margarine
3 egg yolks
1 teaspoon vanilla extract
1 1/3 cups flaked coconut

Beat oil and sugar in mixer bowl until smooth. Add egg yolks; beat well. Stir in hot water. Sift dry ingredients together. Add to sugar mixture; mix well. Stir in next 3 ingredients. Fold stiffly beaten egg whites into batter. Spoon into greased and floured cake pans. Bake for 25 minutes. Cool in pans for 15 minutes. Remove to wire racks to cool completely. Combine evaporated milk and next 4 ingredients in small saucepan. Cook over medium heat for 12 minutes or until thickened, stirring constantly; remove from heat. Stir in coconut. Beat until cool and of spreading consistency. Frost cooled cake.

Approx Per Serving: Cal 804; Prot 9 g; Carbo 83 g; T Fat 50 g;
  Chol 133 mg; Potas 288 mg; Sod 321 mg.

JoAnn Seguin, Duncanville, Texas
Friend of Northwood

WINE CAKE

| Yield: 16 servings | Pan Size: bundt | Preheat: 350 degrees |

1 2-layer package butter recipe cake mix
1 4-ounce package vanilla instant pudding mix
4 eggs, slightly beaten
1/2 cup white wine

1/2 cup oil
1/2 cup water
1 cup sugar
1/4 cup water
1/2 cup margarine
1/4 cup white wine

Combine cake mix, pudding mix, eggs, 1/2 cup white wine, oil and 1/2 cup water in mixer bowl. Beat for 6 minutes. Pour into greased and floured pan. Bake for 45 minutes. Cool slightly. Invert onto cake plate. Pierce top of cake with fork. Combine sugar, remaining 1/4 cup water, margarine and remaining 1/4 cup white wine in small saucepan. Heat until margarine is melted and sugar is dissolved, stirring constantly. Bring to a boil. Cook for 5 minutes, stirring constantly. Spoon glaze gradually over top of cake until all glaze is absorbed. May substitute apricot Brandy or rum for white wine.

Approx Per Serving: Cal 304; Prot 3 g; Carbo 37 g; T Fat 16 g; Chol 53 mg; Potas 27 mg; Sod 263 mg.

Mrs. R. E. L. (Cappi) Gowan, Houston, Texas
Friend of Northwood

FABULOUS ZUCCHINI CAKE

| Yield: 18 servings | Pan Size: four 8 inch | Preheat: 300 degrees |

1 1/4 cups oil
4 eggs
3 cups shredded unpeeled zucchini
3 cups sugar
3 cups flour
2 teaspoons baking powder
1 teaspoon soda

1 1/2 teaspoons cinnamon
1 cup chopped pecans
1 cup butter, softened
3 ounces cream cheese, softened
2 cups confectioners' sugar
1 teaspoon vanilla extract

Combine oil, eggs, zucchini and sugar in mixer bowl; beat well. Combine flour, baking powder, soda and cinnamon. Add to zucchini mixture; beat well. Stir in pecans. Pour into greased and floured pans. Bake for 50 minutes. Remove to wire racks to cool completely. Cream butter, cream cheese, confectioners' sugar and vanilla in mixer bowl until light and fluffy. Spread between layers and over top and side of cake.

Approx Per Serving: Cal 562; Prot 5 g; Carbo 65 g; T Fat 33 g; Chol 80 mg; Potas 125 mg; Sod 199 mg.

Mrs. Robert (Genie) Parker, Phoenix, Arizona
Founding Member and Chairman 1985-1988, Valley of the Sun Chapter

NANA'S DATE ROLL CANDY

Yield: 24 servings   *Pan Size: saucepan*

2 cups sugar
1 cup milk
1½ cups chopped pecans

1 8-ounce package chopped dates
¼ cup butter

Combine sugar and milk in saucepan. Cook over medium heat to 234 to 240 degrees on candy thermometer, soft-ball stage. Remove from heat. Add pecans, dates and butter. Beat until mixture is creamy and loses its luster. Pour onto dampened tea towel; shape into roll. Chill in refrigerator until cooled completely. Cut into 24 slices. This is an old family recipe we have made for Christmas gifts for the last 60 years.

Approx Per Serving: Cal 163; Prot 1 g; Carbo 25 g; T Fat 7 g;
    Chol 7 mg; Potas 106 mg; Sod 21 mg.

Louise "Nana" Hagood, Lubbock, Texas
Friend of Northwood

PRALINES

Yield: 24 servings   *Pan Size: 2 quart saucepan*

1 teaspoon soda
1 cup buttermilk
3 cups sugar
2 tablespoons light corn syrup

½ cup butter
¼ teaspoon salt
3 teaspoons vanilla extract
4 cups pecan halves

Dissolve soda in buttermilk in saucepan. Add sugar, corn syrup, butter and salt; mix well. Cook over medium heat to 234 to 240 degrees on candy thermometer, soft ball stage. Remove from heat. Add vanilla and pecan halves; beat lightly. Drop by spoonfuls onto waxed paper.

Approx Per Serving: Cal 271; Prot 2 g; Carbo 30 g; T Fat 17 g;
    Chol 11 mg; Potas 96 mg; Sod 101 mg.

Carmalee DeGeorge, Houston, Texas
Houston Women's Board

PECOS PRALINES

Yield: 12 servings   *Pan Size: heavy saucepan*

1 4-ounce package butterscotch pudding and pie filling mix	½ cup packed brown sugar ½ cup evaporated milk 1 tablespoon butter
1 cup sugar	1½ cups chopped pecans

Combine pudding mix, sugar, brown sugar, evaporated milk and butter in saucepan; mix well. Cook over medium heat to 234 to 240 degrees on candy thermometer, soft-ball stage; remove from heat. Add pecans; beat with spoon until thickened. Drop by spoonfuls onto waxed paper. Pralines will be soft but will become firm overnight. This is a "can't miss" praline recipe.

Approx Per Serving: Cal 255; Prot 2 g; Carbo 38 g; T Fat 12 g;
    Chol 6 mg; Potas 123 mg; Sod 87 mg.

Northwood Cookbook Committee, Dallas, Texas

ENGLISH TOFFEE

Yield: 9 servings   *Pan Size: 9-inch heavy skillet*

1 cup butter	3 16-ounce chocolate candy bars, softened
1 cup sugar	
½ teaspoon vanilla extract	¼ cup finely chopped almonds
1 tablespoon water	
1 cup almonds	

Melt butter in skillet over medium heat. Add sugar and mixture of vanilla and water, stirring constantly. Cook to 234 to 240 degrees on candy thermometer, soft-ball stage, stirring constantly. Add almonds. Cook until rich brown color, stirring constantly. Pour into greased 9-inch pan. Spread with half the chocolate while warm but not hot. Invert onto waxed paper sprinkled with half the chopped almonds. Spread with remaining chocolate; sprinkle with remaining chopped almonds. Cool. Break into pieces.

Approx Per Serving: Cal 1154; Prot 15 g; Carbo 111 g; T Fat 79 g;
    Chol 87 mg; Potas 666 mg; Sod 297 mg.

Natasha Rawson, Houston, Texas
Houston Women's Board

TEXAS CHOCOLATE FUDGE

Yield: 36 servings   *Pan Size: 9x13 inch*

2 cups chocolate chips,
 softened
1 cup margarine, softened
1 12-ounce can evaporated
 milk

4¹/2 cups sugar
2 cups chopped pecans
Salt to taste
1 teaspoon vanilla extract

Combine chocolate chips and margarine in large mixer bowl. Bring evaporated milk and sugar to a boil in saucepan; reduce heat. Simmer for 6 minutes, stirring constantly. Pour into chocolate mixture; mix well. Add pecans, salt and vanilla. Stir until creamy. Pour into pan. Chill in refrigerator for 2 to 3 hours or until fudge is firm. Cut into squares.

Approx Per Serving: Cal 246; Prot 2 g; Carbo 33 g; T Fat 14 g;
 Chol 3 mg; Potas 91 mg; Sod 72 mg.

Ms. Kimula S. Holmes, Dallas, Texas
Dallas Women's Board

KAHLUA BROWNIES

Yield: 36 servings   *Pan Size: 9x13 inch*   *Preheat: 350 degrees*

1 22-ounce package
 double-fudge brownie mix
2 eggs, slightly beaten
¹/4 cup Kahlua

¹/2 cup chopped pecans
1 cup semisweet chocolate
 chips

Combine brownie mix, chocolate syrup from brownie mix, eggs and Kahlua in medium bowl; beat about 50 strokes just until moistened; do not use a mixer. Fold in pecans and chocolate chips gently. Spread in baking dish. Bake for 35 minutes or until brownies test done; do not overbake. Cool completely. Garnish with sprinkle of confectioners' sugar. Cut into squares.

Approx Per Serving: Cal 120; Prot 2 g; Carbo 18 g; T Fat 5 g;
 Chol 12 mg; Potas 27 mg; Sod 65 mg.

Mrs. Robert H. (Penny) Holmes, II, Dallas, Texas
Dallas Women's Board

TURTLE BROWNIES

Yield: 36 servings	Pan Size: 9x13 inch	Preheat: 350 degrees

1 14-ounce package vanilla caramels	1¹/₃ cups water
¹/₂ cup evaporated milk	³/₄ cup margarine, softened
1 2-layer package German chocolate cake mix	3 eggs, slightly beaten
	1 cup chopped pecans
	1 cup chocolate chips

Melt caramels with evaporated milk in double boiler, stirring constantly until smooth. Combine cake mix, water, margarine and eggs in mixer bowl; mix until smooth. Pour half the batter into greased baking dish. Bake for 10 minutes. Spread caramel mixture over baked layer. Sprinkle with pecans and chocolate chips. Spoon remaining batter over top. Bake for 30 to 35 minutes longer. Cool in pan. Cut into squares.

Approx Per Serving: Cal 166; Prot 2 g; Carbo 20 g; T Fat 9 g; Chol 19 mg; Potas 55 mg; Sod 146 mg.

Mrs. Charles (Anne) Trevino, LaPorte, Texas
Friend of Northwood

CHOCOLATE CHIP COOKIES

Yield: 24 servings	Pan Size: cookie sheet	Preheat: 375 degrees

1 cup flour	¹/₂ cup packed brown sugar
¹/₂ teaspoon soda	¹/₂ teaspoon vanilla extract
¹/₂ teaspoon salt	1 egg, slightly beaten
¹/₂ cup butter, softened	1 cup chocolate chips
¹/₂ cup sugar	1 cup chopped pecans

Combine flour, soda and salt. Cream butter, sugar, brown sugar and vanilla in medium bowl until light and fluffy. Add egg; mix well. Add flour mixture; mix well. Stir in chocolate chips and pecans. Drop by level tablespoonfuls onto ungreased cookie sheet. Bake for 9 minutes. Remove to wire rack to cool.

Approx Per Serving: Cal 158; Prot 2 g; Carbo 18 g; T Fat 10 g; Chol 19 mg; Potas 69 mg; Sod 100 mg.

Ellie Abranovic, Irving, Texas
Friend of Northwood

WHITE CHOCOLATE CHIP COOKIES

Yield: 48 servings   *Pan Size: cookie sheet*   *Preheat: 350 degrees*

1/2 cup butter, softened
1/2 cup shortening
3/4 cup sugar
3/4 cup packed brown sugar
3 eggs, slightly beaten
1 teaspoon vanilla extract
2 1/2 cups flour

1 teaspoon soda
1/2 teaspoon salt
1 cup flaked coconut
1/2 cup oats
1/2 cup pecans
1 cup white chocolate chips

Cream butter, shortening, sugar and brown sugar in mixer bowl until light and fluffy. Add eggs 1 at a time, mixing well after each addition. Add vanilla; mix well. Sift flour, soda and salt into bowl. Add to creamed mixture gradually, mixing well after each addition. Beat at medium speed for 2 minutes. Stir in coconut, oats, pecans and white chocolate chips. Drop by teaspoonfuls onto greased cookie sheet. Bake for 10 to 12 minutes. Cool on cookie sheet for 1 minute. Remove to wire rack to cool completely.

Approx Per Serving: Cal 126; Prot 2 g; Carbo 15 g; T Fat 7 g;
    Chol 19 mg; Potas 48 mg; Sod 66 mg.

Lisanne Korsmeier, Dallas, Texas
Friend of Northwood

CHOCOLATE COCONUT COOKIES

Yield: 60 servings   *Pan Size: cookie sheet*   *Preheat: 300 degrees*

1 14-ounce can sweetened
  condensed milk
3 tablespoons (heaping)
  baking cocoa

2 3-ounce cans coconut
1 tablespoon vanilla extract
1 cup chopped pecans

Combine condensed milk and cocoa in bowl; mix well. Add coconut, vanilla and pecans; mix well. Mixture with be very stiff. Drop by spoonfuls onto greased cookie sheet. Bake for 20 minutes. This recipe is 50 years old.

Approx Per Serving: Cal 48; Prot 1 g; Carbo 5 g; T Fat 3 g;
    Chol 2 mg; Potas 45 mg; Sod 9 mg.

Mrs. William W. (Lorraine) Bland, Houston, Texas
Houston Women's Board/Distinguished Woman

Lorraine B. Bland

EVERYONE'S FAVORITE COOKIES

Yield: 36 servings   *Pan Size: saucepan*

1/2 cup butter
30 large marshmallows
4 cups cornflakes

Assorted candies for
decorating

Melt butter and marshmallows in saucepan; mix well. Pour mixture over cornflakes in large bowl; mix until well coated. Shape quickly by spoonfuls into cookies; place on waxed paper to cool. Decorate with candies appropriate to any special occasion.

Approx Per Serving: Cal 51; Prot 0 g; Carbo 7 g; T Fat 3 g;
  Chol 7 mg; Potas 4 mg; Sod 58 mg.
  Nutritional information does not include candies for decorating.

Wanda C. Shelton, Rochester Hills, Michigan
Distinguished Woman

LEMON BALLS

Yield: 48 servings   *Pan Size: large bowl*

1 12-ounce package vanilla
  wafers
1 cup chopped pecans
2 cups confectioners' sugar

1/2 cup frozen lemonade
  concentrate, thawed
1/2 cup melted butter
1 1/2 cups coconut

Crush vanilla wafers into crumbs. Combine with pecans, confectioners' sugar, lemonade concentrate and butter in bowl; mix well. Let stand for 5 minutes. Shape by level tablespoonfuls into balls. Roll in coconut; place on waxed paper. Chill in refrigerator.

Approx Per Serving: Cal 102; Prot 1 g; Carbo 13 g; T Fat 6 g;
  Chol 10 mg; Potas 29 mg; Sod 43 mg.

Florence Doswell, Dallas, Texas
Dallas Women's Board

LEMON SQUARES

Yield: 16 servings | *Pan Size: 8 inch* | *Preheat: 350 degrees*

½ cup butter, softened
¼ cup confectioners' sugar
1 cup flour
2 eggs

1 cup sugar
¼ teaspoon baking powder
¼ teaspoon salt
2 tablespoons lemon juice

Cream butter and confectioners' sugar in bowl until light and fluffy. Add flour; mix well. Press mixture into baking dish. Bake for 20 minutes. Combine eggs, sugar, baking powder, salt and lemon juice in bowl; mix well. Spread over baked layer. Bake for 20 to 25 minutes. This delicious and light dessert is suitable for casual as well as formal dining.

Approx Per Serving: Cal 145; Prot 2 g; Carbo 21 g; T Fat 7 g;
Chol 42 mg; Potas 20 mg; Sod 96 mg.

Mrs. David M. (Natalie) Taylor, Dallas, Texas
Dallas Women's Board

AUNT MIMI'S CHEWY OATMEAL COOKIES

Yield: 36 servings | *Pan Size: cookie sheet* | *Preheat: 375 degrees*

2 cups packed light brown
   sugar
1 cup shortening
2 eggs
1½ cups flour

1 teaspoon soda
½ teaspoon salt
3 cups oats
¼ cup confectioners' sugar

Cream brown sugar and shortening in mixer bowl until light and fluffy. Add eggs; mix until smooth. Add flour, soda, salt and oats; mix well. Shape into walnut-sized balls. Roll in confectioners' sugar. Place on ungreased cookie sheet. Bake for 8 to 10 minutes; do not overbake. Cool on cookie sheet for several minutes. Remove to wire rack to cool completely.

Approx Per Serving: Cal 148; Prot 2 g; Carbo 21 g; T Fat 6 g;
Chol 12 mg; Potas 74 mg; Sod 62 mg.

Paula Ulmer, Dallas, Texas
Northwood Arts Programs Administrator/Distinguished Woman
Campus Arts Coordinator, Texas/Dallas Women's Board

NANA'S OATMEAL COOKIES

Yield: 60 servings　　　*Pan Size: cookie sheet*　　　*Preheat: 325 degrees*

1 cup sugar	1 teaspoon soda
1 cup packed brown sugar	1/2 teaspoon salt
1 cup oil	3 cups oats
1 teaspoon vanilla extract	1 cup coconut
2 eggs	1 cup chopped pecans
1 cup flour	

Combine sugar, brown sugar, oil, vanilla and eggs in mixer bowl; beat until well blended. Add flour, soda, salt and oats; mix well. Stir in coconut and pecans. Drop by teaspoonfuls 2 inches apart onto cookie sheet. Bake for 10 to 12 minutes or until golden brown.

Approx Per Serving: Cal 103; Prot 1 g; Carbo 12 g; T Fat 6 g;
　　　Chol 7 mg; Potas 43 mg; Sod 39 mg.

Louise "Nana" Hagood, Lubbock, Texas
Friend of Northwood

PECAN BARS

Yield: 36 servings　　　*Pan Size: 9x13 inch*　　　*Preheat: 350 degrees*

2/3 cup confectioners' sugar	1/2 cup packed brown sugar
2 cups unbleached flour	1/2 cup honey
1 cup cold unsalted butter, sliced	3 tablespoons whipping cream
2/3 cup butter	3 1/2 cups chopped pecans

Combine confectioners' sugar and flour in food processer container. Add unsalted butter. Process with metal blade until crumbly. Press into baking dish. Bake for 20 minutes or until edges are lightly browned. Melt 2/3 cup butter with brown sugar, honey and whipping cream in saucepan, stirring frequently. Add pecans; stir until well coated. Spread over baked layer. Bake for 20 to 25 minutes or until light golden brown. Cool completely before cutting into squares.

Approx Per Serving: Cal 216; Prot 2 g; Carbo 16 g; T Fat 17 g;
　　　Chol 25 mg; Potas 69 mg; Sod 31 mg.

Northwood Cookbook Committee, Dallas, Texas

ROBYN'S DELIGHTS

Yield: 36 servings   *Pan Size: 9x13 inch*   *Preheat: 350 degrees*

1 2-layer package yellow
   cake mix
1/2 cup melted butter
1 egg
2²/₃ cups confectioners' sugar

2 eggs
1 teaspoon vanilla extract
8 ounces cream cheese,
   softened

Combine cake mix, butter and 1 egg in bowl; mix well. Press into baking dish. Combine confectioners' sugar, 2 eggs, vanilla and cream cheese in mixer bowl; beat until smooth. Spread cream cheese mixture over baked layer. Bake for 30 to 40 minutes or until set. Cool completely before cutting into squares.

Approx Per Serving: Cal 126; Prot 1 g; Carbo 17 g; T Fat 6 g;
    Chol 32 mg; Potas 14 mg; Sod 104 mg.

Mrs. J. Gilbert McElreath, Dallas, Texas
Dallas Women's Board

GRANDMOTHER'S CHERRY ICEBOX PIE

Yield: 6 servings   *Pan Size: 9 inch*

1 cup whipping cream
1 14-ounce can sweetened
   condensed milk
Juice of 2 lemons
1/2 cup chopped pecans

1 16-ounce can
   water-packed tart cherries,
   drained
1 9-inch graham cracker pie
   shell

Whip cream in bowl until very stiff. Add condensed milk gradually, blending well. Add lemon juice several drops at a time, blending well after each addition. Stir in pecans. Fold in cherries. Spoon into pie shell. Chill for several hours to overnight.

Approx Per Serving: Cal 713; Prot 10 g; Carbo 81 g; T Fat 41 g;
    Chol 74 mg; Potas 490 mg; Sod 422 mg.

Dottie Aiken, Dallas, Texas
Dallas Women's Board

BUTTERMILK CHESS PIE

Yield: 6 servings   Pan Size: 9 inch   Preheat: 350 degrees

3¹/2 cups sugar
1 cup melted butter
1 cup buttermilk
6 eggs

¹/2 cup flour
1¹/2 teaspoons vanilla extract
¹/8 teaspoon salt
1 unbaked 9-inch pie shell

Blend sugar, butter and buttermilk in mixer bowl. Beat in eggs 1 at a time. Add flour, vanilla and salt; mix well. Pour into pie shell. Bake for 1 hour.

Approx Per Serving: Cal 1004; Prot 11 g; Carbo 140 g; T Fat 47 g; Chol 297 mg; Potas 166 mg; Sod 601 mg.

Gwen White, Dallas, Texas
Friend of Northwood

LEMON CHESS PIE

Yield: 6 servings   Pan Size: 9 inch   Preheat: 350 degrees

4 eggs, slightly beaten
2 cups sugar
¹/2 cup melted butter
4 teaspoons grated lemon rind

¹/4 cup lemon juice
¹/4 cup milk
2 tablespoons cornmeal
1 unbaked 9-inch pie shell

Beat eggs and sugar in bowl until light and fluffy. Beat in butter, lemon rind, lemon juice, milk and cornmeal. Pour into pie shell. Bake for 40 minutes.

Approx Per Serving: Cal 615; Prot 7 g; Carbo 84 g; T Fat 30 g; Chol 185 mg; Potas 98 mg; Sod 364 mg.

Mrs. Joan Schnitzer, Houston, Texas
Houston Women's Board

CHOCOLATE ICE BOX PIE

Yield: 6 servings   *Pan Size: 9 inch*

1 4-ounce package chocolate instant pudding mix	1 pint home-style vanilla ice cream, softened
1 cup milk	1 baked 9-inch pie shell

Combine pudding mix and milk in mixer bowl; beat until blended. Add ice cream; beat until thickened. Pour into pie shell. Chill for several hours or until set. Garnish with whipped cream and grated chocolate.

Approx Per Serving: Cal 335; Prot 5 g; Carbo 43 g; T Fat 16 g;
    Chol 25 mg; Potas 156 mg; Sod 365 mg.

Gina and John Marston, Dallas, Texas
Friends of Northwood

WINNER'S CIRCLE CHOCOLATE CHIP AND PECAN PIE

Yield: 6 servings   *Pan Size: 9 inch*   ≈M≈

1 tablespoon melted butter	1/2 cup melted butter
1 tablespoon vanilla extract	1 cup chopped pecans
1 unbaked 9-inch pie shell	1 cup chocolate chips
2 eggs, slightly beaten	1 teaspoon vanilla extract
1 cup sugar	1/2 cup coconut
1/2 cup flour	

Spread mixture of 1 tablespoon butter and 1 tablespoon vanilla over pie shell. Microwave on High for 4 minutes. Cool. Combine eggs and sugar in bowl; mix well. Add flour, remaining 1/2 cup butter, half the pecans, half the chocolate chips, remaining 1 teaspoon vanilla and coconut; mix well. Pour into cooled pie shell. Sprinkle with remaining chocolate chips and pecans. Microwave on Medium for 12 to 15 minutes or until set. Cool.

Approx Per Serving: Cal 799; Prot 8 g; Carbo 77 g; T Fat 55 g;
    Chol 118 mg; Potas 251 mg; Sod 358 mg.

Northwood Cookbook Committee, Dallas, Texas

CUSTARD PIE

Yield: 6 servings   *Pan Size: 9 inch*   *Preheat: 350 degrees*

2 cups milk	¼ cup softened butter
¾ cup sugar	1½ teaspoons vanilla extract
4 eggs	1 unbaked 9-inch pie shell

Combine milk, sugar, eggs, butter and vanilla in blender container. Process at low speed for 3 minutes. Pour into pie shell. Let stand for 5 minutes. Bake for 40 minutes or until filling is set and crust is brown.

Approx Per Serving: Cal 417; Prot 9 g; Carbo 42 g; T Fat 24 g;
    Chol 174 mg; Potas 171 mg; Sod 328 mg.

Florence Doswell, Dallas, Texas
Dallas Women's Board

GRAHAM CRACKER PIE

Yield: 6 servings   *Pan Size: 9 inch*   *Preheat: 350 degrees*

14 graham crackers	1 teaspoon baking powder
1 cup sugar	3 egg yolks, beaten
½ cup finely ground pecans	1 teaspoon vanilla extract
⅛ teaspoon salt	3 egg whites, stiffly beaten

Crush graham crackers into fine crumbs. Combine with sugar, pecans, salt and baking powder in bowl; mix well. Fold into mixture of egg yolks and vanilla. Fold into stiffly beaten egg whites gently. Spoon into pie plate. Bake for 40 minutes. This pie will puff during baking and settle after it is removed from oven. Garnish with whipped cream or ice cream. It is delicious hot or cold. My 90 year old mother can't remember who gave her this recipe but it is of New England origin.

Approx Per Serving: Cal 305; Prot 5 g; Carbo 48 g; T Fat 11 g;
    Chol 106 mg; Potas 113 mg; Sod 230 mg.

Carolyn A. Rabidoux, Palm Beach, Florida
Chairman, Palm Beach Chapter

GREEN TOMATO PIE

Yield: 6 servings	Pan Size: 9 inch	Preheat: 250 degrees

6 to 8 green tomatoes	1/2 teaspoon cinnamon
1 recipe 2-crust pie pastry	1 tablespoon vinegar
1 1/2 cups sugar	1/4 cup (about) flour
1/2 teaspoon nutmeg	1/2 cup butter

Peel, core and thinly slice tomatoes. Layer in pastry-lined pie plate, mounding in center. Combine sugar, nutmeg, cinnamon and vinegar in bowl. Add flour according to moisture of tomatoes; mix well. Sprinkle evenly over tomatoes. Dot with butter. Top with remaining pastry, sealing edge and cutting vents. Bake for 1 hour or until brown.

Approx Per Serving: Cal 529; Prot 4 g; Carbo 74 g; T Fat 26 g;
    Chol 41 mg; Potas 369 mg; Sod 327 mg.

Evelyn Franklin, Midlothian, Texas
Northwood Staff, Texas Campus

LEMON SHAKER PIE

Yield: 6 servings	Pan Size: 9 inch	Preheat: 300 degrees

5 lemons, peeled, thinly sliced	1 recipe 2-crust pie pastry
2 cups sugar	2 tablespoons melted butter
5 eggs, beaten	2 tablespoons Milnot

Combine lemon slices and sugar in bowl; mix until sugar is dissolved. Let stand overnight in refrigerator. Add lemon mixture to beaten eggs; mix well. Pour into pastry-lined pie plate. Top with remaining pastry, sealing edge and cutting vents. Brush with butter. Bake for 1 hour and 10 minutes. Increase oven temperature to 350 degrees. Brush pie with Milnot. Bake until crust is light brown.

Approx Per Serving: Cal 711; Prot 9 g; Carbo 95 g; T Fat 27 g;
    Chol 188 mg; Potas 175 mg; Sod 465 mg.

Mrs. Kenneth D. Owen, New Harmony, Indiana
Red Geranium Restaurant

CHIFFON MAPLE AND PECAN PIE

Yield: 8 servings   *Pan Size: 9¹/2 inch deep-dish*

1 cup packed brown sugar	¹/2 teaspoon maple flavoring
3 egg yolks	3 egg whites
5 tablespoons flour	¹/2 cup sugar
2 cups milk	¹/8 teaspoon salt
2 tablespoons unflavored gelatin	1 baked 9-inch deep-dish pie shell
¹/4 cup cold water	¹/2 cup chopped pecans

Combine brown sugar, egg yolks, flour and milk in saucepan; mix well. Cook over low heat until thickened, stirring constantly. Bring to a full boil; remove from heat. Soften gelatin in cold water. Add maple flavoring; mix well. Add to brown sugar mixture; stir until dissolved. Cool. Beat egg whites in mixer bowl until soft peaks form. Add ¹/2 cup sugar and salt gradually, beating until stiff. Fold into cooled brown sugar mixture gently. Spoon into pie shell. Sprinkle with pecans. Chill for 3 hours or until set. This is a favorite from my childhood that is still a favorite.

Approx Per Serving: Cal 404; Prot 8 g; Carbo 57 g; T Fat 17 g;
    Chol 88 mg; Potas 245 mg; Sod 232 mg.

Mrs. Arthur E. (Johann) Turner, Palm Beach, Florida
Midland and G.P.B./Wife of Co-founder A.E.T.

REFRIGERATOR PEACH PIE

Yield: 6 servings   *Pan Size: 9 inch*

1 pound peaches	8 ounces cream cheese, softened
¹/2 cup sugar	
2 teaspoons lemon juice	1 teaspoon vanilla extract
1 envelope unflavored gelatin	1 9-inch graham cracker pie shell
³/4 cup sour cream	

Reserve 1 peach for garnish. Dip peaches in boiling water for several seconds; peel and chop. Combine chopped peaches, sugar and lemon juice in bowl. Chill, covered, for 20 minutes. Drain ¹/2 cup liquid from peaches. Soften gelatin in liquid in small saucepan. Heat to dissolve gelatin completely, stirring constantly. Add gelatin to peaches; mix well. Chill until slightly thickened. Blend sour cream, cream cheese and vanilla in bowl. Fold in peaches. Spoon into pie shell. Chill until firm. Garnish with reserved peach slices. May substitute frozen peaches for fresh and omit sugar.

Approx Per Serving: Cal 567; Prot 8 g; Carbo 62 g; T Fat 34 g;
    Chol 54 mg; Potas 322 mg; Sod 447 mg.

Mrs. R. J. (Aline) Byrd, Dallas, Texas
Dallas Women's Board

HOLIDAY MINCEMEAT FOR PIES

Yield: 32 servings   *Pan Size: four 9 inch*   *Preheat: 425 degrees*

4 pounds apples, peeled,
   chopped
4 pounds pears, peeled,
   chopped
2 pounds raisins
2 cups packed brown sugar
1 cup orange juice
1/2 cup grated orange rind

2/3 cup lemon juice
1/3 cup grated lemon rind
4 teaspoons cinnamon
2 teaspoons cloves
1 teaspoon allspice
1 teaspoon nutmeg
1 teaspoon ginger
4 recipes 2-crust pie pastry

Combine apples, pears, raisins, brown sugar, orange juice and rind, lemon juice and rind and spices in large saucepan; mix well. Cook for 1 hour, stirring frequently to prevent sticking. Fill each pastry-lined pie plate with 4 cups mincemeat. Top with remaining pastry, sealing edges and cutting vents. Bake for 35 minutes or until brown. May can mincemeat by ladling into 8 hot sterilized 1-pint jars, leaving 1/4-inch headspace. Remove air bubbles with nonmetallic spatula. Seal with 2-piece lids. Process in boiling water bath canner according to manufacturer's instructions.

Approx Per Serving: Cal 460; Prot 4 g; Carbo 72 g; T Fat 14 g;
   Chol 0 mg; Potas 449 mg; Sod 285 mg.

Edmund F. Ball, Muncie, Indiana
Outstanding Business Leader Awardee

MYSTERY PECAN PIE

Yield: 6 servings   *Pan Size: 9 inch*   *Preheat: 375 degrees*

8 ounces cream cheese,
   softened
1/3 cup sugar
1/4 teaspoon salt
1 teaspoon vanilla extract
1 egg

1 unbaked 9-inch pie shell
1 1/4 cups chopped pecans
3 eggs
1/2 cup sugar
1 cup light corn syrup
1 teaspoon vanilla extract

Combine cream cheese, 1/3 cup sugar, salt, 1 teaspoon vanilla and 1 egg in bowl; mix well. Spread in pie shell. Sprinkle with pecans. Beat remaining 3 eggs in bowl until light and fluffy. Add remaining 1/2 cup sugar, corn syrup and vanilla; beat well. Pour gently over pecans. Bake for 35 to 40 minutes or until center is firm and crust is brown.

Approx Per Serving: Cal 758; Prot 11 g; Carbo 88 g; T Fat 44 g;
   Chol 183 mg; Potas 211 mg; Sod 456 mg.

Sharon A. Snyder, Grosse Pointe, Michigan
Director of External Affairs, Greater Detroit Area

TEXAS PECAN PIE

Yield: 8 servings	Pan Size: 9 inch	Preheat: 350 degrees

3 eggs, slightly beaten
1 cup sugar
1 cup light corn syrup
1 teaspoon vanilla extract

1/8 teaspoon salt
2 tablespoons melted butter
1 1/2 cups pecans
1 unbaked 9-inch pie shell

Combine eggs, sugar, corn syrup, vanilla, salt and butter in bowl; mix well. Stir in pecans. Pour into pie shell. Bake for 50 to 55 minutes or until knife inserted halfway between center and edge comes out clean. Cool.

Approx Per Serving: Cal 527; Prot 5 g; Carbo 70 g; T Fat 28 g;
Chol 88 mg; Potas 132 mg; Sod 207 mg.

Mrs. R. J. (Sandy) Smith, Jr., Dallas, Texas
Dallas Women's Board

SPICY RICH AND SMOOTH PUMPKIN PIE

Yield: 6 servings	Pan Size: 10 inch	Preheat: 450 degrees

3 cups canned pumpkin
1 cup sugar
1 cup packed brown sugar
1 teaspoon salt
1/4 teaspoon cloves
1 teaspoon nutmeg
1 teaspoon cinnamon

1 teaspoon ginger
1/4 teaspoon allspice
1/2 cup Jack Daniels Bourbon
4 eggs, beaten
1/4 cup melted butter
1 unbaked 10-inch pie shell

Combine pumpkin, sugar, brown sugar, salt, spices and Bourbon in mixer bowl; beat well. Add eggs and butter; mix well. Pour into pie shell. Bake for 10 minutes. Reduce oven temperature to 350 degrees. Bake for 40 minutes longer or until center is set. May use egg substitute in place of eggs.

Approx Per Serving: Cal 470; Prot 5 g; Carbo 79 g; T Fat 12 g;
Chol 163 mg; Potas 426 mg; Sod 489 mg.

Paula Ulmer, Dallas, Texas
Campus Arts Coordinator, Texas/Distinguished Woman
Northwood Arts Programs Administrator

Desserts

Lambert Commons
Cedar Hill, Texas

BANANA PUDDING

Yield: 16 servings   *Pan Size: 9x13-inch*

1 4-ounce package banana cream instant pudding mix	1 cup sour cream
2 4-ounce packages vanilla instant pudding mix	13 ounces whipped topping
5 cups milk	1 16-ounce package vanilla wafers
	6 to 8 bananas, sliced

Combine pudding mixes, milk, sour cream and half the whipped topping in bowl; mix until thick. Layer vanilla wafers, bananas and pudding mixture 1/2 at a time in glass dish. Spread remaining whipped topping over top. Chill until serving time.

Approx Per Serving: Cal 413; Prot 5 g; Carbo 63 g; T Fat 17 g; Chol 34 mg; Potas 389 mg; Sod 294 mg.

Mary Kay Ash, Dallas, Texas
Dallas Women's Board/Distinguished Woman

BREAD PUDDING

Yield: 15 servings   *Pan Size: 9x12-inch*   *Preheat: 350 degrees*

1 16-ounce loaf French bread	1/2 teaspoon nutmeg
1 cup whipping cream	1/2 teaspoon cinnamon
3 cups milk	1 1/2 cups raisins
3 eggs, beaten	1 2-ounce package slivered almonds
1 cup sugar	
1 teaspoon vanilla extract	

Tear bread into pieces; place in large bowl. Add cream and milk. Let stand for several minutes. Beat eggs until frothy. Add sugar and vanilla; beat well. Add spices, raisins and almonds; mix well. Stir into bread mixture. Pour into greased baking dish. Bake for 30 minutes.

Approx Per Serving: Cal 310; Prot 7 g; Carbo 45 g; T Fat 12 g; Chol 71 mg; Potas 270 mg; Sod 218 mg.

Mrs. Leonard (Mary Tullie) Critcher, Dallas, Texas
Dallas Women's Board

CHRISTMAS PUDDING WITH SAUCE

Yield: 15 servings   *Pan Size: steamer*

1 cup packed dark brown
  sugar
1 cup molasses
3 eggs
1 cup (heaping) minced suet
1½ cups buttermilk
1½ teaspoons (heaping)
  cinnamon

½ teaspoon (heaping) cloves
⅛ teaspoon salt
1 teaspoon vanilla extract
3 cups flour
3½ teaspoons baking powder
1 teaspoon soda
1 16-ounce package dates,
  chopped

Combine brown sugar, molasses, eggs, suet and buttermilk in bowl; mix well. Add spices, salt and vanilla; mix well. Add flour, baking powder and soda; mix well. Stir in dates. Pour into 3 greased steamer inserts. Place inserts in steamer over boiling water. Steam for 3 hours. Serve hot with Christmas Pudding Sauce. Pudding may be frozen. Reheat by slicing and reheating in microwave. My great-great grandmother brought this recipe with her from Denmark. It is still a holiday tradition.

Approx Per Serving: Cal 301; Prot 5 g; Carbo 69 g; T Fat 2 g;
    Chol 44 mg; Potas 947 mg; Sod 217 mg.

CHRISTMAS PUDDING SAUCE

Yield: 15 servings   *Pan Size: 2 quart*

1 cup sugar
1 cup packed brown sugar
3 tablespoons (heaping) flour
½ teaspoon salt

2 tablespoons vinegar
3 tablespoons butter
2 cups boiling water

Combine sugar, brown sugar, flour and salt in small saucepan. Add vinegar and butter. Stir in water gradually. Cook mixture over low heat until thickened to desired consistency, stirring constantly. Serve hot sauce over hot Christmas Pudding.

Approx Per Serving: Cal 132; Prot 0 g; Carbo 29 g; T Fat 2 g;
    Chol 6 mg; Potas 55 mg; Sod 97 mg.

Mrs. Charles V. (Judy) Shepard, Dallas, Texas
Dallas Women's Board

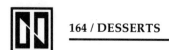

INDIAN CARROT DESSERT

Yield: 8 servings	*Pan Size: 3 quart*

1¹/₂ pounds carrots	**¹/₄ cup white raisins**
4 cups milk	**6 cardamom pods, peeled,**
1¹/₄ cups sugar	**crushed**
¹/₂ cup unsalted butter	**¹/₄ cup blanched almonds**

Grate carrots. Combine carrots and milk in heavy saucepan. Cook over medium heat for 1 hour or until mixture is very thick. Add sugar, butter and raisins. Cook for 15 to 20 minutes or until mixture begins to form ball, stirring constantly. Pour into 9x13-inch dish. Sprinkle with cardamom and almonds. Serve warm or at room temperature. May store in refrigerator for up to 3 days.

Approx Per Serving: Cal 376; Prot 6 g; Carbo 50 g; T Fat 18 g;
Chol 48 mg; Potas 516 mg; Sod 84 mg.

Mrs. M. A. (Rose Mary) Gibson, Houston, Texas
Houston Women's Board

AMARETTO CHEESECAKE

Yield: 12 servings	*Pan Size: 9-inch springform*	*Preheat: 375 degrees*

1¹/₂ cups graham cracker	**4 eggs**
crumbs	**¹/₃ cup Amaretto**
2 tablespoons sugar	**1 cup sour cream**
1 teaspoon cinnamon	**4 teaspoons sugar**
6 tablespoons melted butter	**1 tablespoon Amaretto**
24 ounces cream cheese,	**¹/₄ cup sliced toasted almonds**
softened	**12 ounces milk chocolate,**
1 cup sugar	**grated**

Combine crumbs, 2 tablespoons sugar, cinnamon and butter in bowl; mix well. Press over bottom and up side of springform pan. Beat cream cheese in mixer bowl until light and fluffy. Add 1 cup sugar gradually, beating constantly. Add eggs 1 at a time, beating well after each addition. Blend in ¹/₃ cup Amaretto. Pour into prepared pan. Bake for 45 to 50 minutes or until set. Increase oven temperature to 500 degrees. Combine sour cream, 4 teaspoons sugar and 1 tablespoon Amaretto in small bowl; blend well. Spoon over cheesecake. Bake at 500 degrees for 5 minutes. Let stand until cooled to room temperature. Chill for 24 to 48 hours before serving. Garnish with almonds and chocolate.

Approx Per Serving: Cal 661; Prot 11 g; Carbo 55 g; T Fat 44 g;
Chol 163 mg; Potas 293 mg; Sod 366 mg.

Margie August, Dallas, Texas
Dallas Women's Board/Northwood Arts Programs Special Projects Director

FABULOUS CREAMY CHEESECAKE

Yield: 12 servings   *Pan Size: 9-inch springform*   *Preheat: 400 degrees*

15 graham crackers, crushed
1/4 cup melted butter
1/2 cup packed brown sugar
5 egg whites
12 ounces cream cheese
5 egg yolks
1 cup sugar
1 teaspoon vanilla extract
1 cup sour cream
3 tablespoons confectioners' sugar
1 teaspoon vanilla extract

Mix cracker crumbs with butter and brown sugar in bowl. Press over bottom and side of buttered springform pan. Bake for 5 minutes. Reduce oven temperature to 350 degrees. Beat egg whites in bowl until foamy; set aside. Beat softened cream cheese, egg yolks, sugar and vanilla in bowl until smooth. Fold in egg whites. Pour into prepared pan. Bake for 40 minutes or until set. Blend remaining ingredients in small bowl. Spread over cheesecake. Bake for 5 minutes. Cool to room temperature. Chill in refrigerator. Serve plain or decorate with berries or sliced almonds.

Approx Per Serving: Cal 350; Prot 6 g; Carbo 36 g; T Fat 21 g;
    Chol 139 mg; Potas 142 mg; Sod 209 mg.

Carla Anderson Hills, Washington, D. C.
U.S. Trade Representative/Distinguished Woman

BETTER-THAN-SEX CHOCOLATE CHEESE DESSERT

Yield: 20 servings   *Pan Size: 9x13 inch*   *Preheat: 350 degrees*

1 cup flour
1 1/2 cups chopped pecans
1/2 cup melted butter
8 ounces cream cheese, softened
1 1/2 cups confectioners' sugar
1 1/2 cups whipped topping
1 4-ounce package chocolate instant pudding mix
1 6-ounce package chocolate instant pudding mix
4 cups cold milk
1 8-ounce milk chocolate and almond candy bar

Combine flour, pecans and butter in bowl; mix well. Press into baking dish. Bake for 15 minutes or until light brown. Cool. Combine cream cheese, confectioners' sugar and whipped topping in mixer bowl; beat until smooth. Spread over baked crust. Combine pudding mixes and milk in bowl; mix well. Spoon over cream cheese layer. Top with desired amount of additional whipped topping. Grate candy bar over top. Chill until set.

Approx Per Serving: Cal 365; Prot 6 g; Carbo 39 g; T Fat 22 g;
    Chol 35 mg; Potas 191 mg; Sod 199 mg.

Donald B. Tallman, Cedar Hill, Texas
Provost, Texas Campus

PRALINE CHEESECAKE

Yield: 12 servings   *Pan Size: 10-inch springform*   *Preheat: 250 degrees*

1 recipe graham cracker crust	1 cup milk
24 ounces cream cheese, softened	5 egg whites
2 tablespoons cornstarch	1 cup sugar
5 tablespoons flour	1/2 cup butter
1/8 teaspoon salt	2 cups packed light brown sugar
1/4 teaspoon almond extract	1 cup packed dark brown sugar
1 teaspoon vanilla extract	
1 egg	1 tablespoon vanilla extract
1/2 cup sour cream	3/4 cup milk
1 tablespoon melted butter	1/2 cup corn syrup
1 cup sugar	1 cup chopped pecans

Press crust mixture into springform pan. Process cream cheese with next 10 ingredients in food processor until creamy. Beat egg whites until soft peaks form. Add 1 cup sugar gradually, beating until stiff. Fold into cream cheese mixture gently. Pour into prepared pan. Bake for 2 hours. Combine 1/2 cup butter, brown sugars, 1 tablespoon vanilla, 3/4 cup milk and corn syrup in saucepan. Bring to a boil over high heat, stirring constantly; reduce heat. Cook until thickened, stirring constantly. Stir in pecans. Pour over cheesecake.

Nutritional information for this recipe is not available.

Ellen Weinstein, Dallas, Texas
Dallas Women's Board

CHOCOLATE MOCHA MOUSSE

Yield: 6 servings   *Pan Size: double boiler*

6 eggs, at room temperature	1 tablespoon instant coffee powder
1 1/2 cups semisweet chocolate chips	1 teaspoon sugar
1 tablespoon vanilla extract	9 ounces whipped topping

Separate eggs. Combine chocolate chips, vanilla and coffee powder in double boiler. Heat over hot water until chocolate melts, stirring occasionally. Cool. Beat a small amount of cooled chocolate mixture with egg yolks. Stir into remaining chocolate mixture. Beat egg whites in mixer bowl until stiff peaks form. Beat in sugar gradually. Fold chocolate mixture into egg whites. Fold in whipped topping. Chill for 6 hours or longer.

Approx Per Serving: Cal 433; Prot 8 g; Carbo 36 g; T Fat 32 g;
    Chol 213 mg; Potas 243 mg; Sod 86 mg.

Mrs. George Randolph (Rosalie) Hearst, Sr., Palm Springs, California
Distinguished Woman

Rosalie Hearst

CHOCOLATE MOUSSE

Yield: 8 servings   *Pan Size: 8-inch mold*

¹/₂ cup chopped Brazil nuts	¹/₂ cup sugar
¹/₂ cup chocolate cookie crumbs	¹/₄ teaspoon salt
1 envelope unflavored gelatin	¹/₂ cup milk
¹/₄ cup cold water	3 egg yolks, beaten
1 cup semisweet chocolate chips	3 egg whites, stiffly beaten
	2 cups whipped cream

Rinse mold with cold water. Line with waxed paper; press to secure. Toss nuts and crumbs in small bowl. Sprinkle half the mixture into prepared mold. Soften gelatin in cold water. Combine chocolate chips, ¹/₄ cup sugar, salt and milk in double boiler. Cook over hot water until blended, stirring frequently. Stir a small amount of hot mixture into beaten egg yolks; stir egg yolks into hot mixture. Cook over boiling water until thickened, stirring contantly. Remove from heat. Add gelatin; stir until dissolved. Beat ¹/₄ cup sugar gradually into egg whites. Fold in chocolate mixture and whipped cream. Spoon into prepared mold. Top with remaining crumb mixture. Chill until firm. Unmold onto serving plate.

Approx Per Serving: Cal 251; Prot 5 g; Carbo 24 g; T Fat 17 g; Chol 85 mg; Potas 160 mg; Sod 101 mg.

Mrs. Maurice (Winifred) Hirsch, Houston, Texas
Founding Chairman, Distinguished Woman/Honorary Degree Recipient
Houston Women's Board

CHOCOLATE ORANGE MOUSSE

Yield: 8 servings   *Pan Size: medium bowl*

8 ounces bittersweet chocolate, broken	5 egg yolks
¹/₂ teaspoon instant coffee	2 tablespoons Grand Marnier
¹/₃ cup water	5 egg whites
	¹/₄ teaspoon cream of tartar

Combine chocolate and coffee dissolved in water in small heatproof bowl. Place over simmering water. Heat until chocolate melts, stirring constantly; remove from heat. Add egg yolks and Grand Marnier; beat with wire whisk until blended. Beat egg whites with cream of tartar in mixer bowl until stiff but not dry peaks form. Fold into chocolate mixture. Pour into serving dish. Chill for 2 hours or longer. Garnish with coffee-flavored whipped cream and chocolate curls.

Approx Per Serving: Cal 207; Prot 5 g; Carbo 19 g; T Fat 14 g; Chol 133 mg; Potas 140 mg; Sod 41 mg.

Terry Carder, Dayton, Ohio
Outstanding Business Leader
Chairman of Reynolds & Reynolds

CORONET OF COFFEE MOUSSE

Yield: 12 servings   *Pan Size: 9-inch springform*

2 tablespoons unflavored
  gelatin
1/2 cup cold strong coffee
1 cup sugar
11/2 cups hot strong coffee
12 ladyfingers
1/2 cup semisweet chocolate
  chips, melted

2 cups whipping cream,
  whipped
1 tablespoon rum extract
1 cup chopped pecans
2 teaspoons instant coffee
  powder
2 teaspoons sugar

Soften gelatin in cold coffee. Dissolve 1 cup sugar in hot coffee. Add gelatin; stir until dissolved. Chill until thickened. Split 9 or 10 ladyfingers; dip one end of each into chocolate. Arrange chocolate end up around springform pan. Fold whipped cream into chilled gelatin mixture gently. Fold in rum extract and pecans. Split remaining ladyfingers. Pour 1/3 of the gelatin mixture into prepared pan. Add layer of half the remaining ladyfingers. Repeat layers of gelatin and ladyfingers, ending with gelatin. Chill until firm. Place on serving plate; remove side of pan. Sprinkle with mixture of coffee powder and sugar. Garnish with additional whipped cream.

Approx Per Serving: Cal 279; Prot 3 g; Carbo 31 g; T Fat 17 g;
  Chol 66 mg; Potas 99 mg; Sod 22 mg.

Mary Jane Bostick, Birmingham, Michigan
Distinguished Woman/National Chair 1983-1985

CHOCOLATE SIN DESSERT

Yield: 20 servings   *Pan Size: 9x13 inch*   *Preheat: 375 degrees*

1 pound bittersweet chocolate
1 cup unsalted butter
1/3 cup strong coffee
4 eggs

11/2 cups sugar
1/2 cup flour
2 cups chopped walnuts

Line baking pan with 2 thicknesses of foil; butter foil. Combine chocolate, butter and coffee in double boiler over simmering water. Heat until melted, stirring constantly. Cool for 10 minutes. Beat eggs in mixer bowl at high speed until foamy. Add sugar gradually, beating constantly. Beat for 2 minutes or until light and fluffy. Add chocolate mixture gradually, beating constantly at low speed. Add flour; beat until blended. Stir in walnuts. Pour into prepared pan. Bake for 30 minutes. Cool. Chill for several hours. This is a very rich dessert. The longer it is refrigerated, the smaller the pieces can be cut.

Approx Per Serving: Cal 358; Prot 4 g; Carbo 33 g; T Fat 26 g;
  Chol 67 mg; Potas 161 mg; Sod 20 mg.

Mrs. Russell K. (Susan) Smith, Houston, Texas
Houston Women's Board

BLACK FOREST ICE CREAM

Yield: 8 servings   *Pan Size: ice cream freezer*

2¹/2 ounces unsweetened
  baking chocolate
1 13-ounce can evaporated
  milk
2 eggs
1 cup sugar

2 13-ounce cans evaporated
  milk
2 to 4 tablespoons Kirsch
1 17-ounce can pitted dark
  sweet cherries, drained

Melt chocolate with 1 can evaporated milk in saucepan, stirring frequently to blend well. Beat eggs with sugar in large mixer bowl. Add chocolate mixture gradually, mixing well. Stir in 2 cans evaporated milk, Kirsch and cherries. Chill in refrigerator. Pour into ice cream freezer container. Freeze using manufacturer's directions.

Approx Per Serving: Cal 429; Prot 12 g; Carbo 57 g; T Fat 17 g;
   Chol 94 mg; Potas 597 mg; Sod 167 mg.

Mrs. R. H. (Beverly) Holmes, Dallas, Texas
Chairman, Dallas Women's Board

ICE CREAM BLAIR PACHA

Yield: 4 servings   *Pan Size: medium bowl*

4 peaches, peeled, sliced
Juice of 1 lemon
3 tablespoons (about) sugar

¹/4 teaspoon cardamom
1 quart vanilla ice cream

Toss peaches with lemon juice in bowl. Add sugar and cardamom; mix well. Spoon ice cream into serving dishes. Spoon peaches over ice cream. Garnish with whipped cream and fresh raspberries. I made up this recipe in memory of my late husband who loved peaches and the flavor of cardamom.

Approx Per Serving: Cal 345; Prot 5 g; Carbo 52 g; T Fat 14 g;
   Chol 59 mg; Potas 443 mg; Sod 116 mg.

Mrs. Robert Rush (Carine) Blair, Dallas, Texas
Dallas Women's Board

LEMON MERINGUE PUDDING

Yield: 8 servings *Pan Size: 9 inch* *Preheat: 350 degrees*

1 cup sugar	1/4 cup lemon juice
3 tablespoons cornstarch	Grated rind of 1 lemon
1 1/2 cups cold water	1 tablespoon melted
1/2 cup egg substitute,	margarine
slightly	3 egg whites
beaten	1/3 cup sugar

Mix 1 cup sugar and cornstarch in 2-quart saucepan. Blend in water gradually. Stir in egg substitute. Bring to a boil over medium heat. Cook for 1 minute, stirring constantly; remove from heat. Stir in lemon juice, lemon rind and margarine. Cool. Spoon into greased baking dish. Beat egg whites in mixer bowl until foamy. Add 1/3 cup sugar gradually, beating until stiff peaks form. Spread meringue around edge of pudding, sealing to edge of dish; fill in center. Bake for 15 to 20 minutes or until light brown. Cool. May prepare in individual ramekins or in baked 9-inch pie shell if preferred.

Approx Per Serving: Cal 174; Prot 3 g; Carbo 37 g; T Fat 2 g;
    Chol 0 mg; Potas 84 mg; Sod 64 mg.

Mrs. L.F. (Eleanor) McCollum, Houston, Texas
Distinguished Woman/Houston Women's Board

LEMON SPONGE

Yield: 8 servings *Pan Size: 2 quart* *Preheat: 400 degrees*

1/4 cup flour	2 tablespoons melted butter
1 cup (scant) sugar	1 cup milk
2 egg yolks, beaten	2 egg whites
Juice and grated rind of 1	
lemon	

Mix flour and sugar in mixer bowl. Add egg yolks; mix well. Add lemon juice, lemon rind, butter and milk; mix well. Beat egg whites in mixer bowl until stiff peaks form. Fold into lemon mixture gently. Spoon into baking dish. Place in pan of hot water. Bake at 400 degrees for 10 to 15 minutes. Reduce oven temperature to 300 degrees. Bake for 45 minutes. Chill in refrigerator. Garnish servings with whipped cream. May prepare in individual custard cups if preferred.

Approx Per Serving: Cal 177; Prot 3 g; Carbo 30 g; T Fat 5 g;
    Chol 65 mg; Potas 72 mg; Sod 52 mg.

Leslie A. Gowan, Dallas, Texas
Director of External Affairs, Dallas

MANDARIN ORANGE CASSEROLE DESSERT

Yield: 6 servings	Pan Size: 2 quart	Preheat: 350 degrees

1/2 cup butter, softened
1 cup sugar
4 eggs
1 11-ounce can mandarin
oranges

1 8-ounce can crushed
pineapple
6 slices Pepperidge Farm
white bread with crusts,
cubed

Cream butter and sugar in mixer bowl until light and fluffy. Beat in eggs 1 at a time. Add undrained mandarin oranges and pineapple; mix well. Fold in bread cubes. Spoon into greased baking dish. Bake for 50 to 60 minutes or until set.

Approx Per Serving: Cal 453; Prot 7 g; Carbo 63 g; T Fat 20 g;
Chol 183 mg; Potas 161 mg; Sod 323 mg.

Sharon A. Snyder, Grosse Pointe, Michigan
Director of External Affairs, Greater Detroit Area

PAVLOVA

Yield: 8 servings	Pan Size: baking sheet	Preheat: 225 degrees

4 egg whites
1 cup sugar
Salt to taste
2 tablespoons cornstarch
1/2 teaspoon vinegar

1 cup whipping cream
1/2 teaspoon vanilla extract
2 tablespoons confectioners'
sugar
2 cups strawberries

Grease baking sheet and sprinkle with cornstarch, shaking off excess. Beat egg whites in mixer bowl until stiff peaks form. Beat in sugar and salt gradually. Fold in 2 tablespoons cornstarch and vinegar. Spoon into 8 mounds on prepared baking sheet; shape into cups with rims. Bake for 1 to 1 1/2 hours or until firm but not brown; cover with greased paper if necessary to prevent browning. Turn off oven; let meringues stand in closed oven until cool. Whip cream in mixer bowl until soft peaks form. Add vanilla and confectioners' sugar gradually, beating constantly. Place meringues on serving plates. Fill with whipped cream. Top with strawberries. May substitute kiwifruit or peaches for strawberries if desired. This dessert, topped with kiwifruit, was created by the chef of the Prime Minister of Australia to honor the first visit of the famous ballerina, Anna Pavlova, to Australia.

Approx Per Serving: Cal 233; Prot 3 g; Carbo 32 g; T Fat 11 g;
Chol 41 mg; Potas 108 mg; Sod 37 mg.

Mary-Jo Stevenson, Dallas, Texas
Cedar Hill Women's Board

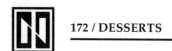

PUFF PASTRY SHELLS

Yields: 6 servings   Pan Size: 3¹/₂-inch muffin cups   Preheat: 350 degrees

2 cups flour
Salt to taste
3 tablespoons unsalted butter
¹/₂ cup (about) ice water

1 teaspoon lemon juice
13 tablespoons unsalted
butter, softened but still cool

Mix flour and salt in food processor. Add 3 tablespoons butter; process until crumbly. Add mixture of ice water and lemon juice. Process for 2 minutes or knead until dough forms ball. Roll into 8x13-inch rectangle on chilled lightly floured marble surface. Place 13 tablespoons butter in center of rectangle. Fold dough over ¹/₃ at a time from short side; press edges lightly to seal. Roll and refold, taking care that butter does not break through dough. Chill, wrapped in plastic wrap, for 15 minutes or longer. Repeat rolling, folding and chilling 5 more times. Chill for 1 hour. Roll as thin as possible on chilled and lightly floured surface. Cut six 6-inch circles. Fit into muffin cups. Line with small coffee filters or parchment. Fill with pastry weights or dried beans. Bake for 20 minutes or until crisp and golden brown. Remove weights and paper. Cool to room temperature. May stand in dry place for up to 3 hours before filling.

Approx Per Serving: Cal 423; Prot 5 g; Carbo 32 g; T Fat 31 g; Chol 83 mg; Potas 51 mg; Sod 5 mg.

Dean Fearing, Dallas, Texas
Executive Chef at the Mansion on Turtle Creek

INDIANA PERSIMMON PUDDING

Yield: 12 servings   Pan Size: 8x8 inch   Preheat: 350 degrees

1 cup sifted flour
³/₄ cup sugar
¹/₂ teaspoon soda
¹/₄ teaspoon (or more) cinnamon
¹/₄ teaspoon nutmeg

Allspice to taste
¹/₂ teaspoon salt
1 cup persimmon pulp
2 eggs, well beaten
1¹/₂ tablespoons melted butter
1 cup milk

Sift dry ingredients into bowl. Blend persimmon pulp and eggs in bowl. Mix in butter and milk. Add to dry ingredients; mix well. Spoon into greased baking pan. Bake for 30 minutes or until set. Serve warm with whipped cream. Use only Indiana persimmons for the proper flavor. Frozen pulp is available from Dillman Farm Inc., 4955 West State Rd. 45, Bloomington, Indiana 47401. Telephone: (812)-825-5248.

Approx Per Serving: Cal 146; Prot 3 g; Carbo 27 g; T Fat 3 g; Chol 42 mg; Potas 107 mg; Sod 156 mg.

Mrs. William J. (Harriet) Stout, Indianapolis, Indiana
National Chairman, Northwood Women's Board/Board of Trustees

ROYAL SUMMER PUDDING

Yield: 16 servings   *Pan Size: custard cups*   *Preheat: 400 degrees*

4 pints blueberries	2 teaspoons vanilla extract
4 pints raspberries	1 teaspoon lemon emulsion
4 pints strawberries	14 tablespoons cake flour
4 pints pitted cherries	1 tablespoon baking powder
2 cups sugar	1 teaspoon salt
8 egg yolks, beaten	1/2 cup water
1/2 cup oil	3/4 cup egg whites
1 cup plus 2 teaspoons sugar	1/2 teaspoon cream of tartar

Combine berries, cherries and 2 cups sugar in deep heavy saucepan. Bring to a boil over high heat. Cook for 20 minutes. Strain, reserving fruit and juice. Chill in refrigerator. Blend egg yolks, oil, 1 cup plus 2 teaspoons sugar, vanilla and lemon emulsion in mixer bowl. Sift in flour, baking powder and salt; mix well. Add water. Beat for 5 minutes. Scrape bowl. Beat for 5 minutes longer. Beat egg whites with cream of tartar in mixer bowl until stiff peaks form. Fold gently into batter. Pour into greased and baking parchment-lined 10x15-inch cake pan. Bake for 15 minutes. Cool on wire rack. Cut circles and strips of cake to line bottoms and sides of custard cups; place in cups. Fill center with fruit mixture. Pour fruit juice over cake and fruit. Chill for 8 hours to overnight. Garnish with fresh berries.

Approx Per Serving: Cal 411; Prot 5 g; Carbo 78 g; T Fat 11 g;
     Chol 106 mg; Potas 474 mg; Sod 222 mg.

Mrs. Cloyd (Vivian) Young, Dallas, Texas
Distinguished Woman/Dallas Women's Board

PUNCH BOWL CHOCOLATE DESSERT

Yield: 20 servings   *Pan Size: punch bowl*   *Preheat: 350 degrees*

1 2-layer package chocolate cake mix	3 cups milk
	1/2 cup Amaretto
2 4-ounce packages chocolate instant pudding mix	16 ounces whipped topping
	6 Heath candy bars, frozen, crushed

Prepare and bake cake mix using package directions. Cool. Break or cut cake into small pieces. Prepare pudding mixes with milk. Blend in Amaretto. Layer cake, pudding, whipped topping and candy 1/2 at a time in punch bowl. Chill until serving time.

Approx Per Serving: Cal 299; Prot 3 g; Carbo 39 g; T Fat 14 g;
     Chol 5 mg; Potas 71 mg; Sod 229 mg.

Mrs. LeRoy B. (Henrietta) McInally, Grosse Point, Michigan
Distinguished Woman

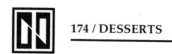

SOUFFLÉ AUX FRAMBOISES - RASPBERRY SOUFFLÉ

Yield: 10 servings   *Pan Size: 10 small molds*   *Preheat: 425 degrees*

2 10-ounce packages frozen
    raspberries, thawed
2 tablespoons sugar
1 tablespoon Kirsch
1½ tablespoons melted butter
2 tablespoons sugar
3 cups fresh raspberries

Juice of ¼ lemon
6 tablespoons sugar
3 egg yolks
12 egg whites
Salt to taste
⅓ cup confectioners' sugar

Press thawed raspberries through fine sieve into small bowl with back of spoon. Stir in 2 tablespoons sugar and Kirsch. Store in refrigerator for up to 1 week or freeze for up to 2 months. Brush individual soufflé molds with melted butter. Sprinkle with 2 tablespoons sugar, coating lightly; shake out excess sugar. Combine 3 cups fresh raspberries, lemon juice and 6 tablespoons sugar in blender container. Blend to a smooth purée. Add egg yolks; blend for 15 seconds. Combine egg whites and salt in copper bowl. Beat with wire whisk until soft peaks form. Add confectioners' sugar, beating constantly until stiff peaks form. Mix ¼ of the egg whites into raspberry purée. Fold purée into egg whites. Fill prepared soufflé molds completely. Smooth top; make groove around top edge with spatula. Bake for 12 minutes. Serve at once. Serve with raspberry sauce.

Approx Per Serving: Cal 199; Prot 6 g; Carbo 37 g; T Fat 4 g;
    Chol 69 mg; Potas 182 mg; Sod 78 mg.

Mrs. Jack. S. (Gretchen) Josey, Houston, Texas
Chairman, Houston Chapter/Distinguished Woman

SPA STRAWBERRY DESSERT

Yield: 4 servings   *Pan Size: compote*

2 cups fresh strawberries
8 ounces low-fat vanilla
yogurt

Sugar substitute to taste

Cut strawberries into halves. Toss with yogurt and sugar substitute in compote. Garnish with mint leaves. May substitute raspberries for strawberries if desired.

Approx Per Serving: Cal 71; Prot 3 g; Carbo 13 g; T Fat 1 g;
    Chol 3 mg; Potas 248 mg; Sod 39 mg.
    Nutritional information does not include sugar substitute.

Northwood Cookbook Committee, Dallas, Texas

Et Cetera

Recipe For A Happy Home

1 House, ripe for occupancy
1 Husband, fully mature
1 Wife, affectionate
Add children as desired
2 measures of consideration
1 tablespoon of sympathy (heaping)
1 pinch of privacy mixed
    with a bushel of shared secrets
2 hours of laughter, sprinkled
    throughout the day
10 minutes of prayer, carefully placed
    on top of each day's portion
Garnish liberally with love
    and keep cool until it sparkles....

This is a recipe I found 29 years ago and it has always had
a special place in my "recipe file".... *Margie August*

Dietary Fiber in Foods

		Amount	Weight (grams)	Fiber (grams)
BREADS	Graham cracker	2 squares	14.2	0.4
	Pumpernickel bread	3/4 slice	24	1.4
	Rye bread	1 slice	25	1.7
	Whole wheat bread	1 slice	25	1.9
	Whole wheat cracker	6 crackers	19.8	2.1
	Whole wheat roll	3/4 roll	21	1.5
FRUIT	Apple	1/2 large	83	2.1
	Apricot	2	72	1.4
	Banana	1/2 medium	54	1.1
	Blackberries	3/4 cup	108	7.3
	Cantaloupe	1 cup	160	1.6
	Cherries	10 large	68	1.0
	Dates, dried	2	18	1.5
	Figs, dried	1 medium	20	2.2
	Grapes, green	10	50	0.6
	Grapefruit	1/2	87	1.1
	Honeydew	1 cup	170	1.8
	Orange	1 small	78	1.9
	Peach	1 medium	100	1.7
	Pear	1/2 medium	82	2.3
	Pineapple	1/2	78	1.2
	Plum	3 small	85	1.7
	Prunes, dried	2	15	1.4
	Raisins	1 1/2 tbsp.	14	0.8
	Strawberries	1 cup	143	3.7
	Tangerine	1 large	101	2.0
	Watermelon	1 cup	160	0.6
GRAINS	All Bran	1/3 cup	28	8.5
	Bran Chex	1/2 cup	21	3.9
	Corn Bran	1/2 cup	21	4.0
	Corn Flakes	3/4 cup	21	0.4
	Grapenuts Flakes	2/3 cup	21	1.4
	Grapenuts	3 tbsp.	21	1.4
	Oatmeal	3/4 pkg.	21	2.3
	Shredded Wheat	1 biscuit	21	2.2
	Wheaties	3/4 cup	21	2.0

		Amount	Weight (grams)	Fiber (grams)
RICE	Rice, brown, cooked	1/3 cup	65	1.1
	Rice, white, cooked	1/3 cup	68	0.2
MEAT, MILK, EGGS	Beef	1 ounce	28	0.0
	Cheese	3/4 ounce	21	0.0
	Chicken/Turkey	1 ounce	28	0.0
	Cold cuts/Frankfurters	1 ounce	28	0.0
	Eggs	3 large	99	0.0
	Fish	2 ounces	56	0.0
	Ice cream	1 ounce	28	0.0
	Milk	1 cup	240	0.0
	Pork	1 ounce	28	0.0
	Yogurt	5 ounces	140	0.0
VEGETABLES	Beans, green	1/2 cup	64	1.5
	Beans, string	1/2 cup	55	2.1
	Beets	1/2 cup	85	1.7
	Broccoli	1/2 cup	93	3.1
	Brussels sprouts	1/2 cup	78	3.5
	Cabbage	1/2 cup	85	2.0
	Carrots	1/2 cup	78	2.5
	Cauliflower	1/2 cup	90	2.3
	Celery	1/2 cup	60	1.0
	Cucumber	1/2 cup	70	0.8
	Eggplant	1/2 cup	100	3.4
	Lentils, cooked	1/2 cup	100	5.1
	Lettuce	1 cup	55	0.7
	Mushrooms	1/2 cup	35	0.6
	Onions	1/2 cup	58	0.9
	Potato, baked	1/2 medium	75	1.8
	Radishes	1/2 cup	58	1.3
	Spinach, fresh	1 cup	55	1.8
	Sweet potato, baked	1/2 medium	75	2.3
	Tomato	1 small	100	1.5
	Turnip greens	1/2 cup	93	2.9
	Winter squash	1/2 cup	120	3.4
	Zucchini	1/2 cup	65	0.7

Cake Baking Tips

It's All In The Pans...

When you are baking, the specified pan size in a recipe is crucial! There are certain occasions when you are baking a cake that you may want a different shape cake. Most simple shortened cakes adapt well to other than specified pan sizes, but most pound cakes, chiffon, sponge or loaf cakes do not do well in other sizes. Listed below is a substitution chart. It is best not to fill pans more than half full. If you have leftover batter, use it for cupcakes.

Two (8-inch) round layers	=	Two dozen cupcakes
Three (8-inch) round layers	=	Two (9-inch) square pans
One (9-inch) round layer	=	One (8-inch) square pan
Two (9-inch) round layers	=	One (9x13-inch) pan One (10x15-inch) jellyroll pan Two (8-inch) square pans One (9-inch) tube pan Thirty cupcakes
One (9x13-inch) pan	=	Two (8-inch) square pans One (10-inch) tube pan Two (9-inch) round pans Two (10x15-inch) jellyroll pans Two (5x9-inch) loaf pans
One (5x9-inch) loaf pan	=	One (9-inch) square pan Two dozen cupcakes

Cake Baking Guide

Problem...	Cause...	
	Butter-Type Cakes	**Sponge-Type Cakes**
Cake falls	Too much sugar, liquid, leavening or shortening; too little flour; temperature too low; insufficient baking	Too much sugar; over-beaten egg whites; egg yolks underbeaten; use of greased pans; insufficient baking
Cake cracks or humps	Too much flour or too little liquid; overmixing; batter not spread evenly in pan; temperature of oven too high	Too much flour or sugar; temperature too high
Cake has one side higher	Batter spread unevenly; uneven pan; pan too close to side of oven; oven rack or range not even; uneven oven heat	Uneven pan; oven rack or range not level
Cake has hard top crust	Temperature too high; overbaking	Temperature too high; overbaking
Cake has sticky top crust	Too much sugar or shortening; insufficient baking	Too much sugar; insufficient baking
Cake has soggy layer at bottom	Too much liquid; eggs underbeaten; undermixing; insufficient baking	Too many eggs or egg yolks; underbeaten egg yolks; undermixing
Cake crumbles or falls apart	Too much sugar, leavening or shortening; batter undermixed; improper pan treatment; improper cooling	
Cake has heavy, compact quality	Too much liquid or shortening; too many eggs; too little leavening or flour; overmixing; oven temperature too high	Overbeaten egg whites; underbeaten egg yolks; overmixing
Cake falls out of pan before completely cooled		Too much sugar; use of greased pans; insufficient baking

Herbs & Spices

Allspice	Pungent aromatic spice, whole or in powdered form. It is excellent in marinades, particularly in game marinade, or in curries.
Basil	Can be chopped and added to cold poultry salads. If the recipe calls for tomatoes or tomato sauce, add a touch of basil to bring out a rich flavor.
Bay leaf	The basis of many French seasonings. It is added to soups, stews, marinades and stuffings.
Bouquet garni	A must in many Creole cuisine recipes. It is a bundle of herbs, spices and bay leaf tied together and added to soups, stews or sauces.
Celery seed	From wild celery rather than domestic celery. It adds pleasant flavor to bouillon or a stock base.
Chervil	One of the traditional *fines herbes* used in French-derived cooking. (The others are tarragon, parsley and chives.) It is good in omelets or soups.
Chives	Available fresh, dried or frozen, it can be substituted for raw onion or shallot in any poultry recipe.
Cinnamon	Ground from the bark of the cinnamon tree, it is important in desserts as well as savory dishes.
Coriander	Adds an unusual flavor to soups, stews, chili dishes, curries and some desserts.
Cumin	A staple spice in Mexican cooking. To use, rub seeds together and let them fall into the dish just before serving. Cumin also comes in powdered form.
Garlic	One of the oldest herbs in the world, it must be carefully handled. For best results, press or crush garlic clove.
Marjoram	An aromatic herb of the mint family, it is good in soups, sauces, stuffings and stews.
Mustard (dry)	Brings a sharp bite to sauces. Sprinkle just a touch over roast chicken for a delightful flavor treat.
Oregano	A staple herb in Italian, Spanish and Mexican cuisines. It is very good in dishes with a tomato foundation; it adds an excellent savory taste.

Paprika	A mild pepper that adds color to many dishes. The very best paprika is imported from Hungary.
Rosemary	A tasty herb important in seasoning stuffing for duck, partridge, capon and other poultry.
Sage	A perennial favorite with all kinds of poultry and stuffings. It is particularly good with goose.
Tarragon	One of the *fines herbes*. Goes well with all poultry dishes.
Thyme	Used in combination with bay leaf in soups and stews.

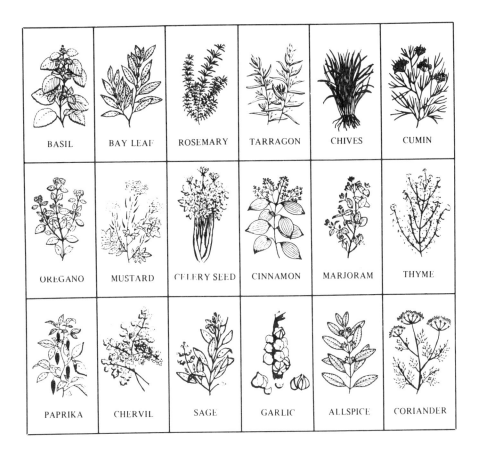

Cheese Chart

CHEESE	GOES WITH	USE FOR	FLAVOR, TEXTURE
Bel Paese (Italy)	Fresh fruit French bread	Dessert Snack	Spongy, mild, creamy yellow interior
Bleu (France)	Fresh fruit Bland crackers	Dessert Salads	Marbled, blue-veined, semisoft, piquant
Brie (France)	Fresh fruit	Dessert Snack	Soft, edible crust, creamy
Brick (U.S.)	Crackers Bread	Sandwiches Snack	Semisoft, mild, cream-colored to orange
Camembert (France)	Apples	Dessert Snack	Mild to pungent, edible crust, yellow
Cheddar (England)	Fresh fruit Crackers	Dessert Cooking	Mild to sharp, cream-colored to orange
Cottage (U.S.)	Canned or Fresh fruit	Fruit salads Cooking	Soft, moist, mild, white
Cream (U.S.)	Crackers and Jelly	Dips Cooking	Soft, smooth, mild, white
Edam (Holland)	Fresh fruit	Dessert Snack	Firm, mild, red wax coating
Feta (Greece)	Greek salad	Salad Cooking	Salty, crumbly, white
Gorgonzola (Italy)	Fresh fruit Italian bread	Dessert Snack	Semisoft, blue-veined, piquant
Gouda (Holland)	Fresh fruit Crackers	Dessert Snack	Softer then Edam, mild, nutty

CHEESE	GOES WITH	USED FOR	FLAVOR, TEXTURE
Gruyère (Switzerland)	Fresh fruit	Dessert Fondue	Nutty, bland, firm, tiny holes
Liederkranz (Germany)	Onion slices Dark bread	Dessert Snack	Edible light orange crust, robust, soft
Limburger (Belgium)	Dark bread Bland crackers	Dessert	Soft, smooth, white, robust, aromatic
Mozzarella (Italy)	Italian foods	Cooking Pizza	Semisoft, delicate, mild, white
Muenster (Germany)	Crackers Bread	Sandwiches Snack	Semisoft, mild to mellow
Parmesan (Italy)	Italian foods	Cooking	Hard, brittle, sharp, light yellow
Port Salut (France)	Fresh fruit Crackers	Dessert Snack	Buttery, semisoft
Provolone (Italy)	Italian foods	Cooking Dessert	Salty, smoky, mild to sharp, hard
Ricotta (Italy)	Italian foods	Cooking Fillings	Soft, creamy, bland, white
Roquefort (France)	Bland crackers Fresh fruit	Salads Dessert	Semisoft, sharp, blue-veined, crumbly
Stilton (England)	Fresh fruit Bland crackers	Salads Dessert	Semisoft, sharp, blue-veined
Swiss (Switzerland)	Fresh fruit French bread	Snack Sandwiches	Sweetish, nutty, holes, pale yellow

Equivalent Chart

	When the recipe calls for	Use
Baking	½ cup butter	4 ounces
	2 cups butter	1 pound
	4 cups all-purpose flour	1 pound
	4½ to 5 cups sifted cake flour	1 pound
	1 square chocolate	1 ounce
	1 cup semisweet chocolate chips	6 ounces
	4 cups marshmallows	1 pound
	2¼ cups packed brown sugar	1 pound
	4 cups confectioners' sugar	1 pound
	2 cups granulated sugar	1 pound
Cereal – Bread	1 cup fine dry bread crumbs	4 to 5 slices
	1 cup soft bread crumbs	2 slices
	1 cup small bread cubes	2 slices
	1 cup fine cracker crumbs	28 saltines
	1 cup fine graham cracker crumbs	15 crackers
	1 cup vanilla wafer crumbs	22 wafers
	1 cup crushed cornflakes	3 cups uncrushed
	4 cups cooked macaroni	8 ounces uncooked
	3½ cups cooked rice	1 cup uncooked
Dairy	1 cup shredded cheese	4 ounces
	1 cup cottage cheese	8 ounces
	1 cup sour cream	8 ounces
	1 cup whipped cream	½ cup heavy cream
	⅔ cup evaporated milk	1 small can
	1⅔ cups evaporated milk	1 13-ounce can
Fruit	4 cups sliced or chopped apples	4 medium
	1 cup mashed bananas	3 medium
	2 cups pitted cherries	4 cups unpitted
	3 cups shredded coconut	8 ounces
	4 cups cranberries	1 pound
	1 cup pitted dates	1 8-ounce package
	1 cup candied fruit	1 8-ounce package
	3 to 4 tablespoons lemon juice plus 1 tablespoon grated lemon rind	1 lemon
	⅓ cup orange juice plus 2 teaspoons grated orange rind	1 orange
	4 cups sliced peaches	8 medium
	2 cups pitted prunes	1 12-ounce package
	3 cups raisins	1 15-ounce package

When the recipe calls for	Use
Meats 4 cups chopped cooked chicken 3 cups chopped cooked meat 2 cups cooked ground meat	1 5-pound chicken 1 pound, cooked 1 pound, cooked
Nuts 1 cup chopped nuts	4 ounces shelled 1 pound unshelled
Vegetables 2 cups cooked green beans 2¹/₂ cups lima beans or red beans 4 cups shredded cabbage 1 cup grated carrot 8 ounces fresh mushrooms 1 cup chopped onion 4 cups sliced or chopped potatoes 2 cups canned tomatoes	¹/₂ pound fresh or 1 16-ounce can 1 cup dried, cooked 1 pound 1 large 1 4-ounce can 1 large 4 medium 1 16-ounce can

Measurement Equivalents

1 tablespoon = 3 teaspoons 2 tablespoons = 1 ounce 4 tablespoons = ¹/₄ cup 5¹/₃ tablespoons = ¹/₃ cup 8 tablespoons = ¹/₂ cup 12 tablespoons = ³/₄ cup 16 tablespoons = 1 cup 1 cup = 8 ounces or ¹/₂ pint 4 cups = 1 quart 4 quarts = 1 gallon	1 6¹/₂ to 8-ounce can = 1 cup 1 10¹/₂ to 12-ounce can = 1¹/₄ cups 1 14 to 16-ounce can = 1³/₄ cups 1 16 to 17-ounce can = 2 cups 1 18 to 20-ounce can = 2¹/₂ cups 1 20-ounce can = 3¹/₂ cups 1 46 to 51-ounce can = 5³/₄ cups 1 6¹/₂ to 7¹/₂-pound can or Number 10= 12 to 13 cups

Metric Equivalents

Liquid	Dry
1 teaspoon = 5 milliliters 1 tablespoon = 15 milliliters 1 fluid ounce = 30 milliliters 1 cup = 250 milliliters 1 pint = 500 milliliters	1 quart = 1 liter 1 ounce = 30 grams 1 pound = 450 grams 2.2 pounds = 1 kilogram

NOTE: The metric measures are approximate benchmarks for purposes of home food preparation.

Substitution Chart

	Instead of	Use
Baking	1 teaspoon baking powder	1/4 teaspoon soda plus 1/2 teaspoon cream of tartar
	1 tablespoon cornstarch (for thickening)	2 tablespoons flour or 1 tablespoon tapioca
	1 cup sifted all-purpose flour	1 cup plus 2 tablespoons sifted cake flour
	1 cup sifted cake flour	1 cup minus 2 tablespoons sifted all-purpose flour
	1 cup dry bread crumbs	3/4 cup cracker crumbs
Dairy	1 cup buttermilk	1 cup sour milk or 1 cup yogurt
	1 cup heavy cream	3/4 cup skim milk plus 1/3 cup butter
	1 cup light cream	7/8 cup skim milk plus 3 tablespoons butter
	1 cup sour cream	7/8 cup sour milk plus 3 tablespoons butter
	1 cup sour milk	1 cup milk plus 1 tablespoon vinegar or lemon juice or 1 cup buttermilk
Seasoning	1 teaspoon allspice	1/2 teaspoon cinnamon plus 1/8 teaspoon cloves
	1 cup catsup	1 cup tomato sauce plus 1/2 cup sugar plus 2 tablespoons vinegar
	1 clove of garlic	1/8 teaspoon garlic powder or 1/8 teaspoon instant minced garlic or 3/4 teaspoon garlic salt or 5 drops of liquid garlic
	1 teaspoon Italian spice	1/4 teaspoon each oregano, basil, thyme, rosemary plus dash of cayenne
	1 teaspoon lemon juice	1/2 teaspoon vinegar
	1 tablespoon mustard	1 teaspoon dry mustard
	1 medium onion	1 tablespoon dried minced onion or 1 teaspoon onion powder
Sweet	1 1-ounce square chocolate	1/4 cup cocoa plus 1 teaspoon shortening
	1 2/3 ounces semisweet chocolate	1 ounce unsweetened chocolate plus 4 teaspoons granulated sugar
	1 cup honey	1 to 1 1/4 cups sugar plus 1/4 cup liquid or 1 cup corn syrup or molasses
	1 cup granulated sugar	1 cup packed brown sugar or 1 cup corn syrup, molasses or honey minus 1/4 cup liquid

Homemade Household Cleaners

Drain Cleaners	Try a plunger first. If that doesn't work, try a handful of baking soda and 1/2 cup of white vinegar down the drain and cover tightly for one minute. The chemical reaction produces pressure, forcing the clog down the drain. Rinse with lots of hot water. Another option is pouring 1/2 cup of salt and 1/2 cup baking soda down the drain and following with hot water.
All-Purpose Cleaners .	Mix one teaspoon of liquid soap or borax to one quart of warm or hot water in a spray bottle or bucket. Add a few drops of lemon juice or vinegar to cut grease.
Oven Cleaners	Mix two tablespoons of liquid soap and two teaspoons of borax with enough warm water to fill a spray bottle. After the mixture has completely dissolved, spray it into the oven, holding bottle very close to the surface so that it does not get into the air–it may irritate your eyes. Leave the solution on for 20 minutes and then scrub with steel wool and a non-chlorine scouring powder.
Disinfectants	Dissolve 1/2 cup borax in a gallon of hot water. Use this as a germ killer and disinfectant.
Wall Cleaners	Make a paste of water and cornstarch and cover stain. Let stand for one hour. Brush off and repeat if necessary.
Furniture Polish	Try plain mineral oil. You may also rub mayonnaise on furniture with a soft cloth, or use one teaspoon of olive oil mixed with the juice of one lemon, one teaspoon of brandy or whiskey and one teaspoon of water. (Make this fresh each time.) For scratches, mix equal amounts of lemon juice and salad oil. Rub into wood until scratches disappear. For water spots, use 10 drops of lemon oil with 2 cups of vodka.
Scouring Powders	Use baking soda, borax or table salt with a wet sponge as an effective abrasive for scouring.
Silver and Other Metal Cleaners	Try toothpaste and warm water. Use like regular silver polish and rinse well. Dry and buff to a shine. For brass and copper, use lemon juice. Apply with a soft cloth, rinse with water and dry. If that is not strong enough, make a paste of lemon juice and salt or lemon juice with cream of tartar. Leave on for five minutes and rinse with hot water and dry well.
Mold and Mildew Cleaners	Mix borax and water or vinegar and water in a spray bottle. Spray your walls with this mixture, or sprinkle borax under the sink cabinets to prevent mildew, since borax inhibits its growth.

INDEX

For additional copies of
Distinguished Recipes from Distinguished Cooks,
please send $10.95 plus
$2.00 shipping and handling

Northwood Institute
3100 Monticello Suite 775
Lock Box 7
Dallas, TX 75205
(214) 521-2666